Walks on
South Cambri
Border

Cambridge Group of
The Ramblers' Association

Walks on the South Cambridgeshire Borders

Published by the
Cambridge Group of The Ramblers' Association

Acknowledgements

Editor – Jill Tuffnell.

Drawings – Ron Wilbraham.

Typesetting, layout and maps – Nigel Balchin.

The following contributed and checked walks:
David Allard, Nigel Balchin, Adrian Best, Des Cheale, Carole Dougan, Margaret English, Ron English, John Fuller, Margaret Graham, Dave Harrison, Betty Jenkins, Norman Jenkins, Lynne Jenkins, Sheila Kidman, Janet Moreton, Roger Moreton, Pat Motherwell, Janet Pake, Margaret Rishbeth, David Shepherd, Harriet Snape, Jill Tuffnell.

The maps in the booklet are based upon the Ordnance Survey Landranger map Sheets 153, 154, 166 and 167, under licence number MC87959M from the Ordnance Survey. The grid on these maps is the National Grid taken from the Ordnance Survey maps with the permission of The Controller of Her Majesty's Stationery Office.

First edition 1997.

ISBN 0 9522518 2 5

Ramblers' Association National Office
  1–5 Wandsworth Road, London SW8 2XX
Ramblers' Association Cambridge Group contacts at time of printing:
  John Capes, 30 Queensway, Sawston, Cambridge
    CB2 4DJ
  R & J Moreton, 23 Emery Street, Cambridge CB1 2AX
  Jill Tuffnell, 62 Beche Road, Cambridge CB5 8HU

Contents

Introduction

The Cambridge Group of the Rambler's Association has compiled this and previous books of walks to encourage others to join us in exploring and enjoying the attractive countryside.

The southern borders of the county with Bedfordshire, Hertfordshire, Essex and Suffolk provide interesting and varied scenery with its own gentle hills. The walks explore tracks and paths which show the area at its best, following chalk escarpments, giving excellent views and visiting ancient woodlands. Scenic villages also offer some excellent refreshment! This book describes 28 walks, some with alternative routes, of different lengths, which should help those new to the area, or to rambling, find their way to enjoyable excursions.

Location map

showing the area of the walks

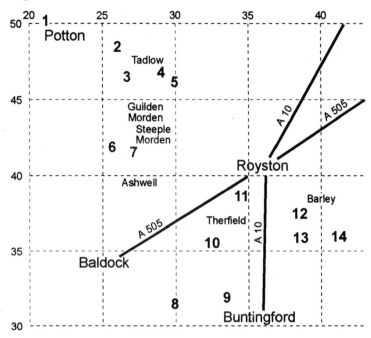

Walk		miles	page
1	Sutton, Sandy Warren, Gamlingay	15	15
2	Wrestlingworth figure of eight	7	20
3	Tadlow, Guilden Morden, Dunton, Wrestlingworth		
		15	23
4	Guilden Morden, Tadlow	6	29
5	Steeple Morden, Shingay, Croydon	12	32
6	Ashwell, Dunton, Guilden Morden	13	37
7	Ashwell, Guilden Morden, Steeple Morden	9	41
8	Sandon, Clothall, Cottered	13	45
9	Buntingford, Cottered, Buckland, Wyddial	14	49
10	Therfield, Sandon	9	56
11	Royston, Therfield	7	60
12	Royston, Barkway, Nuthampstead, Barley	13	63
13	Barley, Reed, Buckland, Nuthampstead	12½	68
14	Barley, Nuthampstead, Langley	11	74

The list on these pages shows only the overall distance for the longest option – see overleaf for a more detailed list.

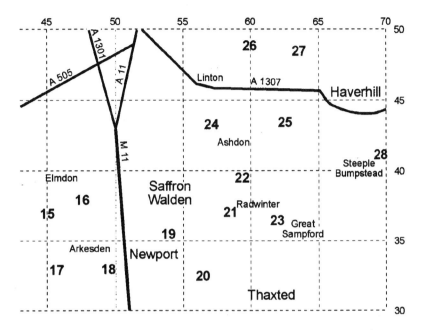

Walks

Walks

Other published walks

These are available at Tourist Information Centres, and at some bookshops in the area.

Walks in South Cambridgeshire, third edition:
Cambridge Group of the Ramblers Association, 1995

Walks in East Cambridgeshire:
Cambridge Group of the Ramblers Association, 1993

The Icknield Way – A Walkers' Guide:
Icknield Way Association, third edition 1993

The Harcamlow Way:
Fred Matthews and Harry Bitten, third edition 1992

The following two titles are out-of-print, but some outlets or libraries may have copies.

Country Walks around Cambridge:
Cambridge City Council

More Country Walks around Cambridge:
Cambridge City Council, 1980

Leaflet series, published by
Cambridgeshire County Council:

Enjoy the Cambridgeshire Countryside
(a general leaflet on where to go and what to see, without detailed route descriptions)
The Clopton Way
The Devils Dyke Walks
Giants Hill, Rampton
Quy Fen
Roman Road Walks
Linton – Hildersham
Stapleford – Wandlebury
The Wimpole Way

How to use this Guide

Information to help you to choose the kind of walk you want appears in the list on pages 4 to 7, with location, length, and whether the walk can be shortened, or varied in other ways.

The following pages give general notes; the descriptions of each walk list the starting point, maps, transport where appropriate, and where refreshments may be obtained. Notes on points of interest are in smaller type.

Public paths

The various paths – footpaths, bridleways and byways – used on the walks in this book are nearly all public rights of way, but their condition may vary; the exceptions are 'permitted paths' used with the landowner's permission, and usually in good condition.

Where paths cross farmland, the farmer must not obstruct them with fences, hedges or crops. In general, paths along field boundaries may not be ploughed, and must be at least 1.5 metres wide for footpaths, or 3 metres for bridleways. Paths across fields may be ploughed, but must be restored to be visible and convenient for walking within two weeks of the first cultivation, and kept clear of crops for a width of 1 metre. These duties are laid down in the Rights of Way Act, 1990. Overgrown paths need to be cleared by the County Council.

All the walks were checked during 1996 or 1997, and any problems reported to the appropriate County Council, who are responsible for keeping all public paths clear (a duty which may be delegated to District Councils). With limited resources, it cannot be guaranteed that all paths will be in perfect condition at all times. If you do encounter difficulties, please inform the relevant County Council (details from the telephone directory or a local library), or the local Footpath Secretary of the Ramblers' Association (see the reverse of the title page for addresses of the Cambridge Group). If you would like to help the Ramblers' Association improve footpaths, why not join? You could also take an active part in waymarking and path clearance.

Circular walks

All the walks described in this booklet are 'circular walks', starting and ending at the same point. The 'figure of eight' walks have two loops, each returning to the starting point.

Public transport

Information on public transport is available from council transport departments, libraries, Tourist Information Centres, etc. Some of these are listed below, with telephone numbers.

Bedfordshire County Council
  Dept. of Transport Engineering   01234 228337

Cambridgeshire County Council
  Passenger Transport Section   01223 717740

Essex County Council
  Public Transport Section   0345 000333

Hertfordshire County Council
  Passenger Transport Unit   0345 244344

Suffolk County Council
  Public Transport Team   0645 583358

Cambridge Tourist Information Centre   01223 322640

Saffron Walden Tourist Information Centre   01799 510444

Stevenage Tourist Information Centre   01438 369441

Rail

Stations in the area include Newport, Audley End (for Saffron Walden), Royston, and Ashwell Station (about 2 miles from Ashwell village). They are served by two lines running from Cambridge to London Liverpool Street and to London King's Cross, operated by West Anglia Great Northern (WAGoN). Information is available in leaflets from stations etc., or from the national rail enquiry line, 0345 484950.

Car parking

Please observe any restrictions on location and duration of parking, and charges.

In rural areas, be careful not to obscure the view of other road users, and do not obstruct farm and field entrances.

Refreshments

Where appropriate, villages with pubs, restaurants, tea rooms or shops in 1997 are listed under the heading 'Refreshments'. Such facilities often close at short notice, so it may be worth checking in advance that food will be available. Most pub landlords welcome walkers, provided they leave their muddy boots outside, but a few do not.

The abbreviation PH is used for a Public House.

Waymarks

Small arrows of various colours on special posts or on stiles, or painted on walls, indicate routes which may be used by walkers and others. The Countryside Commission code is:

Yellow – public footpath
Blue – public bridleway
Red – public byway, may be used by vehicles
White – permitted route, the landowner allows the public to
    walk

A number of walks follow sections of long distance paths which have individual waymarks, e. g. the Greensand Ridge and the Icknield Way.

The waymarks mentioned in the text were in place when the walks were checked.

Maps

Each walk description has a sketch map, on which the route is shown by arrows. Roads are shown by single lines, and footpaths, bridleways and tracks by a dashed line.
Alternative routes are shown by a dotted line. Letters like **H** in bold in the text indicate points on the walk which are marked on the map. Villages etc. identified by a sub-heading

---

shown on the maps in bold type. North is at the top of the page.

Map scale 1:50 000

Our aim has been to make it possible to follow the routes with the aid of this booklet alone, but a map will help, enabling the location of features of interest or the choice of alternative routes.

For each walk, we give the sheet numbers of appropriate Ordnance Survey maps from the Landranger 1:50 000 and Pathfinder 1:25 000 series as listed below; numbers in brackets, as (1025), mean that only a short length of the route falls on that sheet. The Landranger maps are almost essential for finding the more isolated starting points.

The Ordnance Survey has started to replace the Pathfinder series by Explorer Maps (orange covers) and Outdoor Leisure Maps (yellow covers). These are also at 1:25 000 scale, but with more flexible sheet lines, and more details. No information is yet available about plans for the area covered by this book. The maps in the booklet are based upon the Landranger maps – see note on reverse of title page.

Pathfinder 1:25 000 (green covers)

1002	*TL 05/15*	Bedford (North) and St. Neots (South)
1003	*TL 25/35*	Gamlingay & Comberton
1004	*TL 45/55*	Cambridge & Balsham
1005	*TL 65/75*	Dullingham & Chedburgh
1025	*TL 04/14*	Bedford (South) & Biggleswade
1026	*TL 24/34*	Royston (Herts)
1027	*TL 44/54*	Duxford & Great Chesterford
1028	*TL 64/74*	Haverhill & Clare
1029	*TL 84/94*	Sudbury & Lavenham
1049	*TL 23/33*	Letchworth & Barkway
1050	*TL 43/53*	Saffron Walden
1051	*TL 63/73*	Thaxted & Sible Hedingham
1073	*TL 22/32*	Stevenage & Buntingford

Landranger 1:50 000 (mauve covers)
- 153   Bedford & Huntingdon
- 154   Cambridge & Newmarket
- 166   Luton & Hertford
- 167   Chelmsford

While much more detail is shown on the Pathfinder maps, the Landranger series is updated much more frequently, and is therefore more likely to show recently-diverted paths.

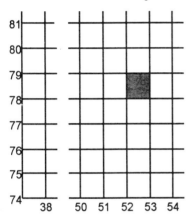

National grid references for starting points are given in square brackets, for example [523781] – the letters 'TL' precede the 6 figures given here for the full reference. The point can be located on an Ordnance Survey map by looking for the first two digits, 52 in the example above, along the lower edge, and the fourth and fifth digits, 78, up the side; lines from these points meet at the bottom left-hand corner of the grid square, as shown in the diagram.

Please note that the wire binding of this booklet may affect compass readings.

Safety and comfort

Suitable footwear is advisable to cope with muddy or uneven paths. Allow extra time for slow going on muddy surfaces. Chalk, for example on Royston Heath, can become very slippery when it is wet and needs special care. Footbridges may be slippery and/or narrow. In summer, nettles and

---

thistles grow in profusion on some paths – long trousers and/or a stick are recommended.

Please take care when crossing roads and especially railways. Make sure that you are visible on roads – wear bright clothing, and carry a light at dusk or in misty weather.

Horses should be treated with caution, and quiet behaviour is advised, especially with mares and foals. It is best to keep dogs on leads, especially on paths through fields with livestock.

1 Sutton, Sandy Warren, Gamlingay

15 miles / 24 kilometres

Start: Sutton, Beds., John O'Gaunt PH **A** [222473].

Maps: Landranger 153.
Pathfinder (1002), 1003, 1025, 1026.

Transport: Bus – occasional.
Car – the ford in Sutton means that it is more practicable to approach from Potton or Eyeworth; parking on roadside.

Refreshments: Sutton, John O'Gaunt PH.
Everton, Thornton Arms PH.
Gamlingay (detour), various.

Points of interest:

A walk through varied countryside, including the RSPB bird sanctuary at Sandy Warren, along the Greensand ridge and through Potton Wood. Generally well-drained surfaces, so good in winter!

Sutton

From the John O'Gaunt PH **A** turn left to walk west, towards the church. After 70 yards look out for a Public Bridleway sign on the left, partly hidden in a tree, but opposite a stile and footpath sign on the opposite (north) side of the road. Take this grassy track south for a mile. Just after a small belt of trees on the left, pick up a hard track, still walking south. Cross a stream and turn right, still on the track (note that the route has been diverted officially onto this track from a cross field path). Where the track turns left towards farm buildings keep straight on – and on again at the next junction, passing under power lines. At the mature hedge ahead turn right, then after 50 yards, turn left over a bridge and stile into a grassy common with hawthorn bushes. It can be muddy!

Keep in the common, going initially west and gradually swinging away from the hedge on your left. After 300 yards you meet the hedge again at a sharp corner – but immediately leave it, going north-west towards a cottage with a tiled roof, which you pass by on your left. You can see the trees of Sandy Warren on the hillside ahead. Cross the stile

in the corner of the field and go over the road **B**, picking up the footpath opposite (Public Footpath sign and stile). Cross the corner of the field half left, behind buildings and over another stile. Now you pick up a field edge grass track (hedge and nursery buildings on your left). At a T-junction of tracks (signposted) turn right to Furzenhall Farm. Pass through a gate between buildings and into a lane. This swings gently right, through another gate, into the large meadow making up Biggleswade Common. Follow the track diagonally right across the Common, leading to a footbridge. Cross it into the woodland, keeping north on the clear path. You soon meet the grounds of the RSPB reserve at Sandy Warren.

Sandy Warren

A number of routes are waymarked through the Warren – but the RSPB charges non-members for a more extensive look round the reserve. From the wall follow the blue arrow (public bridleway) up the hill through trees. Eventually you meet the main drive. Turn right onto it and follow it to the road ahead. There are toilets by the 'Bird Shop' near the entrance.

At the road **C**, cross over and pick up the track ahead, passing under power lines once more. Soon the track forks – keep left. Just before the next road, which can be busy, it is possible to turn left and walk parallel to the road for about 300 yards. Eventually you must cut through to the road – keep walking west until you come to a left bend. Here keep ahead, following first the cycleway sign to Sandy, but looking out on your right – after 30 yards – for your first 'Greensand Ridgeway' path sign – a route we follow through to Gamlingay. The logo is the muntjac deer which are now common in the area.

The sign points invitingly downhill through a grassy field. Follow the waymarked bridleway through fields and then a field edge track. This may be the muddiest part of your walk! When you reach the outlying buildings of Waterloo Farm on your left, look out for a Public Footpath sign on your right. Turn right and follow the track uphill. After crossing a stile turn half right, continuing uphill towards Everton Village. On reaching the road **D**, turn left.

Everton

You soon see the Thornton Arms pub ahead. Take the lane ahead (pub on your right) and pass the church, to enter the grounds of Woodbury Hall. Keep to the drive – you should have excellent views on your left. After passing several buildings, the drive eventually swings left to the Home Farm; you keep straight ahead across grass (waymarked). Pass through a kissing gate and follow the path through a field and over a stile into a narrow lane. Turn right, and in 20 yards left, walking along a field edge path past Tetworth Hall. Just past the Hall cross a drive and cattle grid to enter the next field through a white gate. Keep in the same direction, north-east, through a second gate onto a track, immediately passing a thatched cottage on your right. Very soon you pass another cottage on your left. Follow the edge, through more fields, to the road. This is the end of the Greensand Ridge – 48 miles from its start in Leighton Buzzard!

Gamlingay

The route now skirts Gamlingay to the west and south. If you want refreshments in the village you must make a detour. But – keeping to this route – at the road **E** turn right and go straight over the crossroads ahead into Cinques Road. You will soon see a new route waymarked on your right, the Clopton Way. The walk follows these signs to and through Potton Wood. Cross the rough ground in the direction of the sign (half right). The route continues (right) on a track running between cottages (mailbox on left). It swings right, then, just past a house on the left, it meets a T-junction of tracks (signposted). Turn left along a path which soon becomes a hedge-lined lane (Park Lane on the Pathfinder map). If it's really muddy you can keep in the open grassy field on the right for several hundred yards (view of reservoir on the right). Eventually the lane meets a tarmac road. Turn left, then right at the next junction at Dennis Green. The route follows a lane and is waymarked left, then right. When you meet the next major road at a T-junction, turn right. Now follow the Biggleswade Road south. After Millbridge Farm you will see a Public Footpath/Clopton Way sign on the left. Take this track and follow it as far as Potton Wood **F**.

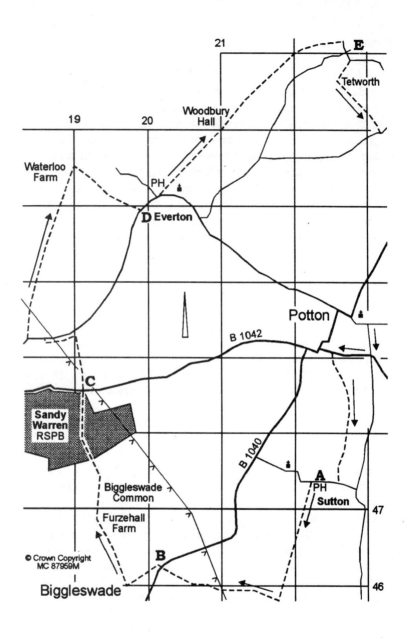

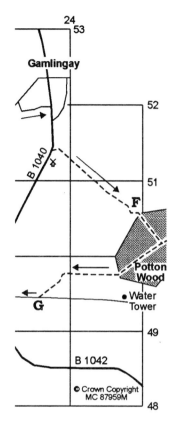

Potton Wood

Go into the wood at its corner (sharp right turn) and follow the clear path to an open ride. Keep to the Clopton Way. Turn left down the ride. At the next junction with another broad ride look out for a Clopton Way waymark on a telegraph pole; turn right and follow this ride to a wooden barrier at the western edge of Potton Wood. Turn left along the track skirting the wood for 50 yards – as far as a crossing hedge. Next turn right along a grassy field edge track going west, with a hedge on your right – do **not** go towards the water tower. Just before you reach the belt of conifers ahead you meet another track. Turn left and follow the waymarked path as far as the lane **G**.

Turn right onto the lane and follow it to the next junction – beware traffic, there isn't much but it can go very fast! At the junction turn left, (signposted Wrestlingworth), crossing over to use the footway. At the next road junction turn right (signposted Potton town centre). In 350 yards cross over, turning left onto a signposted footpath (Sutton 1), passing alongside and then swinging left behind the Telephone Exchange. Cross the stile in the corner of the field and pick up a footpath half left in this new poplar plantation, Pegnut Wood. Go through the hedge on the other side of the wood and turn right, following a field edge path with trees on your right. The path goes gently uphill towards trees on the skyline ahead. Keep on this clear path back into Sutton, turning right when you get to the road, and return to your starting point at the pub **A**.

2 Wrestlingworth figure of eight

a North-east loop 4 miles / 6 kilometres
b South-west loop 3 miles / 5 kilometres
c Total 7 miles / 11 kilometres

Start: Wrestlingworth, Beds., church **A** [259474].
Maps: Landranger 153. Pathfinder 1026.
Transport: Car – parking with discretion in
                    Wrestlingworth.
Refreshments: Wrestlingworth, The Chequers PH,
                    village shop.

Points of interest:

> Wrestlingworth church. Cockayne Hatley church (off the route).
> From near Hatley Gate, good view over to Therfield Heath.
> The route uses part of the Clopton Way.
> On the south-western loop, major path diversions in 1995 moved paths
> away from Manor Farm, now waymarked.

a North-east loop 4 miles / 6.5 kilometres

Wrestlingworth

From Wrestlingworth Church **A**, walk back down Church
Lane to the main street and turn right (north) to Braggs Close
on the right. The tarmac of Braggs Close gives out at its end
to a bridleway running east-north-east with a tall hedge on
the left. Follow this, crossing a ditch on a culvert, and follow
the path round to the right on a grassy headland to meet a
deep stream with tree-lined banks **B**. Here, turn left, north-
east, on a grassy headland beside the stream, and cross the
wooden bridge at the county boundary into Tadlow Parish.
Continue with the now smaller ditch on the right towards
New England Farm. Near the farm, when the way forward is
impeded by a crossing ditch, turn left beside some market
garden plots, right over a culvert bridge, then, shortly, left to
follow the right-hand-side of a ditch running north up the hill
towards a tall hedge line (in common use, but not quite the
right of way).

At the hedge line **C**, turn left along the grassy headland,
crossing the ditch by a small concrete bridge. Continue east
to a junction of paths at the County Boundary, called Hatley

Gate, and continue straight on along a waymarked grassy path, the Clopton Way with hedge on the right. Follow the Clopton Way on first grass, then a hard farm track round right and then left bends into the single street of Cockayne Hatley **D**. (To visit the Church, it is necessary to make a half-mile detour off the route).

Cockayne Hatley

In Cockayne Hatley, pass a few houses on the left, then an open field, and look for a signpost on the left in front of the next house. Turn left down the headland path running generally south, first past tall conifers edging a garden, then beside a ditch for nearly a mile, veering left for a 50 yards, then resuming a south direction at a bulge in a crossing hedge. On meeting a cross-track, turn right for 50 yards, then left (south) at a green metal signpost down a narrow path with tall hedge to left, and a paddock to the right – do **not** go down the gravel farm track, which is just before the tall hedge. Follow the path to the road in Wrestlingworth, turn left, and walk through the village, passing, or pausing at the Chequers PH on the right.

Church Lane leads back on the left to the church **A**, and the end of the north-eastern loop.

b South-west loop 3 miles / 5 kilometres

Wrestlingworth

Go down the main street to Water End, **E**. Turn right (west) down the lane at Water End. At a side branch, with open field on left and hedge on right (signposted), go through the wide gap in the hedge, and continue in the same direction (west) down the other side of the hedge. Continue past an isolated cottage, and along a track through fields to the road between Eyeworth and Sutton, near a lodge **F**. Rights of way around Manor farm were diverted in 1988; the diverted right of way now continues along the track.

Turn right up the road for 100 yards, to find a new signpost and bridge giving entry on the right to a wide gap in a roadside tree belt. Go through the tree-belt, and immediately turn left in the field. At the corner, follow the hedge round to the right, and later to the left (waymarked) and then to the

right again on grassy headlands. At a waymarked T-junction, the turning on the left indicates the (undiverted) bridleway towards Sutton **G**. This gives you a reference point on your map, but continue forward north-east with hedge on the left to the next field boundary, where a further waymark indicates the turning right (east-south-east) to follow another hedge on left. Follow the hedge briefly south, and then turn east to rejoin the old line of a right of way. Since leaving the road, you have been progressing clockwise round the distant buildings of Manor Farm. Follow the bridleway **E** with a hedge on left to a stile giving access to a pasture field. Do not enter the field, but follow the track round to the right, to return to Water End **E**, and turn left back to Wrestlingworth church **A**.

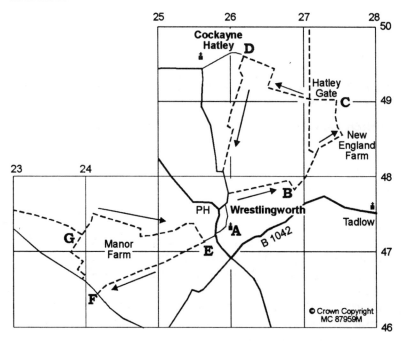

3 Tadlow, Guilden Morden, Dunton, Wrestlingworth

a via East Hatley 15 miles / 24 kilometres
b shorter route 12 miles / 19 kilometres

Start: Tadlow, Cambs., village street **A**
(signposted off B 1042) [282472].

Maps: Landranger 153. Pathfinder 1026.

Transport: Car – parking on roadside in village street.

Refreshments: Guilden Morden, Edward VII PH,
Three Tuns PH.
Dunton, March Hare PH.
Wrestlingworth, The Chequers PH.

Points of interest:

A pleasant walk in varied scenery straddling the border between Cambridgeshire and Bedfordshire. Crosses the River Cam twice.

Tadlow

Walk along the street **A**, away from the B1042, to the edge of the village development. Turn right just before the electricity sub-station onto a track which first passes a field on the right, with a high hedge and ditch on your left. This track may be signed at the road end as a Public Bridleway – but the sign has been reported missing in 1997. At the hedge end turn left along a grassy track. After 20 yards the track forks – take the left branch, keeping generally south. You now have a ditch on your right. At the T-junction with a farm track turn right. After 120 yards look out for a turning on the left through the trees. This turns into a green lane between hedges. Soon you cross a sturdy bridge over the Cam – keep a look out for a waymarked post in the hedge on your right. Turn right off the track onto the field headland, with a ditch and hedge on your left. The headland swings gently ahead to pass Low Field Barn on your left, picking up a gravel track ahead. Continue south on the track passing by a large metal gate before continuing to the road on the edge of Guilden Morden (Public Footpath sign here) **B**.

Guilden Morden

At the road turn right and continue to a T-junction. At the
Potton Road turn left and keep on it until the road forks –
take the right branch, Dubbs Knoll Road, (signposted
Ashwell). Continue until you reach the Congregational
Church on your left. Here take the tarmac road opposite, on
your right. Within 100 yards you come to a Public Footpath
sign. Turn left over a sleeper bridge into a grass field. Pick up
a field path which skirts the garden of the house on your
right, turning right until you reach a cross track. The right of
way now goes across the open field in a south-westerly
direction, at right angles to the track. If the path is not clearly
marked out, turn left and follow a straight line for 700 yards
until you meet another cross track. Here turn right. Continue
on this track until it swings right – you go straight on.
Normally the route is clearly marked across the open field
ahead. On reaching the tree line at the field edge look out for
a strong wooden bridge, which you cross into the field
beyond. Here cross the field diagonally half right to the
hedge. Use the taller trees at the right end of the hedge as a
guide. You should find a gap in the hedge to the road beyond,
with a footpath sign **C**.

Turn right and follow the road as it swings left. In about 200
yards look out for a Bridleway sign left. Take this track (note
that the route has been officially diverted from that shown on
the Pathfinder maps, replacing a cross-field route by the farm
by nearby tracks). Follow the track for 600 yards and turn
with it when it bends sharp right. Keep on the track as far as
the road on the edge of Dunton, about 1½ miles distant.

Dunton

When you reach the road **D** at Dunton, turn left. You might
like to take a detour to the pub, which is near the church.
Our route takes a residential street on the right (after 300
yards). Go to the end of the road to the open field beyond.
Keep on the same line as the road and cross the field to a
waymark post in the hedge ahead. The right of way crosses
the next field in the same north-westerly direction to a track
(but most locals appear to use a good headland path as an
alternative – right then left at the corner).

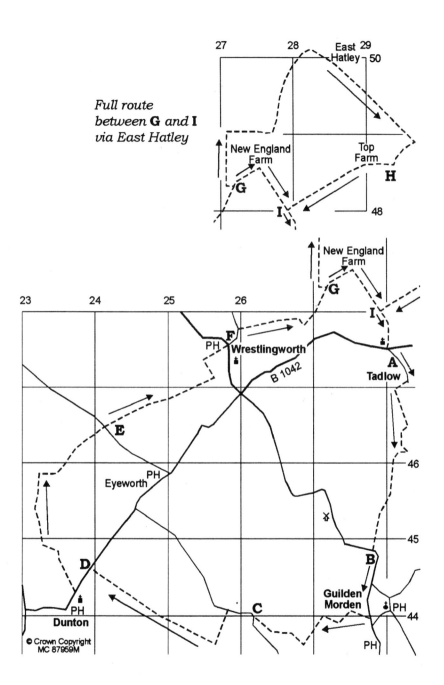

*Full route between **G** and **I** via East Hatley*

At the track turn right to a post by a hedge. Follow the waymarks left, keeping on a field headland with a hedge on your right. At the main ditch ahead on the edge of the field, turn right over a sleeper bridge. Now follow the headland for about 1,200 yards (keeping a ditch on your left). At the next field corner, turn right, joining a waymarked path on the headland (ditch on left). **Don't** cross the wooden bridge on your left.

After 200 yards look out for a waymark footpath post. Your route goes left, over a sleeper bridge, picking up a headland path again (still with a ditch on your left). Continue on this headland until you meet the Eyeworth – Sutton minor road. As you approach the road, keep on the headland as it swings right until you can safely cross a bridge over the ditch on your left to the road **E**.

Turn right and take the bridleway signposted on your left, just beyond Lodge House. (Major changes to the rights of way network in this area were approved in 1995 – so maps may be out of date.) This route is a good wide grassy bridleway which soon passes an old moat on the right. Keep walking in an east-north-east direction on field headlands. After 1¼ miles you come to a house at Water End. The bridleway keeps on the headland with a hedge on your right, rather than joining the roadway. You soon reach a cross track near a signpost. Turn left onto the track for 300 yards. Cross a waymarked stile on your right and cross a grassy field to another stile ahead. Follow a path through grass, aiming for the road. The **exact** route to the road is not clear, as no signpost is in place to identify the access point for this bridleway. If you keep to the left of the cottage you will have to turn to turn right at the road, bringing you to the High Street, shop and the Chequers pub.

Wrestlingworth

After visiting the pub, retrace your steps to the junction and keep on High Street, soon passing the end of Church Lane. Turn right into Braggs Lane **F**, and take the signposted bridleway at the end. You are on a broad grassy track with a hedge on your left. At the hedge end, keep on the track, going in the same direction for around 80 yards, then follow the

track as it turns right down a field edge, crossing a ditch en route. At the tree line ahead turn left onto another good grassy headland. When you get to a stile, wooden bridge and signpost **G**, you must decide whether to follow the 12 mile or 15 mile route. The shorter distance is given as an alternative at the end. Let's assume here that you want to complete the longer route!

a – via East Hatley, 15 miles / 24 kilometres

Don't cross the stile/bridge, but instead turn left. In 100 yards, at the next field corner, cross a sleeper bridge on your right (signposted). Follow the bridleway on the field headland, with a ditch on your left. Keep on this path, almost due north, as far as the trees ahead – Hatley Gate. At the corner turn right onto another wide grassy track. Now keep the tree belt on your left for 600 yards as you walk roughly east. At one point you must take care as you manoeuvre over a concrete culvert top! Avoid the Clopton Way sign right, but keep next to the copse.

Eventually the path turns left – and after 20 yards passes through a hedge on your left to pick up a field edge path which rises gradually uphill, with a hedge on your left. Just past a large building which was built as a hangar look out for a field 'divide' on your right. Turn right onto a track which runs on the north side. Much of the following route from here to beyond Top Farm has been officially diverted – again your map may be out of date. The new route generally keeps to good grassy tracks.

Keep on the track through the hedge ahead. In the next field look out for, and follow, a waymark. The track turns left then right through a hedge into the next field. Here the track turns right, past the hedge ahead, and then sharp left up a slight hill. You should now have a hedge on your left. Follow the track round a tree belt until eventually it swings left through the trees to emerge on the other side, where you turn right. Keep on this headland path, with trees now on your right, until you have passed the wood. Look out for a 'Light aircraft' warning sign (and the aircraft!).

In a dip you reach a waymark sign showing that the official right of way path turns right onto a farm track – into the farmyard. If you decide to go this way, make sure you turn left in the farm to pick up the main access track out. But there is no need to go through the farm. Instead a permitted path has been provided by the farmer, waymarked with white arrows on a red background. If you follow this alternative, ignore the farm track and keep on the field headland downhill. At the field edge at the bottom, turn right, then continue along a ditch on your left as far as a T-junction with the Clopton Way path. Turn right; this path soon meets the drive to Top Farm **H**.

Cross the drive to join a track opposite – or if coming from the farm, turn right. You should have a hedge on your right. Continue on the waymarked Clopton Way – first on a good track, then on a green lane – until you meet the tarmac roadway leading to New England farm **I**. Here look out for a Footpath sign and follow the route left. The path first follows a field edge with a ditch on your left. Go through the hedge ahead and in the next field pick up a diagonal path half right. Cross to the hedge corner; here pick up a path by the side of the churchyard to the church drive, bearing left to the road. Go through the kissing gate and over the busy B1042 to return to Tadlow **A**.

b – Shorter route 12 miles / 19 kilometres

At **G**, cross the stile and bridge and keep on the path, with a ditch on your right, as far as New England Farm. Here turn right, picking up the main farm drive which is now officially used by the Clopton Way. Walk down the drive to the sharp right bend **I**, where you rejoin the longer route.

4 Guilden Morden, Tadlow
6 miles / 9.5 kilometres

Start: Guilden Morden, Cambs., recreation
ground **A** near the church [281443].

Maps: Landranger 153. Pathfinder 1026.

Transport: Bus – occasional to Guilden Morden and to
Tadlow church.
Car – some parking at start.

Refreshments: Guilden Morden, Edward VII PH,
Three Tuns PH.

Points of interest:
Guilden Morden, church, Hooks Windmill (derelict).
Tadlow, church, moat at Moat farm. River Cam.

Guilden Morden

Start at Guilden Morden recreation ground **A**, which is
adjacent to the public house.

Walk beside the pavilion, and continue on the grass down the
north edge of the recreation ground to the back. Cross a stile
in the corner, and turn left on a clear path between fields to
the road **B**. Turn left along the road for 100 yards, passing in
front of a cemetery entrance on the right. Just beyond the
cemetery, a signpost indicates a path running north-west
with gardens on the left and an arable field on the right.
Follow this path through to another road, where turn right,
north, to a sharp bend. Here take the narrow road called
'Little Green' **C**.

Follow this minor road north-east past a scattering of houses,
and continue as it becomes a wide green track with a hedge
to the left. At a T-junction turn left, north, along a fine
hedged green lane, Cobbs Lane. This lane runs north for half
a mile to cross the River Cam at Tadlow Bridge **D**.

Follow the clear track beyond the bridge through thickets, to
emerge on a farm road, where you turn right. After 50 yards,
at a field corner where one branch of the track turns left, and
the other proceeds towards Tadlow Bridge Farm, turn half-
left across an arable field to a bridge halfway along the
opposite hedge. Cross this bridge, and continue diagonally

across the next field, to find a stile in front of an Anglian Water enclosure. Emerge onto the farm access road, and turn left into Tadlow's only street.

Tadlow

Part way along the street, look for a signpost on the left, between No. 43 and Littlecroft. This indicates a narrow passage to be followed between garden fences, and over a stile at the back. Emerging into an arable field, turn half-left diagonally across the field towards a stile at the back of a market garden. Do not cross the stile, but leave it on your left, and follow the marked path beside the fence. Where the route branches, take the right-hand branch, to continue half-right across the field towards a house by the B1042. A stile onto the road will be found in the field-corner **E**.

Cross the B1042 with care, and go up the drive almost opposite towards Moat House. Where the drive turns round to the left to enter the gardens, go straight on, just west of north, keeping the tall hedge to the left. When the hedge ends, continue across the arable field, where the line of the path should be marked. Climb the field, making for the line of trees ahead **F**. A gap should be waymarked at the trees, but if not, it is possible to pass through the line in several places. You are now on a pleasant mown bridleway, part of the Clopton Way long distance path. Turn left, and walk along the bridleway as far as the drive to New England Farm. Here turn left, along a field-edge path, running down the field to the corner. Go through the gap into the next field, and follow the trodden cross-field path towards Tadlow Church **G**.

Tadlow Church

After visiting the church, go down the drive, cross the B1042, and return down Tadlow street. Beyond the houses, a sign on the right, 'Public Bridleway, Guilden Morden 1 ¾' indicates a rutted track running with a hedge to the left. Follow this path south-west, shortly leaving the hedge to continue south-west as a farm track between arable fields. After half a mile, you approach the barns of Hooks Mill Farm. Take the track south towards the barns, then across a grass field to the derelict farmyard **H**. Follow the access track south-east, but where it turns east, instead turn right (south-west) with hedge on the

left, along a grassy track to a minor road where it crosses the River Cam.

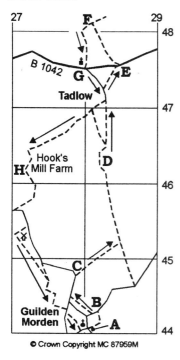

© Crown Copyright MC 87959M

Turn south down the road, towards Guilden Morden, but turn off right down the drive to Hooks Mill – the signpost here should point along the drive, which is a right of way, but often gets damaged or turned round. Where the drive runs into the farmyard, by the Old Windmill **I**, turn left through a gap in the hedge bordering the drive, and seek the cross-field path running generally south-east across arable fields towards Guilden Morden village. This path cuts off a couple of dangerous corners of the road. At the corner of an orchard, do not cross a stile leading into the orchard, but follow the path just south of east along the edge of the orchard, out over a bridge and stiles, through a grass field, and onto Dubs Knoll Road. Cross the road, turn right, go 50 yards, and turn left up a passage between a garden fence and adjacent drive (difficult to see, no signpost at time of writing). Cross a stile, enter a meadow, and walk forward towards the church. Emerge down the church drive. Turn left for 100 yards to the recreation ground and pub **A**.

5 Steeple Morden, Shingay, Croydon

a Steeple Morden, Croydon 12 miles / 19 km
b Steeple Morden, Abington Pigotts 5 miles / 8 km
c Abington Pigotts, Croydon 7 miles / 11 km

Start: Steeple Morden, Cambs., recreation ground car park [285426].
Maps: Landranger 153. Pathfinder 1026.
Transport: Car – parking at start.
Refreshments: Steeple Morden, Waggon and Horses PH. Croydon, Queen Adelaide PH.

Points of interest:

Steeple Morden, church, small Nature Reserve, wood behind recreation ground. Shingay, two new bridges over River Cam. Clopton, Old Village site, ridge and furrow ploughing, Knights Hospital site.
Abington Pigotts, church, Down Hall Farm medieval gateway.

Steeple Morden

From the recreation ground car park **A** in Steeple Morden, cross the recreation field onto Hay Street, and turn left (north). Beyond the last house on the right, opposite the driveway of a bungalow, turn right on a signed path by a tall hedge. Follow the path to the left of the hedge, and in 100 yards, pass through the hedge right, and follow the field boundary right, then left, resuming an east direction. On reaching the lane, turn left, and at the next junction fork right towards Bogs Gap, and follow the signposted bridleway as a track across open fields towards Abington Pigotts.

Ignore the first track on your left. In a further 40 yards, at Bibles Grove, the track veers right towards Down Hall, but continue ahead on a narrow, grassy field-edge path beside the belt of trees towards Abington Pigotts village, passing down the driveway of two cottages.

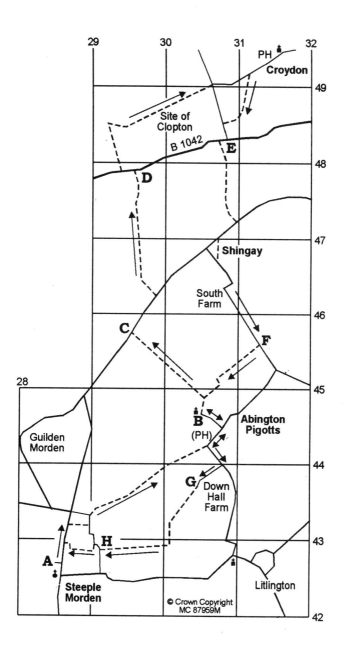

Abington Pigotts

At the road, turn left, and pass the Pig & Abbot PH; although closed during 1997, it is reported to be re-opening at the end of 1997. Take the next turn left to the church **B**. The road forks: you veer round to the right in front of the church and along a grass track between tall hedges. At the signpost, take a bridlepath, diverted 1986, left (north-west) along a field boundary, and follow the path round left, then right, bends to Flecks Lane Farm **C**.

Turn right along Flecks Lane towards Shingay. At the drive to Shingay Gate Farm, turn left by the footpath signpost, along the driveway towards farm buildings. At the buildings, follow the waymarks indicating a right of way north (half-right) across fields towards the River Cam, crossing a bridge over a wide ditch halfway. The high superstructure of the bridge over the Cam (built 1995) is the next point to aim for. Over the bridge, the path to the former Downing Arms on the B 1042 runs first half-right across the corner of a field, and then left up a grassy field-edge track to the road **D**.

Cross the road cautiously, and turn left to walk along the verge, to the drive to Top Farm. Turn right along the bridleway which follows the drive, and right again after about 600 yards on to the waymarked Clopton Way. Follow the path, a good grassy track with excellent views, generally east past the site of Clopton old village (now just a few grassy mounds), to the road at Croydon Hill. There is an interpretative board giving the history of the medieval settlement. Continue across the road and along the High Street into Croydon village, perhaps to visit the Queen Adelaide PH on the left.

Croydon

If not visiting the pub, take the first signed path on the right, running at first south diagonally across a field, over a small bridge and then waymarked around field boundaries right/left/right, to reach Larkins Road. Turn left and walk to the junction with the B1042 **E**. Turn right along the B1042 for 50 yards, and cross the road with care, to find a signposted, stiled, bridged and waymarked path leading through three grass fields. In the first field go forward

---

(south), and look for a stile and footbridge in the hedge ahead. Over this, turn half-right towards a gate and stile in the corner. Cross a farm-drive and immediately over another stile into the third field. Turn half-left aiming for the superstructure of another new bridge over the River Cam ahead. (Note the ridge and furrow in this field). Cross the bridge, and continue south across rough pasture to a small bridge and then two more stiles, to the roadside stile on Flecks Lane, Shingay. Moats and mounds in the adjacent field on the left mark the site of the medieval Knights Templar Hospital.

Turn right along the lane, passing the entrance to Manor Farm on the right. Just beyond the entrance to the drive, a signed, diagonal corner-cutting path on the left should lead to the minor road, with a few houses, at Shingay. (If this corner-cutting path is not reinstated, continue along the road and turn left by the dangerous road corner, signposted to Abington Pigotts.)

Shingay

Follow the road south-east, past the sharp bend at South Farm. After half a mile, take the signed footpath **F** along a farm track, running south-west towards Abington Pigotts. At the end of the track, continue forward into the corner of the field. Turn left, with hedge to right, for 100 yards, then right into a narrow track running through a band of woodland, ignoring crossing tracks. Follow the grassy track, to rejoin your earlier route, soon emerging onto the lane which will lead you back to the church in Abington Pigotts **B**.

Abington Pigotts

Return through the village, but now follow the road where it bends sharp left, and turn next right along the access drive to Down Hall Farm **G**. Admire the medieval gateway, and continue on a signposted path skirting right of the old mill. 200 yards beyond the mill, a signposted path (diverted 1987) crosses the stream on a farm culvert and follows a grass track south, along by a hedge, and then diagonally (waymarked) across a field to join a grass track, on which turn left. After 300 yards, at a junction, turn right (west) on a gravel farm track, back to Brook End, Steeple Morden **H**.

From here there are several possible routes back to the car park: a quiet road leads south. At the next junction, turn west back towards the church and the recreation ground. Alternatively, walk north along the road, and at a sharp bend right, look for a signposted path on the left, pointing up a drive to the right of a house, then over a stile to give access to a network of paths in grass fields, in the very centre of the village. This complex network is worthy of exploration, but is so dense as to be scarcely differentiated on the 1:25,000 scale. We suggest you cross the stile, turn right and follow the field-edge to the next corner. Cross a stile (right) and in 15 yards, turn left down a footpath between gardens, which leads back to the road. Turn left and return to the recreation ground **A**.

6 Ashwell, Dunton, Guilden Morden

13 miles / 21 kilometres

Start:	Ashwell, Herts., High Street **A** [268397].
Maps:	Landranger 153. Pathfinder 1026, 1049.
Transport:	Car – parking on-street.
Refreshments:	Ashwell, pubs, possibly a tea-shop.
	Dunton, March Hare PH.
	Guilden Morden, Hinxworth, pubs
	(diversion).

Points of interest:

The route visits three counties, starting from Ashwell in Hertfordshire, then to Dunton in Bedfordshire, and on to Guilden Morden in Cambridgeshire.

The walk is mainly on tracks – although the bridleways can be muddy in winter. There are excellent views from Newnham Hill, and of Royston Heath.

Ashwell

Walk down the High Street **A** towards the south-west in the direction of Baldock. The road swings left past Farrow's Farm, and then right. At the next road junction, initially take the Hinxworth Road (right fork) but almost immediately leave it by a track on the left (public bridleway sign). This track takes you up Newnham Hill, with a hedge on your left, to the giddy height of 84 metres/275 feet! The route gives excellent views to the north. Over the brow of the hill the track drops down to a hedge ahead **B**. Turn right, keeping to the field edge, with a hedge still on your left – horses can make this a real mess.

Hinxworth

The track leads down to Hinxworth Place; the path passes between a barn on your right and the house on your left. When you come to a cross-track, turn sharp right into a field (yellow waymark). The path skirts the trees/pond on your left and then strikes half-left diagonally across the field – this should be clear and reinstated through crops. Make for the large tree at the end of a hedge. Here turn right, following a grassy, tree-planted strip, between fields to the road. Cross the road and pick up the signposted track, the Ridge Way,

opposite. Follow this for almost 1½ miles. First there are open fields on both sides, then to your left and then to your right. Eventually the path leads between hedges on both sides to a cross-track – Green Lane **C**. Turn left. This route has a strip of woodland on its northern side – and there are routes through the trees, parallel to Green Lane, which can be followed if there is too much mud and water on the main track!

The route now uses Green Lane for a further 1½ miles. Keep a watch out for a couple of gentle swings in the lane; just after them, you should see a post, with a white marker nailed on. by the right-hand side of the track, with a path running north along a field edge, away from the lane. Follow this path, with a hedge on your left. In 400 yards you meet a track; keep going straight ahead, to and through Millowbury Farm, using the farm track. You can see Dunton church ahead.

Dunton

At the next cross-track follow the waymarked path ahead, across a field, using a row of telegraph poles as your guide. On the other side the route continues up towards Dunton, alongside a hedge on your right. At the field end follow the waymark; the route skirts the field first left, keeping the wire fence on your right, then right, passing between house gardens into the village. Turn left and pass the church, emerging onto the main road. Turn right and cross to the safety of a footpath on the other side (unless going into the pub!). Continue along the Cambridge Road through the village. On the other side look out for a 'public bridleway' sign pointing right down a track **D**. Take it and follow it for almost two miles. The route first runs slightly south of east. It passes a small wooded nature reserve – keep on the track to the left of the copse; the route has been officially diverted from the cross-field bridleway shown on older maps. Eventually the track swings sharp left; follow it north to the road, east of Eyeworth Lodge Farm. At the road turn right. In 300 yards the road swings right, over a small bridge. Just beyond look out for a public footpath sign on your left, showing the way across fields beyond, **E**.

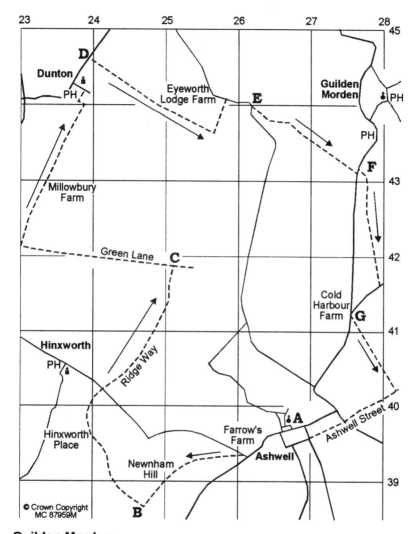

Guilden Morden

The route crosses the first field diagonally (half-right), leading to a new wooden bridge. Cross it, and pick up another diagonal cross-field path beyond. This leads to a hardcore track, which you follow south east. To your left you should see the spire of Guilden Morden church. Where the track swings sharp left you should keep ahead along a grassy strip between open fields, with a hedge and public footpath sign

---

ahead. This leads to a green lane; if you turn left, you can go into the village and seek out refreshment. But our route crosses the lane, picking up a field edge path, with a hedge on your left, to the houses on the road beyond. Follow the path round to the road. here turn left, cross and, just beyond a cottage **F**, turn right onto a public footpath which leads to another field edge path behind some cottages. Follow the waymarked path behind two small rows of cottages on your right to the last cottage garden – then strike almost due south across the fields ahead. The path should be clearly reinstated; in the middle distance ahead is a line of telegraph poles as a guide. After half a mile, you cross a field edge and continue over another field for a further 400 yards. At the next field edge you come to a hedge; follow the grassy path south, with a hedge initially on your left. This leads to a road. Turn right and walk to the next junction, opposite the driveway to Cold Harbour Farm **G**.

The route now follows a byway (no signpost) to your left for 1,200 yards. This broad track runs roughly south-east. When you get to a cross-track you have reached the ancient Ashwell Street – look out for more modern Herts CC boundary stones. Turn right and follow the track into Ashwell. At the first cross lane, go straight over. At the second lane, turn right and walk downhill – watch out for traffic as there is no pavement initially. This brings you back down to the High Street **A**, with pubs on both right and left!

7 Ashwell, Guilden Morden, Steeple Morden

9 miles / 14.5 kilometres

Start: Ashwell, Herts., church **A** [267398].
Maps: Landranger 153 (not recommended).
Pathfinder 1026, (1049).
Transport: Car – parking in residential roads near church.
Refreshments: Ashwell, several pubs and café.
Guilden Morden, Edward VII PH,
Three Tuns PH.
Steeple Morden, Waggon & Horses.

Points of interest:
Churches and thatched cottages in all 3 villages. Ashwell, museum.

Ashwell

From Ashwell churchyard **A,** emerge at the gate to the west of the tower, and turn right to walk north along the residential road towards the River Rhee. Cross the river and continue along the road until it bends right. Take the signed footpath, pointing forward through a kissing gate into a grassy field. Walk up the edge of the field, with a fence and tall trees on the left. Emerge through a kissing gate, cross the road and take the signposted right of way, continuing in the same direction (north-north-east) across the arable field to the County boundary **B**.

Cross the County boundary ditch by a 2-plank bridge, and continue in the same direction towards the buildings of Cold Harbour Farm, along a crop-boundary. Cross the drive to the farm, and take a waymarked path to the right of a farm cottage, through paddocks, over stiles to the right (east) of the farm. Emerge over another stile into an arable field, and cross the field to the signpost on Ashwell Road. Turn right (due south) on the road for 300 yards. At the road junction, turn left along the road towards Steeple Morden. Continue along this road for 500 yards, passing a Farm Shop on the right, to a signpost on the left **C**. Take the path running approximately north for nearly a mile towards Guilden

Morden. Initially this path is on a grassy headland, with hedge on right, but subsequently it continues in the same direction across large arable fields.

Guilden Morden

The path passes behind cottage gardens on the outskirts of Guilden Morden, and reaches the road. At the road, turn left, away from Guilden Morden for 50 yards, and pick up a signposted path on the other side of the road, running north-west as a grassy track zig-zagging round field boundaries. At the intersection with a bridleway (Silver Street), turn right and walk up this attractive, grassy lane between tall hedges, into Guilden Morden, passing the Three Tuns pub on the left. Cross the road and continue forward north-east down a lane opposite. After about 300 yards, on reaching an open space, follow the track as it bends left, to pick up a residential road leading to Guilden Morden church **D**.

In front of the church, turn right at T-junction to visit the Edward VII pub on the opposite side of the road in a few yards. If not stopping, walk in front of the pub, and south-east down Trap Road. On the right, ignore a narrow, signed footpath between trimmed hedges, leading back towards the church, but look for a second signed footpath on the right after 300 yards. Take this footpath through a rough gap in the hedge, to continue south-west along a grassy headland with trees on the right. On reaching a crossing byway (Theobalds Lane), turn left and follow it back to the road. Just short of the road, turn right along a field-boundary with stream on left. Descend to a low-level bridge to cross the stream, and continue south for another 100 yards. (For the Recreation Ground, Nature Reserve, seats and toilet, continue by the stream). Look out for, and take a grassy trod running east across the fields, to emerge between high fences onto Hay Street in Steeple Morden.

Steeple Morden

Turn left (north) for 75 yards along Hay Street, and take the signposted path on the right. A well-used, grassy headland path zig-zags east, south, east, south, following the outside of gardens and paddocks. Over a stile, enter a fenced pasture, which cross to a stile and signpost in the south-west corner,

---

to emerge on Cheyney Street, Steeple Morden. Turn left along Cheyney Street for 75 yards, and look for a surfaced path (Black Lane), which follow round bends to Morden Green. Continue straight on through the hamlet, and on the grassy footpath south towards Lower Gatley End.

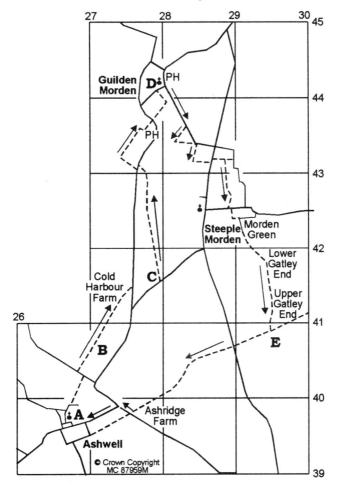

Approaching Lower Gatley End, after about 300 yards, watch out for the path entering some attractive woodland. Follow the waymarked path through the woodland, and straight ahead through the paddocks of Lower Gatley End. (Ignore confusing waymarking directing one right, off the right of

way.) The route crosses stiles and the track to Lower Gatley End, and continues south across fields, veering towards the fence on the left, and crossing a stile to continue along a grassy headland, reaching Ashwell Street **E** at Upper Gatley End.

Turn right along Ashwell Street (here a tarmac road). Cross the road to Steeple Morden by High Farm, and continue on Ashwell Street (now an unsurfaced track), back towards Ashwell. Beyond the caravan site at Ashridge Farm on the outskirts of Ashwell, turn right towards the War Memorial, and then left with playing fields on the right, towards Ashwell. Visit the spring at the Ash Well, which is the source of the River Rhee, and follow the main street back towards the church, turning right by the shops and into Ashwell churchyard **A**.

8 Sandon, Clothall, Cottered
13 miles / 21 kilometres

Start: Sandon, Herts., The Chequers PH **A** [318342].

Maps: Landranger (153), 166. Pathfinder 1049, 1073.

Transport: Car – parking in lay-by south of pub.

Refreshments: Sandon, The Chequers PH. Cottered, The Bull PH.

Points of interest:

The walk starts along the waymarked Icknield Way as far as Wallington, then follows good paths to Clothall, a byway to Luffenhall, more good paths to Cottered and back to Sandon.

There are excellent views across pleasant undulating country.

Sandon

From The Chequers pub **A**, make your way 100 yards down the road south. The Icknield Way is signposted right, over a stile into a grassy field. Follow the waymarked route through fields and over stiles. It takes you first west, half left, then south-west through two fields, over a drive and through two more fields to the open space at Roe Green. At the road turn right, then almost immediately left down a track. You should see the waymarked Icknield Way sign on your right. It crosses a stream and passes between two garages. Cross a stile and over the field ahead, bearing right to another stile in the corner. Cross it and turn right, picking up a good headland path, with a hedge on your right. Follow this path for about three-quarters of a mile, keeping straight ahead when the hedge ends. The path becomes a lane and reaches the road at Redhill **B**.

Turn left, cross the lane and almost immediately take the signposted cross field path on the right. Cross the field and ditch, picking up a path ahead (hedge on right) which leads up a gentle rise. At the next path junction leave the Icknield Way; instead turn right (north) along a headland, now with a hedge on your left. There are good views to your right. In 300 yards you join a lane, still walking north. When the lane turns sharp left, keep straight on, following a waymarked

---

bridleway. The main track soon swings left, but the bridleway goes ahead, with the gardens of Wallington houses passed on your left.

Wallington

After 400 yards you reach cross tracks. Turn left for 100 yards, soon reaching an asphalt lane. Turn left up the hill. Just before the first cottage on your right, take the signposted footpath, right. Now pick up a footpath which skirts the north of Wallington village. Ignore all tempting stiles on your left, and one path on your right. In 500 yards you come to another lane. Cross it and pick up the Icknield Way again!

Follow this bridleway south past the church on your left, bearing right to pick up a track which can become very muddy. At a signpost follow the 'Wallington Common' route ahead. The track bears left, then right behind a hedge. Three hundred yards past this turn look out for a low waymark, indicating a footpath on your right. You pick up a good grassy headland, with a hedge on your right. Follow this for about 700 yards, to reach a wood. Cross the narrow plank bridge into the wood. The route through is well waymarked. Once out of the wood keep straight ahead, passing Clothall Bury buildings on your left. Follow the track to the A507 **C**.

Clothall

Cross the road, picking up the footpath opposite, across a field to a stile and paddock beyond. Cross the paddock to a gate; there is a gap on its right leading into a lane by stables. Pick up the track ahead – first hard surfaced, then soft, past a thatched cottage on your right. In 400 yards this meets a lane; turn left. This can be rutted and muddy, but it is usually possible to find a dry route alongside. As you progress the condition improves. Follow this green lane, signposted Cromer at one point, for just over 2 miles. About 400 yards beyond a substantial bridge over a stream look out for a cross track; turn left between fields. At the fenced field ahead turn right, down into the hamlet of Luffenhall **D**.

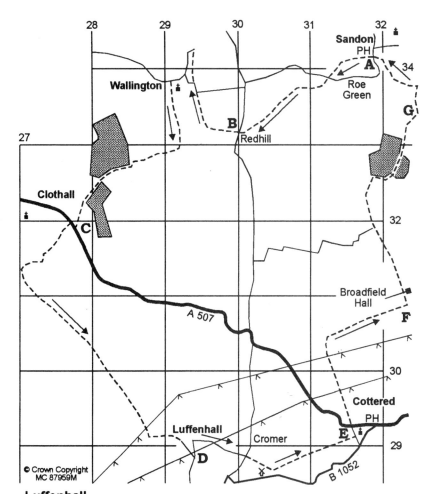

Luffenhall

At the lane turn left, then right, signposted Rushden. Follow
this lane to a T-junction. Go straight over, up a narrow path.
Take a look at the fine post-mill to your right. Keep ahead,
ignoring the track to the mill, and, just before you reach a
road, turn left onto a grass track. There is a 'No Horses' sign
on this footpath. With a wire fence initially on your right,
then a track across open fields, admire the views on your left.
You can also see the spire of Cottered church ahead. When
you meet a path, turn left, soon crossing narrow steps by a
small stream.

Cottered

This path takes you to a lane in the village, opposite the church **E**. Turn left and soon cross the busy A 507 again, picking up a bridleway opposite, signposted Rushden 1¼ miles. The Bull PH is 500 yards right along the main road. Follow the track past the sewage works, turning into an excellent grassy track. Go under one set of power lines, cross a stream just before the second set of pylons and follow the route under the pylons, continuing right up the field ahead. At the field edge turn right, keeping a hedge on your left. Just by a belt of trees turn right again, going slightly downhill, the hedge now on your right. Cross a very narrow field, then a ditch. Follow the track waymarked with black arrows half left, up the rise ahead. In half a mile you come to a track by Broadfield Hall **F**.

Turn left onto it. Follow the track north, first past Lodge Farm, then through Broadfield Lodge Farm. The track becomes a tarmac lane. At the next road junction keep ahead (signposted Wood Farm only). When the lane swings right, keep straight on between high hedges. Ignore the public footpath signposted half left; instead cross over to the wood ahead and turn right. Follow the bridleway which runs first outside the wood, then just inside it. Before you reach the barn turn left, keeping the wood on your left. The path enters the wood a second time, now turning north (Friars Lane on the map). It can be muddy but there are escape routes to avoid the worst problems! The lane leaves the wood after 250 yards and runs along a field edge to Beckfield Farm, passing it on the west/north. Turn left into the lane beyond the farm, **G**.

100 yards further on look out for a path on your left, following a field edge path with a hedge on your right. Follow the field edge round, down the slope, till you come to a gate on your right to Blagrove Common Nature Reserve. Go through the gate, then turn left, crossing a bridge and a stile. Turn left onto the field edge path beyond the stile. Follow the field edge, turning right after 300 yards, and right again at the next corner. 15 yards beyond, cross the bridge and stile on your left. Cross two fields, keeping a red brick cottage on your left, back down to Sandon and your starting point **A**.

9 Buntingford, Cottered, Buckland, Wyddial
14 miles / 22.5 kilometres

Start: Buntingford, Herts., town car park **A** on west of High Street [362297].

Maps: Landranger 154,166. Pathfinder 1049,1073.

Transport: Car – park at start (no vehicle entry from High Street – look for signs).

Refreshments: Buntingford, various. Cottered, The Bull PH.

Points of interest:
Ancient green lanes and good tracks. Excellent views. Historic churches.

Buntingford

From the car park **A**, pick up the tarmac footpath running east/west on the northern boundary, next to the toilets. Go west – and cross the road ahead to pick up another footpath opposite (playing field to your right). At the next road turn left, cross and in 50 yards turn right down a private road (signed 'The Folly'). Turn left with the private road in front of a terrace of cottages. Pass new houses and pick up an alleyway at the end of the tarmac. Cross the next road, continuing along the alley and enter the field ahead. The path crosses the field in the same direction, south-west, to cross stiles and a footbridge over the Buntingford bypass.

Once over the bridge continue south-west through the field to a stile in a hedge. Cross this into a grassy field. Follow the fence on your right downhill to the bottom corner. Cross the stiles/bridge ahead. In the next field carry on ahead, with fence on your right, to a wooden kissing gate. There are fine views of Aspenden Hall on your right.

Aspenden Church

Go through the gate into the churchyard **B**. Follow the path as it goes to the left of the church – emerging onto the lane beyond. Here you turn left (not into the Tudor Stud on your right). At the bottom of the lane turn right – signposted

Public Bridleway and Tannis Court. After 400 yards the track swings to the right – and in a further 100 yards swings left. Follow the track – ignoring the inviting green lane ahead! You keep on the track for 1,000 yards or so. Before you get to the Tannis Court buildings keep a look out for a wooden waymark post near a field edge on your right. Leave the track here and pick up a field edge path (hedge on your left). You are now walking north-west. The route is waymarked, first over a bridge crossing a ditch on your left, then right, initially with the hedge on your right, then across an open field. If this last part hasn't been reinstated it may be easier to walk round the field edge!

On the other side continue along a field edge path, again with a hedge on your right. Just before the next field corner take a waymarked path half left, leading diagonally across to a bridge. Cross it – and cross the track you immediately meet on the other side. Your route continues along the grassy track directly opposite, with a hedge on your right once more. In about 200 yards you should see a ground level wooden bridge through the hedge on your right. Cross it into the next field – then turn half left and make your way diagonally through the new copse of trees and grassland. Some mature trees to your left mark the site of an ancient moat.

Continue past the moat in a north-west direction and go through the bushes in the field corner. Cross another wooden bridge over a ditch. Again pick up a cross field path – if not reinstated, turn one-quarter left and cross. On the other side the path continues between a fence on your left and a hedge. Continue to the tarmac lane ahead (Rumbolds Cottage on your left).

Turn right and continue, picking up a green lane to the right of a cottage called 'The Place'. Cross a stream (in winter anyway!) and you soon come to a signpost groaning with fingerposts! Don't go into the field ahead, but instead take the green lane to your right. This swings to the left. Ignore paths/stiles off it. It continues as a sunken lane, eventually joining a gravel drive. Turn left down the drive, then carry on straight ahead along a 'Public Byway' to the main road C.

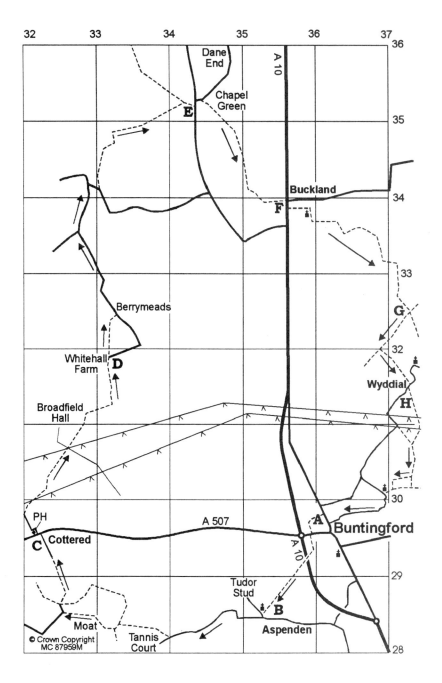

32 33 34 35 36 37

Dane End

Chapel Green

E

Buckland

F

A 10

Berrymeads

G

Whitehall Farm **D**

Wyddial

H

Broadfield Hall

PH

A 507

A Buntingford

C Cottered

A 10

Tudor Stud

B

Moat

Aspenden

Tannis Court

© Crown Copyright
MC 87959M

36

35

34

33

32

30

29

28

Cottered

Turn left at the road as far as the Bull pub. Turn right down Bull Lane which passes in front of the pub. You soon pass a signpost to Broadfield Hall (1¼ miles). The lane swings right, then left round a field and down a gentle slope. The track enters a large field.

Turn right – but in 20 yards turn half left to follow a grassy track diagonally across the field, climbing slowly uphill and under a power line. Continue beyond the pylons with a hedge on your right.

At the hedge beyond, follow a path through it, crossing a low wooden bridge. On the other side of this mature hedge turn left and follow a field edge path (hedge on your left). Follow the field edge round – turning right at the field corner. At the next corner you should come to a substantial wooden bridge. Cross it, picking up a field edge path ahead (hedge now on your right). When you meet a gravel cross track you want to go over it, through a wooden gate into a grassy field. Cross the field and through the gate ahead. You pass quite close to Broadfield Hall on your left. Once through this second gate your path continues through what is in summer grassland, but is at other times of the year very muddy. It should be obvious, passing in a generally north-east direction past ponds/trees on your left. You are making for the right hand corner of Great Wood. When you get to the field corner turn right though the hedge. Carry on straight ahead, north-west, on a cross field path through crops, parallel to a line of pylons on your right.

When you reach the corner of the wood ahead, turn left and follow a field edge path down to the next corner. Here turn left for just 10 yards – then right to pick up another field edge path with a ditch on your left. This takes you to Whitehall Farm. Just before the farm the right of way swings right to pick up a track into the farmyard **D**.

Once in the farmyard turn left, and look for a wooden signpost just behind an open tractor shed. Turn right by the signpost and go over a stile (or through the gate alongside) into a field of pasture. Turn half right, to look for a stile in the hedge opposite. Cross the stile – then the field ahead and

another stile. The waymarked route now turns slightly to the right, aiming for the end of the hedgerow. You should find another stile in the hedgerow. Cross it, and now pick up a field edge path with a hedge on your left. Follow the hedge round to the road.

At the road turn left, passing Berrymeads. Continue along a quiet lane through the settlements of Mill End and Green End. After about one mile, at Rockell's Jersey Farm, there is the option of joining a footpath which continues parallel with the lane (on the west). Follow a signposted route on the left of the road. The path crosses a field, stile and then crosses a second field back to the lane. Or you can just keep on the lane as it forks right past the Farm (ignore Beckfield Lane which branches left).

At the next road junction turn right (signposted Buckland 2). In 50 yards turn left up a drive (Icknield Way). Before you get to the house look out for a green lane forking right, signposted Notley Lane. Take this fork and proceed along a pleasant green lane between hedges. In half a mile you come to a junction of tracks. You should turn right (waymarked post 'Chapel Green') into another attractive green lane. Follow this for a good half mile, until you reach a T-junction of tracks.

Turn right – signposted Chapel Green once more – until you see a white house. Your path goes to the left of this cottage, The Retreat, to the road E. On joining the road turn left, then almost immediately right (Dane End). Look out for a high stile in the hedgerow on your right, just past the junction. Cross the stile into a grassy field; your route keeps to the left side of the field, over to a stile and bridge ahead. Cross these and turn right – but just as far as the field corner. Here turn left and proceed up a gentle hill (hedge on your right). You should find a waymark post near the top. Turn right onto the track which immediately swings left. Continue on the track, first with a wood on your left, then open fields. Follow the track as far as the main road in Buckland. The last few yards go through the middle of an HGV yard!

Buckland

At the busy A10 **F** turn right for 60 yards. Then cross the road to turn left down a lane signposted 'Wyddial 2 miles'. The track is initially tarmac, then grass as it continues into the churchyard. Pass the church by on your right and look out for a grassy lane on the other side of the churchyard. Turn right into the lane – now part of Daws Lane Common.

Turn left at the field corner along Daws Lane – a pleasant track between hedges. At the next T-junction of tracks turn right, now another broad grassy lane. When you come into an open field you should turn left, following a field edge path gently uphill (ditch on your left). This may be ploughed and difficult going. Continue until you meet a cross track. Here turn right, first downhill, straight over at the bottom of the 'dip' and up the track ahead.

Once you have climbed the gentle rise ahead you should see a solitary gate just to the left of your path. Turn left here along a fence for 200 yards (keep it on your right). At the end of the fence – and before the hedgerow bushes – turn right to pick up a reinstated cross-field path. This usually follows a diagonal line to meet up with a hard track **G,** not the exact line shown on the Pathfinder map.

Turn right onto the track – first between open fields, then picking up a hedge on your left. After half a mile look out for a track on your left and turn onto this. It takes you into Wyddial.

Wyddial

At the road junction **H** in the village turn right, then take the next lane on the left (No Through Road). Continue along the lane, passing under power lines. The surface is tarmac as far as the last house, then earth. You should follow first a Public Bridleway sign, then a signpost to Buntingford, where the path goes straight ahead, even if the wonky signpost points left! The path narrows before coming to more open fields. Here it is obvious that people walk either side of a field edge hedge but the right of way stays on the right of it – at least initially!

You will soon notice a number of waymarks – but they do soon guide you to a route on the left of the hedge. When you come to a grassy cross track (with wooden post but no waymarks!) turn right towards a now-derelict church. The track swings to the left and then right, passing to the left of the churchyard. Just past an agricultural building on your right you come to a junction of tarmac lanes. Go straight ahead.

The lane swings left, then right down into Buntingford, marked as The Causeway on the Pathfinder map. At a road junction marked with a 'Ford' sign take the left fork (avoiding the ford!). This takes you over a bridge. Continue down the 'no entry' road ahead, passing the Fox & Duck pub on your right. At the junction with the High Street, cross and turn almost immediately left, under an arch with clock tower and weather vane. This brings you back into the car park **A**.

10 Therfield, Sandon

a 8 miles / 13 kilometres
b extended 9 miles / 15 kilometres
c Therfield, Kelshall 3½ miles / 6 kilometres
d Sandon, Woodcotes 4½ miles / 7 kilometres

Start: Therfield, Herts., Fox & Duck PH **A**
[336372].

Maps: Landranger 153, 154, 166.
Pathfinder 1049.

Transport: Car – parking on roadside.

Refreshments: Therfield, Fox & Duck PH.
Sandon, The Chequers PH.

Points of interest:

Varied terrain allows some panoramic views. The lie of the land and the
nature of the soil make for poor drainage and muddy paths in places. The
Icknield Way Path uses some of the same paths – at L there is a map on a
post.

a via Sandon and Kelshall 8 miles / 13 km

Therfield

From the Fox and Duck PH **A**, turn left to take the road
signposted to Reed and Buckland. After 100 yards, turn right
between hedges by power poles and go over a stile into a
field. Follow the edge of a field with a hedge on your left, then
a line of trees and go over a stile to the left of a gate. Bear
half-right across the next field, over a stile, go diagonally
across the next field to the middle of the long side, go over a
stile into a lane, and turn right.

After half a mile **B**, turn right onto a farm track by a signpost,
and follow it round a right-hand corner. At a junction by a
wood, turn left. Continue in the same general direction for
three-quarters of a mile, signed 'Woodcotes' near end. Where
the mud is impassable, use the edge of the fields on the left.
At the road **C** turn left; where the road turns right, continue
ahead into Park Lane, a track through a narrow wood which
is part of the Icknield Way Path. Where this is muddy, use
the edge of the field on the left, and later look for a footpath
to the right of the stream.

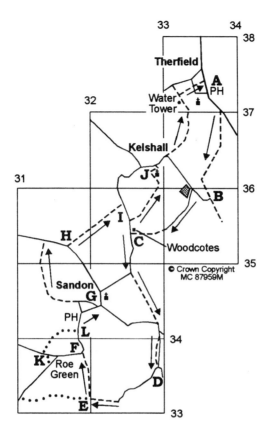

At the road turn left; continue straight ahead at the junction for 100 yards, then go through a gap in the right-hand hedge and to your left across the field to a stile. Cross this, and walk across the meadow, towards the left-hand side of the house. Cross the fence at a stile and cross the lawn to leave the garden by the gate. Turn right on the road, and take the right turn **D** into Beckfield Lane.

Look out for traffic as you walk up the road; where it levels out continue on a track past a farmyard. Where it bends left, just past a hedge on the right turn into a field. Go straight across toward a bend in the hedge on your right, then follow it to a waymark post **E** after 400 yards.

Turn right through the gap in the hedge, straight across the field and to the right of a hedge, then turn left for 5 yards to

reach a stile. Cross this into a meadow; keep to the right-hand side, then go over a stile to the right of a gate. At the road **F** turn right. At **L** there is a map of the Sandon part of the Icknield Way Path on a post. After passing The Chequers PH on the left, at a junction follow the through road to the right to reach the village green **G**, with the church ahead.

Sandon

Turn left over the green and follow the road; where it turns left, carry straight on up along Drift Way. Where the surface is too muddy, use the edge of the field on the right. At the road, turn right; at the top of the hill, just past the house named Gannock Thatch on the right, turn left over a stile **H** to the right of a gate.

Go ahead over grassland planted with trees and climb over a stile beside a pond to go over a stile to the right of a gate. Cross the field, heading 50 yards left of a large tree to a gap in the hedge. In the next field, continue towards Kelsall church ahead and, 20 yards right of a power pole, exit to the road.

Turn right, and at the top of the rise **I** turn left over a plank bridge next to a barn; go diagonally across the field to go over a stile. In the next field go slightly to the left of your previous course to the corner of a fenced enclosure. At the corner follow the fence to the left, crossing over it at a stile, to leave the field by a gate, cross the roadway, and enter the churchyard **J**.

Kelshall

Go to the right rear corner of the churchyard and down a passage. At the road turn left, then right, and at the junction keep straight ahead towards Kelshall. Where the road bears right, turn left into a field. The right-of-way runs parallel to, and 20 yards from, the fence on your right; if the path is not clear, follow this general direction until you come to a mid-field crossing path between two waymark posts, which you turn left onto.

Cross into the next field at a culvert; take the left-hand path, or if it is not clear, head between the water tower and the church towards a waymark post. Continue in the next field,

parallel to the line of the power cables on your left. Turn half-right onto a track, and, at a junction, left towards the water tower. To your right, behind the hedge, is the motte and bailey of a mediaeval castle; you may glimpse the outer ditch.

Look on the right for stiles – ignore the first, and cross one just before you reach the tower. Pass a magnificent thatched house on your left to go over a stile in the corner of the field along a passage to a road; cross it to go over a stile in the hedge, and straight across the field. The 'lumps and bumps' here indicate a mediaeval fortified village; the iron basket on a pole is a beacon, erected in 1988 for the commemoration of the 400th anniversary of the Spanish Armada. Go over the stile to the right of the gate, and turn right to return to the village green **A**.

b – extended version 9 miles / 15 kilometres

At **E**, continue straight ahead, and walk with hedges and ditches on your right for another half-a-mile to reach a road. Turn right, walk to Roe Green and turn left in front of the cricket pavilion. Cross the road ahead to find a footpath **K** which bears right over a series of stiles through fields, often with friendly horses, reaching the road at **L**. The route between **K** and **L** is part of the Icknield Way Path.

c – Therfield, Kelshall 3½ miles / 6 kilometres

At the road by Woodcotes **C**, turn right, and after 100 yards turn right onto the path at **I** to join the return route.

d – Sandon, Woodcotes 4½ miles / 7 kilometres

Start at the village green **G** and follow the return part of the route above via **H** to **I**, continuing on the road to join the outward leg above at **C**.

11 Royston, Therfield
7 miles / 11 kilometres

Start: Royston, Herts., Briary Lane off Baldock Road **A** [352402].

Maps: Landranger 153, 154.
Pathfinder (1029), 1049.

Transport: Car – parking at heath end of Briary Lane.

Refreshments: Royston, pubs. Therfield, Fox & Duck PH.

Points of interest:
Royston and Therfield Heaths. Rare pasque flowers in spring. Good tracks and views.

Royston

Cross Briary Lane **A** onto the open heath. There are lots of paths through the grass: go uphill half-left, making for a large tree by a hedge corner. At the tree turn left and follow a path which skirts the heath, with small trees on your left. Paths fork to left and right – but keep going uphill as far as you can. Eventually you will come to a metal 'squeeze' stile. Don't go through, but turn right, initially alongside a fence on your left. The route round the heath now passes in and out of beech woods and skirts the golf course, which should at all times be kept on your right!

At a T-junction of footpaths, turn left, gently uphill – avoid a tree branch across the path on your right. You soon pass a bench on your left. Ignore paths leading off to the right. At the next T-junction, again keep left, climbing earthen steps. You soon emerge from the trees. Go along the edge of the golf course. At the fence corner turn left onto a track provided for golf carts. Skirt the valley head on your right. The path next passes between trees to reach a lane **B**. Cross the lane and go through the 'squeeze' stile ahead, onto a permissive path through a nature reserve (Therfield Heath). Follow the main path, which can be muddy, through a stand of large beech trees, where the route swings left and gently downhill to the open heath on your right. Follow the path along the spur of a ridge. The path is marked by wooden posts – keep between them. At the prow of the ridge the path swings right, down to a squeeze stile by a track. Go through the stile and turn

right. Pass a tree belt on your left and **then** turn left – don't
go along the track on your left. Your route keeps to the
common land on the edge of the open heath itself, with a
hedge on your left. Now – away from the golfcourse – the
heath is used for exercising racehorses and you can see
considerable evidence of this activity!

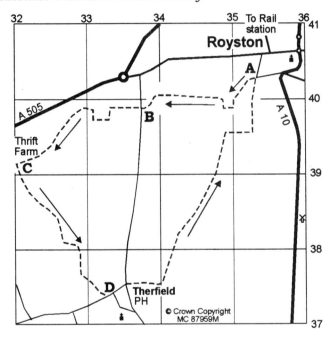

Continue along the heath until you see Thrift Farm ahead on
your left. When you reach the farm drive **C**, turn left along it
and into the farmyard. Continue on the muddy track beyond
– usually passing pigs in the fields on your right. You have a
fence on your left. When the track swings left, you keep
ahead on a field-edge path (hedge on your left). At the field
corner your route involves a turn half right, following a cross-
field path to a hedge ahead. There is a sign warning of a firing
range ahead. The path now passes between the range on
your right in an old chalk pit and a hedge on your left, and
soon continues as a grassy field edge track. The track proper
then turns left and your waymarked route follows between
open fields half-right. On the other side of the field you pick

---

up a signposted track with a hedge on your right, which turns into a green lane as it climbs towards Therfield.

Therfield

At the lane **D**, turn left. Alternatively, to explore the village turn right and then left onto a footpath which leads past the water tower to the church and then left to the pub. At the road turn left again, and look out for Mill Lane on the right.

If you don't want to explore the village, keep ahead and don't turn into Pedlars Lane which you pass on your right. When you meet the main road cross straight over into Mill Lane.

Mill Lane is initially tarmac, then earth. Look out for a signposted bridleway at a left fork of tracks; take it and follow it as it swings left and downhill. Ignore other paths and tracks to both left and right. Eventually the lane becomes less steep and the surface improves. For much of the way it is a very pleasant grass lane. There are some waymarks but they may be rather faded!

After about a mile and a quarter the path begins to climb gently once more. As it flattens out a public footpath is signposted to the left; ignore this and, instead, turn right along a broad grassy track. At the corner turn left with the track, again climbing uphill. Ignore the next track on your right and keep ahead, passing a covered reservoir. This lane is the extension of Briary Way and continuing ahead you soon return to your parking place **A** near the junction with Sun Hill.

12 Royston, Barkway, Nuthampstead, Barley

13 miles / 21 kilometres

Start:	Royston, Herts., car park by bus station [358404].
Maps:	Landranger 154. Pathfinder [1026], 1049, 1050.
Transport:	Buses and trains – from Cambridge. Car – parking by bus station.
Refreshments:	Royston, pubs; Reed, The Cabinet PH. Nuthampstead, The Woodman PH. Barkway, Tally-Ho PH. Barley, Fox & Hounds PH.

Points of interest:

Good views over surrounding countryside.
Nuthampstead, World War II airfield. Horse paddocks. Cokenach estate.

Royston

From the car park **A** walk downhill past the bus station and turn right into Barkway Road. Walk up Barkway Road until you see Beldam Avenue on your right; turn into it and and cross over to turn left into Grange Bottom. Continue to the end of the houses and pick up a bridleway (signed). This climbs gently uphill. At the brow of the hill cross over a track and pick up a usually-grassy downhill track, with sparse trees and bushes on your right. At the next path junction (field corner) keep straight ahead. The path skirts to the left of a farm and paddock beyond. Turn right at the paddock corner, then, by a gate, turn left. There is a fairly well-defined track uphill to the field boundary ahead.

Keep on the track south past the hedges, aiming for a gate on the other side of the field. Go through the gate, cross over a grassy track and go through the hedge ahead. You now pick up a field edge path which can be muddy. Keep straight ahead when you join a track – soon passing a large house on your right. Your route next passes a large 'agro-business' on your left. Just past the yard turn left, off the concrete track and onto a field edge path, with a hedge on your right. This

climbs uphill to the road. In wet weather parts can be very slippery.

At the road **B** turn left. In 100 yards turn onto the signposted footpath on your right. This path takes you to the edge of Reed. Cross a stile and at the road junction beyond keep straight ahead (High Street). You soon pass The Cabinet pub on your right.

Reed

When the road swings to the right keep ahead on a track. Almost immediately you pass a house on your left – Kesten. Next to it look out for a byway on your left; turn into it. Initially it may be muddy – but it soon improves. Cross over the first cross-track and continue on a grass track (ditch on your left). Your route next passes a wood on your right, before continuing as a cross-field path to the next wood; this you also pass by, keeping it on your right.

Barkway

Beyond the wood continue on a grassy track (still in an easterly direction). You eventually come to the edge of Barkway and a road junction **C**. Go straight ahead until you come to a T-junction – Cambridge Road. Cross over and turn right for about 120 yards. Then turn left on a path signposted 'Nuthampstead 1½ miles'. This path starts as a broad green lane between mature trees and hedges, before turning into a cross-field path which leads to the right-hand edge of a conifer belt ahead which it skirts on a left-hand bend, leading to a cross-track. Turn right onto it. Go straight over the next cross-track and continue ahead towards woodland.

The open parkland on your left is part of the Cokenach Estate. Pass a second woodland on your left. At the next waymark post don't turn right, but keep straight ahead. You should be on a grass field edge path, with a ditch and trees on your left. Waymarks direct you over a couple of wooden bridges, so that the ditch is now on your right. The route then crosses a stile by a tree belt – with a second stile soon following. Ignore a waymarked cross-field path and substantial wooden bridge on your right, and continue along the ditch/field edge instead. The path climbs gently uphill to

a copse. At the waymark post turn right – with the copse on
your left. At a sharp corner turn left, **through** the narrow tree
belt. On the other side immediately turn right, so the tree
belt is now on your right, and an open field on your left.
Cross the stile in the field corner and, in 25 yards, cross a
second stile and bridge over a ditch on your right. Turn left
onto a field edge path and continue to the road **D**.

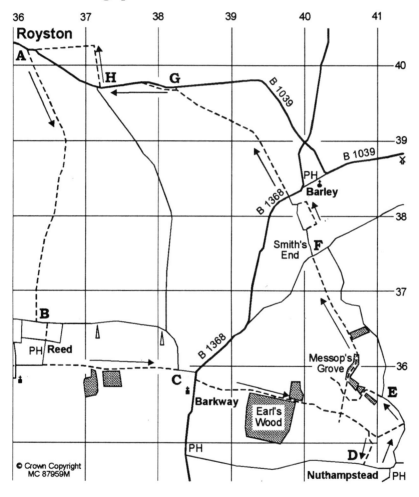

Nuthampstead

At the road turn left and continue to the road junction. If you want refreshment, turn right here and call in at The Woodman pub; otherwise keep left. Ignore the 'No Through Road' fork in 50 yards; instead keep left. Follow this country lane for around 1,000 yards. When the road takes a sharp right turn **E** keep left, picking up a signposted bridleway on a concrete track. Keep on this track for about 600 yards, passing a copse on your right and crossing open fields. Just after the track has crossed a ditch you should take a cross field path signposted on your right. This leads towards the edge of woodland. The path enters the wood, Messop's Grove, and continues through a narrow belt of trees. At the northern boundary turn half left and look out for a cross field grassy track which soon passes to the left of a small wood. Beyond the wood, cross a track and continue in the same direction (north-west). The path is usually reinstated across the field.

At a clump of trees pick up a field edge path with a hedge on your right, and continue to another cross-track. Go straight over to pick up another field edge path, although initially there is a newly planted copse on your left. Beyond the copse the path crosses between open fields. Eventually at a field corner you drop down off the path into a lane **F**. Take the lane ahead and walk through Smith's End, passing a cricket ground on your right. When the lane turns sharp left turn right onto a signposted footpath, skirting the cricket outfield. Just before the corner turn left to cross a waymarked stile. Keep the hedge on your left. Cross the next stile into a narrow path. At the next path junction turn left (ignore the next path on your right) and walk through to a lane. Turn right into the lane and follow it as it swings first left, then right, to the B1368. Cross the road, turning left and then right, following the footpath into Horseshoe Close if you don't want refreshment. If you do, keep on the road for 100 yards more to the pub.

Barley

The track passes right, then left between derelict farm buildings. Keep on a good chalky track for over a mile until it reaches the busy B1039 **G**. At the road junction, by a large

black barn, look out for a good grassy track on your left. This isn't a right of way, but is well-used by walkers and is much preferable to trudging down the road. The track skirts a clump of trees before ending; here you must join the road proper.

About 150 yards before the junction with the Newsells – Barkway road you pass a narrow belt of trees on your right. There is no sign on the road, but there is a long-established 'permissive path' here which takes you back into Royston. Turn right off the road **H**, keeping the tree belt on your right. After 600 yards the path/track turns half left to skirt woodland shielding Burloes Hall. The track turns half-left again and continues for half a mile to the road. Here turn right, and almost immediately take a tarmac path on your right which leads first past a school, then past gardens and houses down to the former A505. Here turn left back into Royston. At the roundabout by the cinema, turn left and follow the road round back to the car park behind the bus station **A**.

13 Barley, Reed, Buckland, Nuthampstead

a   12½ miles / 20 kilometres

b   10 miles / 17.5 kilometres

Start: Barley, Herts., Town House **A** [402385]
                (opposite the church).

Maps: Landranger 154; Pathfinder 1049, 1050.

Transport: Bus – Herts. county contract buses 26, 28.
                Car – parking on Chishill Road,
                or with permission behind the Town House
                (telephone 01763 848276).

Refreshments: Barley, Fox & Hounds PH.
                Nuthampstead, The Woodman PH.
                Reed, The Cabinet PH.

Points of interest:
Barley, Town House. Newsells, paddock, obelisk.
Good views from high paths in Barley, Barkway and Reed.
Nuthampstead, World War II airfield.

Barley

From the Town House **A** turn left, towards the Fox & Hounds
pub. Opposite the pub, just before the war memorial, turn
left, up Crossways (public footpath sign). When the road
swings right keep straight on, along a footpath. This soon
meets a cross-path; turn right along the back gardens of
houses. At the road junction turn left. At the next bend look
out for a Public Footpath sign on your right. The path passes
left behind the barn and then follows a cross field route. This
isn't always reinstated; the correct route swings gently to the
right. Look out for a metal Public Footpath ('PF') sign down on
the road and head for it, crossing a wooden bridge over a
ditch by the roadside.

Cross the road and turn left for about 400 yards. At the next
'PF' sign turn right, crossing 3 stiles and a gate in quick
succession, as the footpath goes downhill, across a paddock,
to another gate and stile on the other side. The route now
enters the copse ahead of you before climbing uphill. At the
top of the rise cross the track and pick up a narrow path

ahead which lies to the **left** of the hedge. This path leads down to a lane (by a war memorial) **B**. Turn left along the lane. Just past a cottage look out for a 'PF' sign on your right. Cross the stile and go half left, cutting the corner of the paddock to another stile. Cross it, then turn right and immediately left, onto a track with a gate. Bypass the gate on the left and proceed for a few yards, before turning left onto a track which continues to a further gate which you bypass at the entrance drive to Newsells. Turn right past a white cottage and then immediately left onto a waymarked bridleway. This can be muddy! Follow this path due south to Barkway, keeping straight on over cross tracks. A large mast can be seen on your right. The track then swings left to join a road **C**.

Barkway

At the road turn right along the pavement. At the next junction turn right (signposted Reed, Royston). When the road swings right, keep straight on, but almost immediately turn left at the end of a wall ('PF' sign). Follow this grassy track and go through a kissing gate into a field. With a fence on your left continue in the same direction almost as far as another kissing gate; instead of going through, turn right and cross to a small gate in the fence. Follow the waymarked route through the next field to pass through another kissing gate. Now pick up a field edge path with a fence on your left. 100 yards before you reach the wood ahead swing left to cross a ditch and meet a track. Here you turn right to pick up a bridleway.

The track continues along the southern boundary of Rokey Wood. At the south-west corner of the wood, keep straight ahead (west) on the track,. At the next tree belt turn left and then right to skirt the south of Bush Wood. Again at the south-west corner go straight ahead as far as the next hedge and T-junction of tracks. Turn right, with the hedge on your right. At the field corner swing left, then right, still keeping to the track which now crosses between open fields. At the hedge ahead look out for a waymarked stile. Cross it and turn half left. In 100 yards or so swing right on a footpath through a gap in the hedge and then turn left, making your way to a stile next to a gate. Cross it. You are now on the outskirts of

Reed. If you want refreshments here, turn right on the track ahead **D** and keep straight on along the road you soon meet, as far as 'The Cabinet' pub.

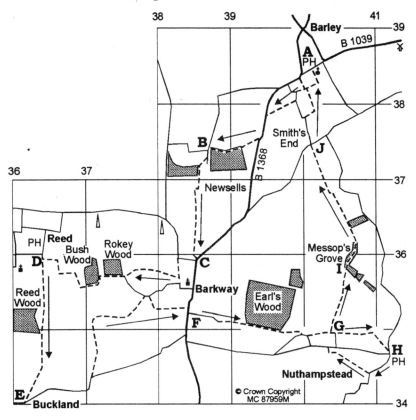

Reed

Otherwise, when you meet the track beyond the stile **D** turn left. Keep ahead on a footpath when the track swings right. This route continues generally south – so keep ahead over any cross tracks you meet. Generally you will have a ditch on your right for the next half mile. The path is sometimes enclosed by hedges, sometimes more open.

At a junction of ditches and field edges, by the south-east corner of Reed Wood, the path continues in the same southerly direction with the ditch still on your right. This may not have a proper headland – but efforts have been made

to improve the path! As you approach Buckland – the church is clearly seen on your right – cross the ditch by an earth bridge where the ditch swings sharply left and continue along the field edge with the ditch on your left until you reach the road **E**.

Buckland

Turn left. In half a mile the road swings left – and then, just as it swings right, keep straight ahead along a signposted Public Bridleway. Note that this is a newly created path which is not shown on older Pathfinder maps. The track swings first right, then left, with a tree belt and then a hedge and ditch on your right. The track continues in a northerly direction between open fields, then tall hedges. 100 yards after the high hedges start, the path swings to the right. Keep on this pleasant enclosed path until it emerges into an open field. Turn left on a field edge track which soon swings right. You should have trees on your left. Look out for a signpost at a cross-roads of tracks/paths; turn right over a wooden footbridge onto a path which crosses a large field. Keep an eye on the hedge parallel to your path which marks the field edge on your left; when it finishes turn left along another cross-field path to meet it, walking in an easterly direction. Keep ahead, with a hedge on your left, to the field corner. Cross the stile on your left and turn right, following a narrow path back to the main road through Barkway **F**.

Barkway

Cross the road and turn right, then left down the signposted footpath. Join a track and continue ahead, with a hedge on your right. The right of way passes to the left of the farm buildings and then swings right to cross a concrete bridge over a ditch. Look out for a waymark post by a power line; here turn left to join a grassy track which skirts to the south of Earl's Wood. At the south-east corner of the wood the path swings left and soon crosses a stile into a field of pasture. The right of way now swings right – head for the farm buildings. Cross two stiles on your right (near a cattle trough) and continue half left to the corner of the field near the buildings (look out for a 'PF' sign). Cross a stile onto a track.

Turn right and then almost immediately left ('PF' signpost), before you reach the houses. A well-waymarked path directs you along a stream and over a substantial wooden bridge into an open field. The cross-field path half-right ahead should be reinstated through crops.

b – Short Route

If you are following the **short route**, avoiding Nuthampstead and its pub, turn **left** in 200 yards at a junction of cross-field paths **G**, and follow the description from point G on the next page.

a – Full Route

If following the full route, continue ahead (east) until you meet a ditch. Don't cross the ditch at the culvert, but turn right along it on a field edge path, so the ditch is on your left.

Just before you reach a strip of woodland ahead cross left over the ditch, then swing right. At the field corner go through the narrow tree belt ahead. From this point, cross the field ahead to a stile just on the left of a farm. From the stile follow a well waymarked route through meadows to reach the road by a stile. Turn right along the road and take the second turning on the left, signposted 'Anstey' as well as 'The Woodman' **H**.

Nuthampstead

If not visiting the pub, pass it by on your left. Keep on the road for another 200 yards until you see a 'PF' sign on your right, just beyond a tree on the roadside. Turn right onto the cross field path, which should be reinstated through crops. This goes north-west, crossing a wooden bridge over a ditch, before approaching the backs of houses. Turn left onto a field edge path and follow this round to an access track to the road on your right.

At the road turn right. In 150 yards or so look out for a roadway into the Nuthampstead Industrial Estate on your left, opposite a house named 'Teanga Cluig'. There **is** a 'PF' sign, but it is almost completely obscured by cupressus trees. The route through the buildings is, however,

waymarked; it skirts to the right of the main buildings and then left behind them, before taking a cross-field path north. In less than 200 yards you cross your earlier route into Nuthampstead at **G**, joining the shorter route.

Keep north, first crossing a ditch by the end of a hedge and then crossing a more substantial wooden bridge and a footpath running east-west. Keep to your cross-field path going north. Next cross a bridleway track, keeping on a cross-field path as far as a wood, Messop's Grove **I**. Your route now runs through the wood, first passing a pheasant-rearing enclosure on your right. On the north side of the wood your path swings to the left, north-west, as a grassy track between open fields, to pass just inside the west end of a copse ahead.

At the end of the trees keep ahead (north-west) over a cross track. Make for the trees on the skyline; when you reach a hedge continue with it on your right. Cross another track and now pass a newly planted copse – this time on your left. Your path passes between fields, and your marker is a cream cottage ahead. Eventually the path reaches a road at Pinners Cross **J**. Cross it to pick up the lane ahead, signposted 'Barley'. You now walk through the settlement of Smith's End.

When the lane swings left, look out for 'PF' sign on your right, which skirts the north side of the recreation ground. Follow the path with a hedge on your left to the hedge corner; here turn left and cross a stile. The path follows the hedge, still on your left, before crossing a second stile. The path is now enclosed and continues back towards Barley. When you meet a cross track turn right; at the next junction with a lane turn left and back down to the Chishill Road through Barley. Turn right to return to the Town House **A**.

·

14 Barley, Nuthampstead, Langley

11 miles / 18 kilometres

Start: Barley, Herts.,
                    Fox & Hounds PH **A** [400385].

Maps: Landranger 154, 167.
                    Pathfinder (1049), 1050.

Transport: Bus – Herts. county contract buses 26, 28.
                    Car – parking on Chishill Road,
                    or with permission behind the Town House
                    [402385] (telephone 01763 848276).

Refreshments: Barley, Fox and Hounds PH.
                    Nuthampstead, The Woodman PH.
                    Anstey, The Chequers PH.
                    Langley Lower Green, The Bull PH.

Points of interest:

This walk passes through the counties of Hertfordshire, Essex and
Cambridgeshire, providing excellent views over rolling countryside.
It circles the wartime airfield of Nuthampstead – see **B**.
Barley, Town House.

Barley

From the Fox and Hounds PH **A**, walk uphill and cross the
road; the war memorial and ancient village lock-up are on
your right. Go up a roadway, then onto a path between
fences; turn left for 10 yards, then right. Go over a stile, then
along the right-hand side of a field, over another stile onto a
cricket ground and turn right to pass to the right of a gate.
On the road, turn left; at a T-junction take the footpath
straight ahead.

The path lies along the boundary between two fields; behind
you to your left is the Great Chishill windmill. At the top of
the hill go right of the hedge, then along the field boundary to
a lane between the end of a wood on your left and a line of
trees on your right, with another field boundary completing
the straight course of one mile from the road.

Bear right into a wood, Messop's Grove, following a path
which passes a pond and a wire mesh enclosure to your left;

when you emerge from the wood, turn half-left towards a post in a dip. Cross the culvert and continue on the same line to another post by a bridge. Turn left along the nearer bank, with the ditch on your right.

At a belt of trees turn right on a waymarked path, and follow this path with the trees on your left until you reach a road. Turn left and walk along the road for 400 yards, then turn right to The Woodman PH **B**. On the left is a memorial to the USAAF 398th Bombardment Group with a map showing the wartime airfield on the back.

Nuthampstead

Continue along the road for a mile. Behind you on your left as you approach the first bend is a large structure resembling a bandstand, a radio beacon for aircraft, which often turn overhead. At the road junction **C**, turn left towards Meesden (The Chequers PH, Anstey, is 200 yards down the road to the right). 200 yards along the road, past two terraces of cottages, turn left along a track to a yard; go to the left of a fence and continue to a wood, Scales Park.

Follow the track to the left of the wood, and where it turns half-right, enter the wood by a bridge over the ditch. Follow a broad straight grassy track through the wood until it turns left, where you continue ahead over a plank bridge, across a field and along a wide headland with the wood on your left. At the far end of the wood turn right for 100 yards with the ditch on your left; at a waymark post turn left over a culvert and follow the ditch on your right.

At a track (public bridleway) turn left along it. After 300 yards, the track bears slightly left at the Essex boundary; continue along it to the bottom of the field. Turn right and then first left, following a hedge on your right. Turn right at the corner of the hedge; ignore the first track on the left, and follow the public bridleway sign as it turns left and then curves right. As you start to descend, the lane itself is often muddy; if it is not passable, walk along the top of the bank on the left. At the road turn left and to a ford (there is a footbridge on the right if necessary) and a T-junction.

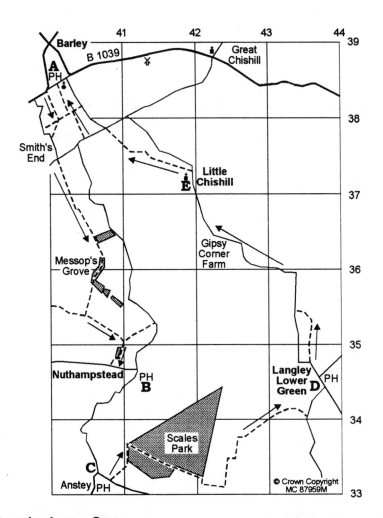

Langley Lower Green

Turn left, pass The Bull PH **D** on your right and continue ahead; part-way round a left-hand bend, branch off to the right up a track into a field. Go left along the edge of the crop; at the corner of the field turn left over a plank bridge then right, going along the edge of a field with a deep ditch on your right. Go right to cross a plank bridge to the road and turn right.

Walks on the South Cambridgeshire Borders

Follow the road round a left-hand bend, past Gipsy Corner Farm, into Cambridgeshire, to a high point with good views. The road is two miles in all to Little Chishill **E**.

Little Chishill

Go up a path on the left into the churchyard, past the church to the far corner. Leave by a stile, cross the field to go over another, cross a track and turn half-left across the next field. Aim for a point 300 yards left of the corner by the road, where two posts mark a bridge.

Cross the bridge into Hertfordshire, up the steps and follow the field edge to the left; at the corner of the field turn right along the top of the bank. When you reach a hedge, turn left alongside it, and turn right at the corner. Keep to the headland on the right of the field until the field narrows in the middle, where you bear left to the opposite corner with a signpost. At the lane bear right, and at the road turn left.

After 300 yards turn right up a track and continue along a footpath; Great Chishill windmill is visible to your right. At the hedge turn left for 20 yards, then right over a stile, across the field to a path between hedges and over a stile onto a path between fences. At the end turn left, pass a churchyard on your right and bear right to emerge onto the road. Turn left under the pub sign, and right to the front of the pub **A**.

15 Elmdon, Langley
9½ miles / 15 kilometres

Start: Elmdon, Essex, post office **A** [464397].

Maps: Landranger 154. Pathfinder 1050.

Transport: Bus – occasional from Saffron Walden.
Car – parking on main street, or in Nature
Trail carpark off Kings Lane (to south-
west).

Refreshments: Elmdon, Kings Head PH.
Duddenhoe End, Woodman PH.
Langley, The Bull PH.

Points of interest:
Upper Pond Street, thatched church. Langley, two huge greens, church.
Elmdon, Nature Trail, Tudor cottages, oldest building Hill Farm with
15th-century wing and two ancient barns on hill below.

Elmdon

Walk south along the unsigned footpath at the side of the
post office **A**, uphill to a T-junction with Freewood Lane. Turn
right, then right again onto a road with a 17th-century
moated building 'Pigots' on your right. Turn left after 250
yards into a footpath, with Elmdon recreation ground on the
right. Continue south between paddocks, crossing a track
and two stiles, before bearing right through some trees and
crossing a stream by a slippery bridge. Turn left and follow
the field-edge footpath to the B 1039. Zig-zag right and left
across the road, and follow the path uphill, next crossing
School Lane, with a thatched church on the right, to
Duddenhoe End. Turn left and follow the minor road, shortly
turning right at a junction, and continue on a quiet lane to
Coopers End **B**.

Bear right and follow Beards Lane, a Roman road, keeping
straight on past Lorking's Lane, and the driveway to Cosh
Farm, both turnings on the right. In winter, cross a ford – or
if it is too deep, detour in and out of the field on the left. In a
few yards, turn right and cross a stile onto a footpath going
west with a ditch on the right, then after one field north-west,
pick up an earthen field-edge track with a hedge on the left,
to reach Langley Upper Green. Turn left passing the cricket

ground, and left again at the road junction in Langley. After 200 yards, turn right by a footpath sign, and follow the path south-west to Langley Lower Green **C**.

Langley Lower Green

Turn right, pass The Bull PH; ignore the road to the right, but carry straight on with the minor road until it swings left. At this point continue straight on by a footpath, and after 50 yards bear right and follow the path to Langley church. Keeping the church on your right, turn north across an arable field, towards a waymark post at a field corner. Cross a track and continue up the field-edge with a hedge on your right to the right-hand end of a belt of trees. Turn left along the edge of the trees, and right through the belt, following yellow waymarks. Continue north along the path, first with a wood to the left, then along a track through open fields, to the delightful moated Chiswick Hall. The path was diverted in 1997 to run round the east and north sides of the buildings; follow it to reach the driveway, where you turn right, down to the B 1039. Zig-zag left and right over the road, across a footbridge, and uphill past some remains of an old hedge, to the wicket gate of Chrishall Church **D**.

Turn right in front of the churchyard, follow the grassy track left and right, and walk east along the edge of Park Wood. Continue beside a tall hedge, and turn left at the T-junction to re-join the eastern edge of Park Wood after 250 yards. Continue for a further 250 yards, to pass through a hedge-gap and join the Elmdon Nature Trail, signed with large, numbered, yellow-topped posts. Turn right, then left at Dewberry Grove, and follow the Nature Trail signs in reverse order, back to number 1, which then takes you through the car park into Kings Lane. Bear left into Kings Lane, and turn left when you reach the Essex Hill road by a telephone box. Walk to the church, and then right to the post office **A**.

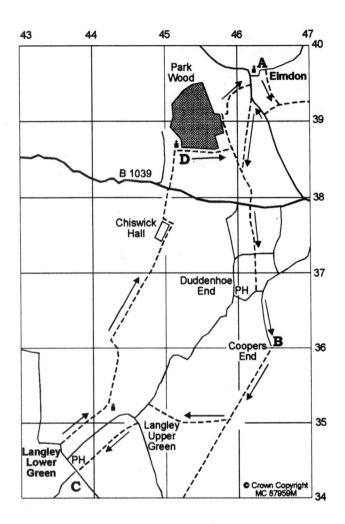

Park Wood

Elmdon

A

D

B 1039

Chiswick Hall

Duddenhoe End

PH

Coopers End

B

Langley Upper Green

PH

Langley Lower Green

C

© Crown Copyright
MC 87959M

43   44   45   46   47
40
39
38
37
36
35
34

16 Elmdon, Littlebury Green

8 miles / 13 kilometres

Start: Elmdon, Essex, church **A** [462396].

Maps: Landranger 154. Pathfinder 1050.

Transport: Bus – occasional from Saffron Walden.
Car – parking on main street, or in Nature
Trail carpark off Kings Lane (to south-
west).

Refreshments: Elmdon, Kings Head PH.
Duddenhoe End, The Woodman PH.

Points of Interest:

Elmdon, Freewood Farm, Nature Trail. Catmere End, hamlet.
Upper Pond Street, thatched church.

Elmdon

From Elmdon Church **A** walk east along Ickleton Road to the
post office. Turn right and go uphill to a T-junction with
Freewood Lane. Turn left and continue through Freewood
Farm with its well-cared for animals until you reach the end
of Free Wood. There turn left, keeping the wood on your left,
and then right along a track. Strethall Church can be seen on
the left and a detour can easily be taken if desired. Continue
to Catmere End and turn right into Birch Lane **B**. At the T-
junction turn right, and then take the next left into Littlebury
Green.

Littlebury Green

Turn right along the main road and then left at the telephone
box. Follow this path, bearing right until it reaches a
T-junction with the open fields beyond. Turn right, then left,
and go downhill to the B1039 Royston – Saffron Walden road.
Turn right and then left at New Farm. Follow the track right,
left and right again which brings you to Rockell's Wood **C**.
Turn left and continue with the wood on your right. At the
end of the wood turn right and go north-west to Bridge
Green. Cross over the junction and continue along a minor
road, turning left into School Lane until a footpath crosses **D**.
If you want to visit the thatched church continue ahead,
otherwise turn right.

Walk north to cross the B1039 and continue on a good grassy
footpath through cereal crops. The path continues with a
wood on your right, then with another wood coming in on
your left. When a field appears ahead turn right and join the
Elmdon Nature Trail (in reverse direction) which brings you
into the Trail's carpark. Continue out into King's Lane and
turn right along to Essex Hill road. Turn right along the road
and then take the footpath on the left, which leads you into
Elmdon Village just east of the church **A**.

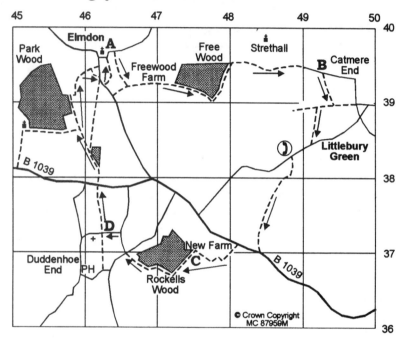

17 Arkesden, Clavering, Brent Pelham, Langley

11½ miles / 18.5 kilometres

Start: Arkesden, Essex, church **A** [482345].

Maps: Landranger 154, 167. Pathfinder 1050.

Transport: Car – parking on roadside, possibly south of church.

Refreshments: Arkesden, Axe & Compasses PH.
Brent Pelham, Black Horse PH.
Langley Lower Green, The Bull PH.

Points of interest:

Clavering, site of former castle and moat.
Ancient green lanes and generally good field paths.
Villages with open streams running through the streets.

Arkesden

From the church **A** walk down the hill to the T-junction. Turn left for 50 yards, cross the road and look for a concrete 'Public Footpath' sign on the right between houses. Follow this field edge path up a gentle hill towards Clavering. You will soon pass a 'No Horses' sign. Cross a private track, keeping to the left hand side of the field beyond (high hedge on your left). At the buildings of Wood Hall you pass a house on your left, picking up a track which you follow downhill, swinging gently round to the right. When the track turns sharp right you go straight ahead, following a field edge path (hedge on your left). At the field corner, turn right, following the path round the field boundary, soon turning sharp left. At the next field corner continue ahead, down a green lane. This takes you into Stickling Green. Continue down a track to the road **B**, turning left along it. In 200 yards look out for a 'Public Byway' sign on the right – turn down it. This is Colehill Lane, which you walk along for half a mile into Clavering.

Clavering

At the road turn right. In just over 100 yards turn left over a pedestrian bridge into a cul-de-sac. Walk to the end, where you turn right, picking up a track towards the church. When

the track turns sharp right into a garden go straight ahead into the churchyard. The path now skirts the churchyard, (fence on your right). This area is the site of a former castle, and the ditch on your right was once the moat. Go through a kissing gate on your right, following the moat edge back to another pedestrian bridge and the road beyond.

Turn left and follow the quiet lane for about 1,000 yards, to just beyond Deer's Green. Look out for a double-headed signpost on the left-hand side of the road **C**; you want to take the footpath which goes down the drive of the house named 'Deers' over a cattle grid on your right. When the track turns right, you should keep ahead, skirting a small fishing lake on your left. Go through a waymarked gate and keep on a path with a stream on your left. You cross a stile and continue to follow the stream – keeping it on your left – through fields. 200 yards after passing farm buildings on your left the path crosses a stile into a lane. Ignore the path continuing into the field on the other side; instead turn left down to the road at Ford End.

At the road turn right. 100 yards on by a telegraph post turn left into Cakebreads Lane, a public bridleway. This is initially a track with enclosed fields on your right. As it climbs gently uphill, the field alongside on the right opens out. At the top enter the wood ahead. Follow the track through the wood (a generally westerly direction). When you see a field ahead keep a look out for a path turning left **just inside** the wood. Follow this – only a few yards from the boundary – south, out of the wood. The path now follows a field edge with a hedge on your right – this can be muddy! At the end of the hedge pass over a crossing track. You should now have a ditch/hedge on your right; over the fields in the distance you can see 'Beeches' – a large white house just over half a mile way. Follow the broad track as it swings right, then left. Keep the woods on your right. Soon after the wood you pass a track on your left; ignore it. Just before you come abreast of 'Beeches' look out for a cross track. Turn right along it, crossing two fields. At the next cross track turn right; at the field edge ahead turn left into a green lane. Follow this into Brent Pelham, ignoring any turns off. The final 100 yards pass through a stable yard to reach a road **D**.

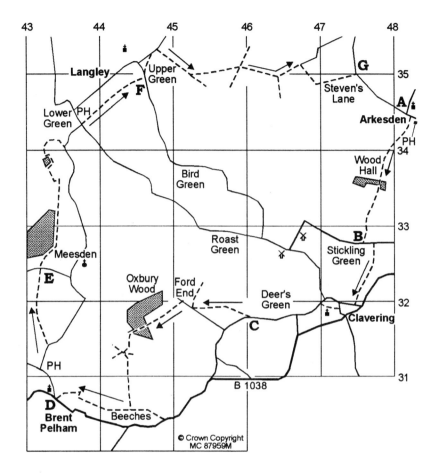

43   44   45   46   47   48

Brent Pelham

Turn right. At the road junction keep right (signposted
Meesden, Anstey). Passing the Black Horse pub on your
right, at the next road junction again keep right (signposted
Meesden). In 200 yards, just beyond some kennels, take the
public bridleway through the gate on your left. Turn half
right, diagonally across the field – this can be slow going in
wet weather! Cross a bridge into the next field and follow a
signposted path across to the hedge ahead. Once through the
gate you enter a green lane, Willoughby Lane. Follow this for
just under half a mile to Meesden **E**. Cross over the road
ahead and follow the track opposite, Wood Lane. When the

track turns left go straight ahead on a wide grassy path. You should have a hedge on your left. At the corner turn left along a much narrower field edge path. At the end of the tree belt (still on your left) pass between hedges into the next field. The path continues with a hedge/ditch on your left. At the next field corner search out a narrow gap through the hedge; continue in the field beyond with a ditch on your left. Next cross a way-marked bridge, turning left and almost immediately right along the field edge. The path skirts the small copse ahead (keeping the copse on your left). There are often deer in this area.

Regain the field edge, and at the next field corner turn right, then almost immediately left onto a grassy track, Roper's Lane. Turn right and follow the lane east to the road. At the road junction turn left and walk through part of Langley – Lower Green. If you would like some refreshments, the Bull public house is just 100 yards to the left at the next road junction.

Langley

Otherwise, at the T-junction turn right – then immediately left (Public Footpath sign). This route takes us through to Upper Green. Where the track turns left go straight ahead along a narrow lane, which emerges to continue along a field edge (ditch on your right). Look out for a footbridge on your right; cross it and turn left. At the road F, turn left. You can now take a path on your right cutting off the corner of the green; this picks up the road again opposite the little cricket pavilion. Turn right onto the road.

In 150 yards, opposite two houses on your left, look out for a public footpath sign on your right. This appears to direct you into an impenetrable hedge, but instead keep the hedge on your right, following an earthen track. Keep on the track for 500 yards. At the field corner the track swings right. Follow it for 10 yards – then turn left and pick up a waymarked footpath along a field edge with a deep ditch on your left and an open field on your right. At the next field corner you meet Beard's Lane byway; turn left. In 15 yards look out for waymarks on a tree on your right. Turn right along a field edge path, with a hedge on your right. At the next corner

cross a stile and turn left along a green lane. At the next junction of tracks ignore the waymarked path right; instead continue straight on, passing buildings on your right. At the next junction with a track turn right – signposted Public Bridleway – into Steven's Lane – and parts can be muddy!

The track climbs uphill and turns sharp left soon after. Follow the track down to the metalled road **G**. Turn right and follow Hampit Lane for just over half a mile back into Arkesden.

18 Arkesden, Rickling, Wicken Bonhunt

8 miles / 13 kilometres

Start: Arkesden, Essex, church **A** [482345].

Maps: Landranger 154, 167. Pathfinder 1050.

Transport: Car – parking on roadside, possibly south of church.

Refreshments: Arkesden, Axe & Compasses PH.
Wicken Bonhunt, Coach & Horses PH.

Points of interest:
Attractive villages, pleasant green tracks and good field edge paths.
St. Helen's Chapel at point **E**.

Arkesden

From the church **A** walk down the hill to the T-junction. Turn left for 50 yards, cross the road and look for a concrete 'Public Footpath' sign on the right between houses. Follow the field edge path up a gentle hill towards Clavering. You will soon pass a 'No Horses' sign. Cross a private track, keeping to the left hand side of the field beyond (high hedge on your left). At the buildings of Wood Hall you pass a house on your left, picking up a track which you follow downhill for 200 yards. At the corner of the tree belt on your left, turn left onto a field edge path (hedge on left). At the next field corner turn right down a field edge path, with a hedge on your left. At the next field corner the Ordnance Survey map shows the right-of-way turning half left across the field ahead; clear footprints show that walkers generally walk round the edge – first left, then right. Look out for a hidden, narrow lane between fences – set back behind the main hedge line about 70 yards beyond the right turn. Turn left down the lane to the road. This is Hill Green **B**.

At the road turn left. In 100 yards take the signposted Public Footpath on the right. This goes over a stile; look out for the two moveable planks across the path in the next field. Follow the field edge beyond (hedge on right). Cross two more stiles, join a lane and continue to the road beyond. Turn right. After 150 yards take the signposted footpath on your left. The track

Walks on the South Cambridgeshire Borders

follows a field edge and hedge initially, then crosses between open fields. Join a track at a junction, keeping in a southerly direction. After a further 150 yards – at the next track junction – turn left, soon passing under a power line **C**.

Go through a hedge next to a trig point (119 metres/390 feet here!). Follow a field edge path straight ahead (hedge on your left). At the large prefabricated farm building turn right, then left, following a waymarked route which is not on the map. This brings you into Coldhams Farm yard. Pick up the farm drive ahead, down to the road, where you turn right. Keep on the road for about a quarter of a mile. Just outside Rickling, look out for a Public Footpath sign on your left. This crosses an open field diagonally towards the church (turn one-quarter right) – but may not be reinstated through crops. Just by the church cross a stile on your right into the churchyard. Keeping the church on your left, walk through to the road **D**.

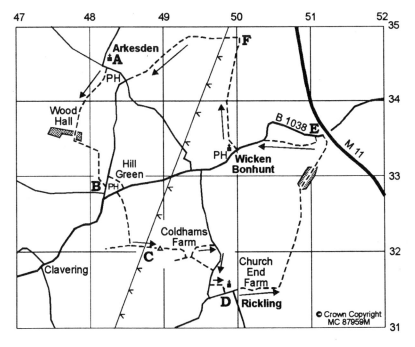

Rickling

At the road turn left. Pass the church on your left and follow
the track (left) past Church End Farm. Just beyond the
house, take the signposted Byway (right fork). After 500 yards
the track swings right, but you should keep straight on,
down a (mainly) green lane. You follow this lane for just over
a mile. The lane continues ahead over two cross-tracks before
turning sharp left just before the M 11.

Turn left down to the road **E**. Do not pass under the M 11,
instead turn left along the road. In 100 yards take the drive
on the left, turning almost immediately right to follow a path
signposted diagonally across a field. Spare a moment to look
at the nearby St. Helen's Chapel (normally kept locked). At
the corner of the field turn to the right, joining a field edge
path, with a hedge on your left. This takes you into Wicken
Bonhunt, first along the field, then joining a lane.

Wicken Bonhunt

At the road turn left. After 250 yards look out for a Public
Footpath on your right – just before the Coach & Horses pub.
A track climbs gently uphill for almost one mile, ignoring first
a track on your right – then one on your left. At a hedge
junction in a field corner **F**, turn left along a waymarked
footpath. Follow a good path, first along a field edge with a
hedge on your right, then through a narrow tree belt, then
along a field edge again. Go through the field corner ahead.
The path now crosses through an open field (diagonally half
left). The path swings right to meet a ditch (on your left).
Follow this now-grassy track back into Arkesden, turning
right into a lane, then right again into the pretty main street.
Follow the path by the stream back to the church **A**.

19 Saffron Walden, Debden

10½ miles / 17 kilometres

Start: Saffron Walden, Essex, Swan Meadow car park **A** [533387] – off B184, signposted to golf club and car park.

Maps: Landranger 154, 167. Pathfinder 1050.

Transport: Bus – regular service from Cambridge. Car – parking at start.

Refreshments: Saffron Walden, pubs and cafes. Debden, White Hart PH, Plough PH.

Points of interest:

Saffron Walden has a wealth of history, and deserves a good exploration. Pleasant undulating countryside with good paths. Audley End House and grounds.

Saffron Walden

Continue along the lane beyond the Swan Meadow car park **A** south towards the town. Soon after it swings left look out for a pathway on your right which goes under an archway between terraced bungalows, 'The Piece'. Take the path through to the next road. Here turn right past the almshouses and continue to the end of the road – and through the pedestrian gate into the park of Audley End House. The public footpath turns half left, south-west, gently climbing uphill to another iron gate in a wall. Go through to Audley End Road beyond. Turn right along a footpath for 600 yards. At the junction by the tea shop and post office cross the road and turn left down a private road between terraced cottages. Beyond the cottages the lane forks; take the left branch, **not** St Mark's College lane. Continue on the lane until it reaches the next main road, Wendons Road. Cross over and pick up the signposted track ahead. After 400 yards look out for a bridge over the stream to your right; cross it and follow a footpath on the right bank of this stream. At the next road, B1052 **B**, cross over and follow a signposted footpath ahead. This path keeps close to the stream and is occasionally waymarked with fading yellow arrows.

After 300 yards the path forks right, through a hedge. The path is now bounded by this hedge on its left – but just

before this hedge widens to a wooded belt, crosses back over a normally dry ditch to continue south as a field edge path, with a hedge now on your right. Follow the path along the wood, then a hedge, on your right, around left and right corners and then over a plank foot bridge, still with a hedge on your right. Continue generally south for 1¼ miles, crossing a further bridge and following a path with hedge to the right, then round a left bend by a ditch, towards Rosy Grove. Cross the ditch over a culvert with Rosy Grove on your left. At the end of the Grove go through a gap in a wide hedge, and resume a southerly direction, with a hedge on your right. Eventually you cross a stile and drop into a steep, attractive valley by Debden Water, a stream liable to disappear in summer! Drop down the field and in the corner **C** turn left, ignoring the stile by the gate on your right. Follow this path through the field as it first narrows to a lane, then enters an open field again. Cut across to a gate and emerge onto a short lane. Turn right, then, at the main road, turn right again. Keep walking along the road for 500 yards.

Just before a sharp right hand bend go through a kissing gate on your left **D**, and follow a grassy track straight ahead for about half a mile. When you meet a gravel 'cross-track' turn left onto it. In 150 yards, just after crossing a bridge and before you reach the stable buildings ahead, turn right onto an earthen path. Follow this as far as a kissing gate; go through it into Debden Churchyard. You can pass either side of the church to the main gate leading to a lane. Go into the lane and follow it to a road junction where you go straight ahead (right fork). If you want refreshments there is a choice of either the first pub on your left, or one 300 yards further on, this time on your right.

Debden

If continuing look out for, and take, a signposted footpath in 200 yards on your right. In 50 yards turn right; then, after a further 200 yards turn down a grassy field edge path on your left. On the far side of the field turn right, down to the field corner. There turn right once more.

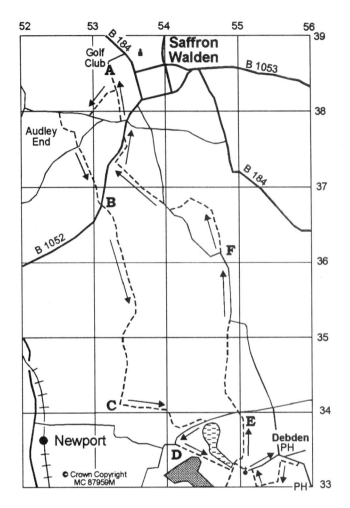

Continue on this track until you reach the lane, where you turn left. This lane leads back to Debden Church and you retrace your steps through the churchyard and the kissing gate on the far side of the church. Follow the path back to the track near the bridge – but when you reach the track turn **right** and pass the stable building.

At the next cross-track junction go straight over, and follow down to the road **E**. Cross the road and pick up the signposted right-of-way opposite – often a muddy track. This climbs gently uphill to a small copse. Here you must look out

for a green lane between hedges on your left, which takes you through Howe Wood. Keep on the lane and the track which it becomes, crossing over other tracks you meet. On the other side of the wood the track continues as a grassy path. Continue along this until you meet the road. Keep ahead down the road for 1,000 yards **F**.

The road then bears sharp left, opposite a track. Our route lies almost straight ahead – after turning right onto the track, turn almost immediately left, to go north, up a field edge path. This good grassy track continues to a field corner, just before a house, 'Herberts' on the map. Here turn left, then right, round the field. Pick up the track from the house going west and follow it to a sharp left bend. Your route goes straight ahead into the recreation ground. Turn half left and walk diagonally across the playing fields. Just before the road look out for a flight of wooden steps on your right. Go down them, and follow a path through a narrow belt of woodland until you come back to the road on your left. Cross the road and turn right. When the road swings more sharply right go straight ahead down Seven Dials Lane. Follow a path which keeps to the left of the houses. The path swings right before reaching the road – cut through to the right to avoid having to walk down the main road. However, you are forced to join it eventually, about a quarter of a mile to the bottom of the hill. Here pick out your next path – the narrow footway on the other side of the road junction, beyond the mini-roundabout, by a disused wall-mounted postbox. Cross the road and go down the alleyway. Continue over the next cross-road. The alleyway brings you back to the lane near Audley End Park. At the lane turn right, then, just beyond the almshouses on your left, turn left, retracing your steps under the archway to the lane near the carpark. Turn left and back to the car park **A**.

20 Newport, Thaxted

15 miles / 24 kilometres

Start: Newport, Essex, railway station **A** [522335].

Maps: Landranger 167. Pathfinder 1050, (1051)
(see note at top of page 97).

Transport: Rail – Cambridge to Liverpool Street line.
Car – parking at railway station free on
Saturdays and Sundays.

Refreshments: Newport, pubs.
Debden, White Hart PH, Plough PH.
Thaxted, pubs, tea shops and restaurants.

Points of interest:

Newport and Thaxted, many medieval timbered buildings.
Thaxted, a fine guildhall, church and windmill.
Widdington, Priors Barn (English Heritage).

Newport

At the railway station **A**, cross lines by the footbridge and
turn right onto the lane. Follow the lane to a quarry and just
before the gate turn left onto a bridleway, which may be
overgrown. Continue, first along a green lane and then the
edge of fields, with hedges on your left, until you meet a road.
Turn left onto the road and after 100 yards – where the road
bends left – turn right at Waldegraves Farm onto a bridleway
track, which you follow to Cabbage Wood. Here take the
middle track, marked 'Footpath only, no cycles or horses'. Go
through the metal gate and continue on the track through
the wood and open fields beyond to cross a bridge over a
lake. Immediately turn right (before the large brick building)
and follow the footpath to Debden Church. Go through the
kissing gate into the churchyard, pass the church by to
continue along a lane into the village **B**.

Debden

At the road junction bear right and cross over to pass the
White Hart pub. Take the left fork 'No Through Road' and go
left again at the next junction to walk out of the village along
Deyne's Farm private road. Beyond the houses, where the
farm road swings left, keep ahead on a grassy field edge path,
with a hedge on your left, as far as the edge of Rowney

Woods. Take the footpath right along the outside of the wood and in 250 yards, at the next corner of the wood, turn left and continue on a good path, still skirting the wood. At the next corner, ignore the path/plank bridge on your left, but look out for a path entering the edge of the woodland. This path swings right, to continue close to the edge of the wood, but just inside it. Take this path to the edge of the wood. As you emerge, look out for a grassy track between fields beyond. Continue on this path, ignoring tracks off. The path crosses a drive and then meets a bridleway, which you turn right onto, soon passing Fellowes Farm **C**.

Carry on along the public byway beyond the farm, next passing Pages Farm. Just by the metal gate beyond the farm on your left, look out for a plank footbridge ahead; cross it. Take the footpath left around the edge of a field. Where the hedge bears sharp left you keep straight ahead across the open field, which should be waymarked. Cross a bridge at the field edge and continue along another field edge ahead, under the power lines, with a hedge on your right. The path leads to a pond, which you pass by on the right to meet Woodhams agricultural machinery works. Pick your way through the machinery to pass the office and a vehicle park beyond. Go through to the track beyond, leading past the farmhouse on your left. Once on the track turn left. Continue on the track to pass barns on your left. Then, just before the track swings left to enter the grounds of Yardley Hall, turn right along a field edge to cross a concrete bridge over a stream, picking up a field edge path beyond, with a fence on your right. Continue, passing by a newly planted copse on your left.

The path now passes through a hedge into an open field. Your route lies straight ahead, passing by two large oaks – this path may not be clear. On the other side of the field turn left onto a green lane/bridleway. Follow this as it skirts fields and eventually becomes a metalled lane (Watling Lane) into Thaxted.

Thaxted

Having looked round Thaxted return to Watling Lane. 100 yards from its start, look out for a concrete Public Footpath

sign on your left, which may be overgrown with creeper, by Piggots Mill **D**. Take the path downhill, cross the stream and turn immediately right. The path follows the stream and emerges onto a track. Turn left onto the track to pass by the red house, Whiteleys. 100 yards beyond the house turn right over a ditch. Turn right for just 10 yards and then left, taking a path along the **right hand side** of the ditch up towards, and under, a pylon. (Note that the power lines were recently moved, and the new route is shown on the 1996 Landranger map, but not on the current Pathfinder map.) At the top corner of the field turn right and at the next corner turn left to join a bridleway. Follow the bridleway to pass Millhill Farm by on your right.

You now join the exit farm track. In just 50 yards you take a bridleway which forks right, gradually moving away from the farm track along a field edge, with a ditch on your left – evidence of use by horses may help here! The bridleway swings gently right down to the road. At the road turn right, to pass Waterhall Farm **E**. Just beyond the farm turn left onto a waymarked footpath which follows a field edge (hedge on your left). Eventually you come to a stile in a hedge by the field corner. Cross it and continue through a field of pasture (hedge now on your right). At the next corner cross a stile on your right, then turn left and follow the path right past a garden and tennis court, then left to meet a cross-lane by a pylon. Turn right and continue past Pinewood Farm. When the track swings sharp left by buildings, continue ahead on a waymarked footpath (hedge on your left). Cross first a small plank bridge, then a more substantial structure. Here turn left and follow a field edge path down to the road. Turn right along the road until the next bend. Cross and take the footpath to the right of a house, Farthings **F**.

Walk along a grassy field edge path as far as a copse on your left. Turn left over a plank bridge and through the hedge, to pick up a path running along the outside of the wood. Continue in the same direction beyond the next corner of the wood on a grassy path, to pass between open fields. The path continues almost as far as a farm 'Witchbars'. Just before the hedgerow ahead turn right and keep alongside the hedge as it bears left. Go through a gap in the hedge to meet a grass

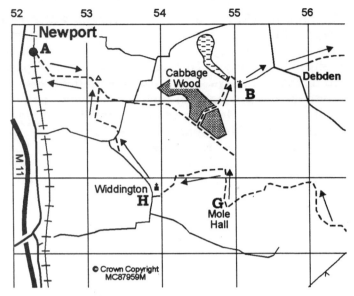

track. Turn right and follow this field edge track around – the map shows the right of way going across this ploughed and cropped field, but the track is commonly used. The track meets a byway on the far side of the field. Turn right along this, approaching and then passing Littley Wood West, on your right. Bear left and some 100 yards beyond the wood ignore the path on your right. Instead keep on a field edge track (can be muddy) which continues in a roughly westerly direction for over a kilometre. At a right bend the track forks – take the right side, first with a hedge on your left, then entering a green lane towards the outbuildings of Swaynes Hall.

Your path meets a farm track, footpath signpost no. 38, **G**. Turn right and bear round to the left for 50 yards, until you meet a hedge line on your right, which should be waymarked. Turn right onto a headland path (hedge on your left). Continue until you meet a shallow ditch, where you turn left along another field edge path. This soon passes by a copse on your left. Just beyond the copse go left through a gap in the hedge and then bear right on a cross field path. On the other side of the field you continue on another field edge track,

---

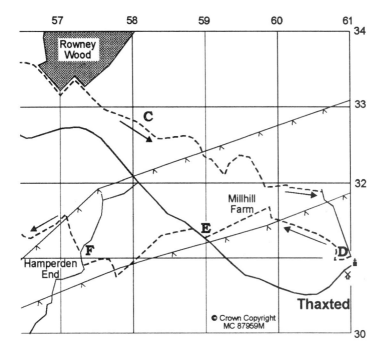

with a ditch on your right. The path swings left, passing
between open fields. At the hedge ahead turn right and
continue along to Widdington Church **H**. At the lane turn
right to pass the church and walk beyond to the road. Turn
right and walk out of the village for just over 400 yards,
passing the lane to Prior's Hall, or Widdington, Barn on your
left.

Look out for a Public Footpath sign on your right, opposite
Belmont Cottage. Cross a stile and follow the path half-left; it
first crosses a field, then a ditch and then a second field
before crossing another stile onto a lane. Turn right along the
lane for 200 yards before crossing and taking a signposted
footpath on the left. The path follows a field edge, with hedge
on left, as far as a grassy cross track. Turn right up the track
and continue to the field corner. Turn left at the corner to
rejoin your route back into Newport – first a bridleway, then
the lane to the station **A**.

---

21 Sewards End, Radwinter

a Sewards End, Radwinter 9½ miles / 15 km
b Sewards End, Wimbish 5½ miles / 9 kilometres
c Radwinter, Wimbish, 4 miles / 6 kilometres

Start: Sewards End, Essex, water tower **A** [569381].
Maps: Landranger 154. Pathfinder 1050, 1051.
Transport: Car – limited parking by water tower,
possible car parking for a group in 'Tylers'.
Refreshments: Radwinter, Plough PH.
Points of interest:
The River Pant and its tributaries are much in evidence.
Radwinter, church.

a Sewards End, Radwinter

Sewards End

From the water tower **A**, take the byway bearing left. Pass the
'Tylers' group of houses on the right. Follow the track straight
ahead for half a mile, then as it turns right, through a gate
and out onto a roadway. Turn left and follow it to a farm,
where you bear right to go round a pond. Continue to a track
with barbed wire on your left and trees on your right. Carry
on along a field headland on the right side of a hedge, then
with a wood on your left. At the end of the wood, follow
straight along the headland, and 10 yards before reaching
another wood turn left through a gap in the hedge **B**. To
follow the rights-of-way, go half-right towards a group of
houses and in the middle of the field turn right onto another
path to reach the road; if the path is not clear, turn right and
go along with the wood on your right to the road. At the road
turn right; where the road bends right turn left onto a
footpath to the right of a wood. Follow the edge of the field
and turn left to cross a bridge with metal railings **C**.

Follow the edge of the next field to the left, and in the corner
turn left over a plank bridge. Turn right and walk along the
right-hand side of the field. After 200 yards cross the ditch to
your right at a culvert and follow the other side. Continue to
follow the ditch where it turns left; after 20 yards, turn left for
10 yards, then right onto a bridge across the river. Turn right

to follow the river bank. Near the church, bear left alongside a fence, then across rough ground, through a dilapidated gate and across a bridge; to your left is the elaborate south porch of the church. Continue to the road **D**, cross it and turn right; just before the bridge, turn left onto a footpath. Cross a bridge to your right, and turn left towards a 'stile' in the middle of a fence, which you climb through. At the end of the field, go over a stile at the left of the gate and over a concrete slab bridge to follow the river bank for 150 yards to **E**. Turn left with a recently-planted hedge on your right. When you reach the road, turn left; the Plough PH is at the road junction **F**.

Radwinter

On leaving The Plough turn right to retrace your steps along the road, then turn right onto the path. At the river bank **E** turn left, and walk to a gate, where you turn right onto a track over a bridge. At the top of the rise, bear left for 10 yards, then turn right in front of two trees. Follow the track across two fields to a road. Turn left along the road; just after it bends right, take a plank bridge on the left and cross the field in a continuation of the line of the road to a signpost where you cross the ditch on a culvert.

Continue along the road, passing Jenkinhogs Farm on your right; 200 yards farther on **G**, turn right to follow a track between old huts. Go ahead into a small field and follow a headland along the right-hand side of another field, crossing a ditch and passing a wood on your right. At the end of this very large field, go over a sleeper bridge to the next field and continue on the headland, past a wood on your right. Follow the headland, passing the plank bridge and the one with metal railings **C** you used on the outward leg, and continue with the river on your right into the next field on a grassy track to reach the road by a stile.

Cross the road and go into a bridleway up to a gate. Go through the gate, then go right over a bridge; Wimbish Hall is on the right. Go half-left and round a fence to reach a track along the right-hand side of a field (note that the path has recently been diverted). Follow this as it narrows to a headland, over a culvert, until it widens once more, where

you follow a track to the right of a ditch. Farther on, a golf course may have been established on the right; follow the track until it becomes a road with Cole Green Farm on the right.

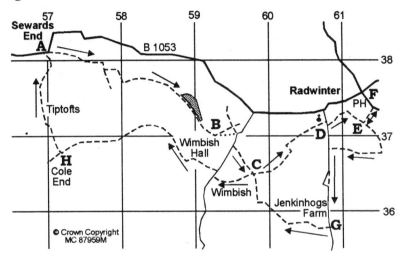

Just after the farm, under a power line, turn right **H** into a field and follow the right-hand side to a stile at the far end. Turn right, follow the headland to the corner and turn left. Where the ditch swings left, bear right and cross over a culvert to follow a grassy headland between two fields to the left of Tiptofts.

Cross the driveway and continue on a field edge path, through a gap in the hedge to the next field. Turn half-right towards The Towers and cross a plank bridge to reach a path with a fence on the right. Emerge onto a driveway and the Tylers' houses, with a small cottage on the left. Just past this, turn half-left down a driveway which is also a public footpath to the main road, and turn right to walk back to your starting point at the water tower **A**.

b Sewards End, Wimbish

After crossing the bridge with metal railings **C**, turn right to follow the later part of the route via **H** to return to Sewards End.

c Radwinter, Wimbish

Start at The Plough PH **F** [612376] and follow the return part of the route above via **G** to **C**; take the plank bridge to join the outward leg above via **D**.

22 Ashdon, Radwinter

10½ miles / 17 kilometres

Start: Ashdon, Essex, church **A** [581417].
Maps: Landranger 154.
                   Pathfinder 1027, 1028, 1050, 1051.
Transport: Car – parking in driveway to church.
Refreshments: Ashdon, Rose & Crown PH.
                   Radwinter, Plough PH.

Points of interest:

Ashdon and Radwinter, many attractive thatched houses.
Paths through varied landscape.

Ashdon

Walk along the church drive, passing to the left of the church
A, and go over a stile into a meadow. Turn right and proceed
downhill, and then over a further stile to reach a farm track.
Continue in the same direction until you enter a field. The
route then follows a good field edge path with a hedge on
your left, which climbs uphill. At the corner of the field path
pass through a hedge gap where the path turns half left – still
with a hedge on the left – to reach a stile. Cross and proceed
downhill to a fourth stile which leads onto a farm track.
Follow the track in the same direction until you reach a road.

Continue in the same direction along the road, keeping a
watch on traffic, passing large thatched houses. At the top of
the hill take a public footpath ('PF') signposted on the right,
pointing left down the path immediately to the right of the
second bungalow. This follows a wide grassy track with
orchards on the left and a hedge on the right. Emerging into
a field, bear slightly right to cross a culvert into the next field
and continue to a stile.

Cross the stile into a narrow pasture and continue south to
another stile at the far end. If there are cattle in the field it is
probably best to keep to one side to avoid a confrontation!
Continue in the same direction, turning left after 20 yards
onto a grassy track with a stream on your left – until you
reach a road. To follow the line of the right-of-way, turn right
along the road for 100 yards, then left into a small wood –

but, as it is currently overgrown, cross the road and take the track with a ditch on your right, around the boundary of the wood, until you come to the far corner where you turn left along the hedge.

After 100 yards, turn left in front of the hedge and ditch to continue south-east and follow this line for half a mile over poor surfaces, passing a wood on your right, through a gap in the hedge, bearing left along a grassy track with a further wood on your left, to reach Stocking Green **B**.

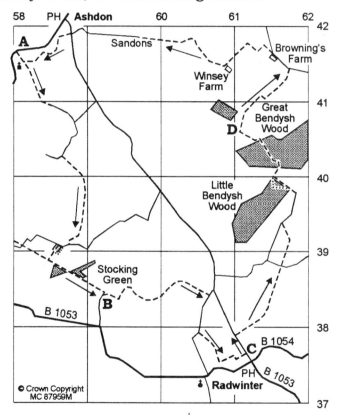

Turn right over the road, and, after a few yards, turn left onto a signposted bridleway which crosses a field to reach a hedge. Continue along the field edge with the hedge on your right to reach a waymarked junction of paths – at which point turn left to cross a further part of the field to enter a green

lane. Then continue in the same general direction for three-quarters of a mile to reach a road by a farm. Turn right to proceed along the road as far as a right hand bend, where there is a signposted footpath which passes over a bridge on the left. Follow the field edge path with a hedge on your left to reach a junction of paths, where you turn left to cross a bridge almost immediately. Then turn right and follow the field edge path with a fence on your right. Turn left after 10 yards by an open barn and follow the track to the road **C**. The Plough pub is 50 yards on your right.

Radwinter

Turn left – or from the pub retrace your steps. After 300 yards, past a dip, turn right and go over a stile by a 5-barred wooden gate into meadows. Continue with a stream on your right through three stiles – through bushes, over another stile and along the edge of fields crossing 2 more stiles until you reach a road. On the other side of the road continue along the right of a ditch. At a waymark post cross the earth bridge, then continue with a ditch on your right for 100 yards. At a junction of paths turn left and proceed towards another post at the edge of a wood. Cross a plank bridge and bear slightly right in a field to an exit between fences to a road.

Turn right. Near the end of the tarmac, after the last house on the left, take a signposted track on the right of a hedge. Continue along the edge of a field, with a ditch and Little Bendysh Wood on your left. If this isn't passable, take the track into the wood and bear right to emerge on another track east. Follow this track into Great Bendysh Wood, then bear left and go uphill to the edge of the wood. Cross a ditch by a bridge into the field to a gap in the hedge on your right. Continue north-east by a cross-field path to reach a farm track **D**.

Turn right on the farm track and continue on it for ¾ mile to reach a road. Turn left, ignoring a road turning to the right, and take a footpath on the left just after Browning's Farm. This soon turns left and then right – and then left again to reach Winsey Farm. Pass to the right of the farm and follow the gravel track which proceeds downhill to the right. Where

the gravelled track turns left, continue ahead on a grassy track. In the valley, bear left and continue with a stream on your right along a track – often muddy – through the yard of Sandons Farm and onto a road which leads back to Ashdon.

When you reach the village street, cross it and then take the footpath at the side of the village hall car park. Then continue diagonally across a meadow to cross a wide wooden bridge over a stream. Next turn left to follow a good field edge path with a hedge on your left. This follows the field round and up towards the church. At the end of the hedge, take the narrow path between a fence on the left and a hedge on the right to reach the stile by the church. This takes you back to your starting point **A**.

23 Great Sampford, Radwinter

8 miles / 13 kilometres

Start: Great Sampford, Essex,
Red Lion PH **A** [643353].

Maps: Landranger 154. Pathfinder 1051.

Transport: Car – parking on street.

Refreshments: Great Sampford, Red Lion PH.
Radwinter, Plough PH.
Free Roberts Koi farm – canned drinks.

Points of interest:

The open landscape includes a former airfield from World War II,
contrasting with more ancient rural activities. Great Sampford and
Radwinter, many fine old thatched cottages.

Great Sampford

From the Red Lion PH **A**, turn right, and at the junction cross
the road to the church and enter the churchyard on the right.
At the rear of the churchyard, go through a hand-gate into a
field. Continue west, straight ahead across an arable field,
sighting a distant lone tree and crossing a bridge with steps.
Cross the next short field to a plank bridge with handrail,
and on the other side follow the headland to the right past
the lone tree – do not cross a second plank bridge, but
continue to the road.

Bear right and follow the tarmac road, taking particular care
at the bends, and passing Bush Lane and Dove House Farm
on the left. Then, on a straight and level stretch, look for
signposts on the left **B**. Turn right and head across an arable
field towards the second power line pole from the left,
continuing to the hedge and following it to the right to a gap
at the corner with a plank bridge. Cross this onto the former
airfield and go forward to a tarmac track; at this turn right,
and after 50 yards turn left to follow the dividing line between
crops. Join a gravelled track at Great Brockholds Barn, pass
the barn on your right and turn right for 50 yards, then left
onto a concrete drive.

At the road turn right and walk to the junction at the top of
the hill – ahead is a World War II pill-box. Take the track to

the left and follow it round 'Mortlocks', then downhill, through left and right turns, and uphill for 200 yards. At the top of the hill turn right and go downhill again on a track to cross a bridge **C** over the River Pant. Turn left and walk with the river on your left for 400 yards. Turn right to go uphill to the left of a recently-replanted hedge. Exit to the B 1053, and turn left to the Plough PH **D**.

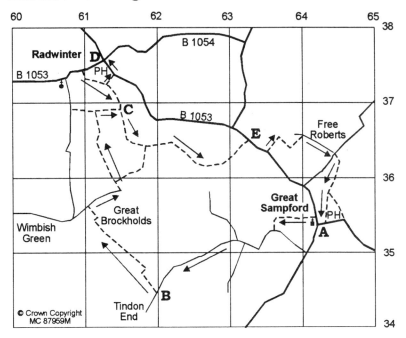

Radwinter

From the pub, retrace your steps to the bridge **C**, or go round through Radwinter village, returning to the riverside path from Bridgefoot. Then go over a stile onto pasture and follow the stream on your right. Go over further stiles and continue, passing a bridge, through a wooded stretch and a field, then over the left-hand of two stiles. Leave this field by the gate to the left far corner, away from the stream. Follow the hedge on your left, then go through another gateway, following the hedge to a corner where you go straight ahead to a stile and bridge. In the next field follow the headland to the left to reach the road by a sewage works **E**.

At the road turn right; after 200 yards turn left up a drive beside Long Thatch, passing through a gate beside a cattle grid. At the top of the hill, to the right of another cattle grid, go through a wooden bridle-gate into a small enclosure, then through another gate into the main field. Carry on along the top edge of the field, out through a third gate and turn left along a field edge. At the road turn right; the Free Roberts Koi farm on the left may be open for the sale of canned drinks. Continue to a T-junction with Howe Lane.

Follow the track opposite, and after 150 yards turn half-right along the power line poles. Walk beside a ditch on your right, and on reaching a hedge, through a gap to your left; cross the lane to go over a stile and bear left. Follow the power line, with barbed wire on your left, to go over a stile. Bear left to walk down the right-hand sides of the sports field and the school playground to the forecourt of the Red Lion pub A where you started.

24 Saffron Walden, Hadstock, Bartlow, Ashdon

18½ miles / 30 kilometres

Start: Saffron Walden, Essex, The Common car park **A** [542385].

Maps: Landranger 154.
Pathfinder 1027, 1028, 1050.

Transport: Bus – regular service from Cambridge.
Car – park at start, or at Catons Lane free car park [538389] (see map).

Refreshments: Saffron Walden, numerous pubs.
Little Walden, The Crown PH. Hadstock, Kings Head PH. Bartlow, Three Hills PH. Ashdon, Rose & Crown PH.

Points of interest:

Excellent views from the chalklands north of Saffron Walden and south of Linton. Bartlow Hills, Roman burial mounds.
Saffron Walden, castle ruins.
Can be muddy, especially where the route follows bridleways.
The route can be shortened by about 3 miles in Ashdon.
Some routes in this area have recently been diverted, so you should follow the route described here.

Saffron Walden

From the Cannon Hill car park A, the route starts north uphill on the B1052, passing the castle ruins on your left. Keep on the road until you come to Byrds Farm Lane. Follow the lane over a couple of cross lanes and ignoring a right fork, as far as the farm. Just past the buildings turn left, entering a field. Follow the field edge path round, with a fence then a hedge on your left. Keep to the headland path until you come to Grimsditch Wood, where you turn right, keeping outside the wood. Follow the wood and field edge beyond gently downhill. At the hedge ahead follow the waymarks right, then soon left, crossing a bridge over a stream. The path goes straight up and across the field ahead. It meets a bridleway along the field edge on the other side. Turn left. The bridleway soon passes between hedges into a green lane, which can be very wet!

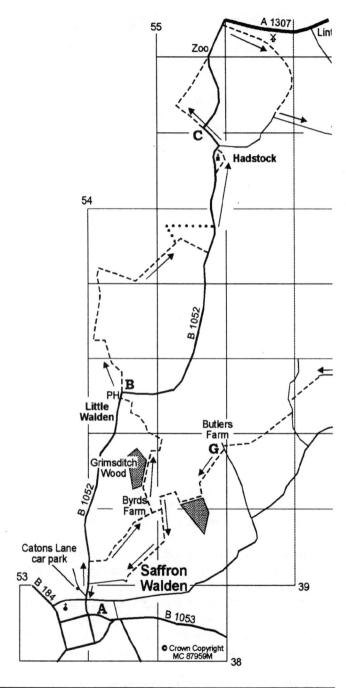

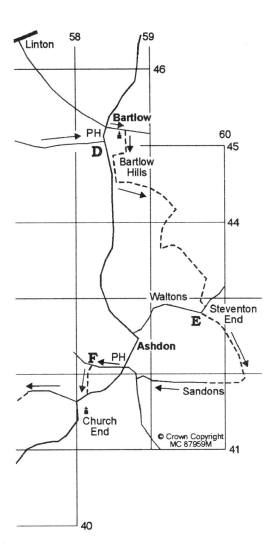

This leads to Little Walden. Before you get into the village proper, the path crosses a stream and soon meets a cross-track. Turn left here, passing a fishing lake on your right. When you get to the road turn right, passing The Crown pub **B**.

Little Walden

The road soon swings right – but take the 'No Through Road' signposted ahead. This forks – take the right arm, Petts Lane. After the track to Home Farm Fishery, when you get to the drive to Home Farm, turn right down it, passing first through the farm and then passing by Burntwood Farm on your left. At the next track junction turn right. After 300 yards look out for a footbridge ahead, and cross it. The path now passes between trees along a field edge, with a hedge on left. If it is overgrown you will have to follow the edge of the crops instead. As you approach farm buildings look out for a waymark post pointing left, onto a concrete track. The tracks are relics from the World War II airfield at Hadstock. The former runways are still popular with local people learning to drive, so watch out! Turn right onto the track, following it past farm buildings. The track swings right, then left, past an old garage. There is a T-junction of concrete tracks ahead. The right of way goes straight over the fields ahead to the Hadstock road; if the cross-field path is reinstated follow it as far as the road and then turn left. If it hasn't been reinstated adequately it is accepted to turn left along the track to the next junction where you pick up a bridleway, and turn right down to the road.

Hadstock

Turn left onto the B1052 and walk first along a road verge, then the road itself, down towards Hadstock. Take care – traffic can move very fast! Before you reach the first buildings of the village, look out for a yellow waymark arrow on a tree trunk on your right. The path goes steeply up the bank between trees, then between hedges. The path comes out into a field. Turn left, following the field edge downhill. Look out now for a simple stile on your left (waymarked). Cross it, the field beyond, and a second stile. This brings you

into Hadstock churchyard. There is a very ancient Saxon doorway – worth a diversion.

Turn right downhill and out of the churchyard. Turn left, then take the Linton road ahead (north-west), past the Kings Head pub. Where the road swings sharp right **C**, follow the right-of-way track ahead. Take the footpath on the right (keep the coal store on your left). The track passes between fields, through a hedge and right, onto the Icknield Way. Follow this down to the road. Turn left, past Linton Zoo. Just before you reach the busy A 604 turn right into Long Lane. Follow this to its end, eventually passing the remains of a former windmill on your left. Just past the old mill the lane turns into a track which can be very muddy. The track swings right to meet a lane. Turn left onto the lane and follow it for almost a mile into Bartlow village.

Bartlow

The road meets a T-junction in the village **D**. Turn left, passing the Three Hills pub. At the next road junction turn right. Look out for the church on your right, and go into the churchyard. Follow the signpost past the church to the three remaining Bartlow Hills. These are Roman burial mounds – the highest in northern Europe! Steps mean you can climb the 45 feet to the top of the highest, with excellent views of Linton to the north west. At one time there were seven mounds – but the ravages of time have reduced what can be seen today.

The walk circles right, round the first hill – picking up a path between wire fencing. Just before you get to the road look out for a path through the tree belt on your left – it runs parallel with the road and is signposted. When you come to a wide gravel drive by buildings turn left along it, passing a strange circular building on your right. You soon meet a field edge track where you turn left, alongside a copse of trees. The path continues along a field edge beyond the trees. When the track turns left, your route goes right, between fields. This too can be waterlogged in winter! Keep right of a hedge/tree belt which divides the path. At the next field corner you come to a junction of tracks. Turn left onto a track (field on your left). Watch out for a gate on your right – go through it, or

over if it is padlocked, and cross the field to a wooden gate. Go through and across the next field to another gate. Both these fields are usually pasture. Go through to enter a third field. The route now involves following a cross-field path (waymarked) up a slight rise (often cropped). At the other side turn right (hedge on your left). Follow the headland round for 250 yards, looking out for a waymark sign pointing over a ditch left. Cross the ditch. The right-of-way follows a hedge line on your right down through gardens to Steventon End, **E**.

Ashdon

At the road turn right, then soon left up Overhall Lane. Keep on the lane, into 'Overhall' grounds, passing a house and gardens on your right. Ignore the track on your right, behind the garden, and continue as far as a T-junction of tracks. Turn right along the track, passing 'Sandons' before it becomes Kate's Lane. Follow the lane down to the road. Turn right and go to the road junction ahead. Turn left, then immediately right, taking the uphill lane next to the Rose & Crown pub.

Near the top of the hill look out for fencing and a gate on your left – opposite a large house **F**. Take the grassy track between fields as far as the next road, where you turn right. (There is a pedestrian pathway for 100 yards or so, just off the road). Follow this road as far as the next turning on the right, Fallowden Lane. Take the lane down to the former Ashdon station (admiring the train topiary work by the house!). Just beyond the buildings take the signposted bridleway left, soon swinging right. Turn right at the gravel track. At the next fork, keep on the footpath (left), ignoring the bridleway signposted off to the right.

Follow the field and stream edge path to another asphalt lane. Turn left. Then, just before some glasshouses, turn right onto a track. This first passes buildings, then becomes a less distinct path along a former track. When the hedge on your left ends, the path follows a more distinct track between open fields down to Butlers Farm **G**. Pass to the right of the farm buildings, ignoring first a track on your right, then one on your left. Keep ahead. The track descends gently, crossing

a ditch to reach the hedge ahead. Turn right, with a hedge now on your right. Just beyond the corner of the field, look out for a gap in the hedge. The path crosses a narrow plank bridge into the next field.

Here the actual route diverts somewhat from the path shown on the Pathfinder map. Instead of taking a diagonal path half-left across the field, go round the edge (hedge on your left). There is a good headland. Once in the far corner you meet a gravel track. Here again the route on the ground has been diverted. So, instead of going straight over the field, keep on a track round three sides – first right, then left and left again. When you have done this, ignore the first waymarked path on the right; instead keep on the track running south. Follow it as it turns right, taking you directly back into Saffron Walden, emerging near the castle. At the road turn left, back downhill to the car park **A**.

25 Castle Camps figure of eight

a North loop to Shudy Camps 5½ miles / 9 km
b South loop to Camps End 5 miles / 8 km
c Total 10½ miles / 16 kilometres

Start: Castle Camps, Cambs., shop/post office **A** [633433].

Maps: Landranger 154. Pathfinder 1028.

Transport: Car – parking in Nosterfield End road.

Refreshments: Castle Camps, The Cock PH, village store open all day Saturday and Sunday.

Points of interest:

Castle Camps, church and medieval moat at Castle Farm.
Shudy Camps, park. Barsey Farm, moated.
Good views from a high point of 126 metres/416 feet!

a North Loop to Shudy Camps 5½ miles / 9 km

Castle Camps

Start outside the shop/PO **A**. Opposite the green bus shelter there is a wide track between cottages; go down it and through a kissing gate by a signpost into a grassy field. The path goes ahead, along the hedge on your left. At the field corner turn left through another kissing gate. The path now follows a ditch on your right. Follow the ditch for 250 yards as it turns first right by a large tree, and then, after a further 150 yards, left. Continue, still with the ditch on your right, until you see Goodwoods Farm. Look out for a stile in the hedge just to your right. Cross the end of the ditch and then the stile and continue ahead to a lane. This is Nosterfield End **B**.

Nosterfield End

At the road turn left for 350 yards, passing buildings on both sides. Before the road swings left – look out for a track on your right, with a signpost set back from the roadside. Take it, soon swinging right and then left. The track becomes increasingly grassy, even overgrown. It goes through a hedge and then becomes a field edge path, with a hedge initially on your right. Soon the path picks up a track from the left – and swings to the right of the hedge. Continue with the hedge on

your left past Barsey Farm and its ancient moat, keeping the house on your right. The grassy path now joins the main drive to the farm. Continue along it away from the farm for just 70 yards. Then, before the drive swings to the right, look out left for a hedge by a field corner. Turn left along a field edge track with a hedge on your left.

At the end of the field swing left onto an earthen track, keeping a mature belt of trees on your right. You can see Shudy Camps water tower ahead. Keep on the track for just over 200 yards, but keep a look out for a short wooden waymark post on your right. Turn right here over a ditch, leaving the track. In 50 yards at the next field corner, turn left. This path has been diverted from the course shown on older OS maps to follow field boundaries.

Continue along a field headland path, with the open fields on your left and hedges/ditches on your right. Eventually you come to a waymark post directing you right through a hedge, then, just 10 yards later, left over a sleeper bridge crossing a ditch. The path now crosses through an open field, aiming for the white gable wall of the cottage on the other side. This path should be obvious if properly reinstated through crops.

The path leads past the cottage to your right to a lane. Turn right for 200 yards. Look out for a signpost 'Public Footpath' on your left, leading down a shady path between hedges. This leads to an open field and the path continues as a field-edge path with a hedge on your left. In the far distance to your right you should see Linton water tower on the horizon.

Keeping the hedge, then a ditch, on your left, continue to the bottom of the hill. You should see a stile in the corner of a hedged field on your left. Cross the bridged ditch and the stile into the field. The path now runs alongside the hedge on your left down to a stile and the road through Shudy Camps beyond **C**.

Shudy Camps

The stile is close to a seat and village sign. Unfortunately the former Post Office opposite has now closed and there is no pub! Turn left past the telephone box. After 150 yards look out for a footpath sign on your left. Take the path which goes

---

across the field ahead, guided by the top of the Shudy Camps water tower. At the road on the other side turn left, soon swinging right. Again look out for the next 'Public Footpath' sign, this time on your right. A pleasant path follows mature poplar trees into the grounds of Shudy Camps Park (house to your left). The route runs south, crossing three stiles and paddocks until it reaches another lane.

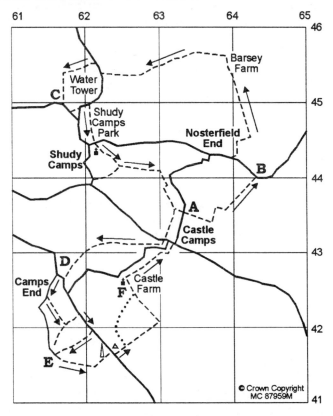

Here turn left and almost immediately right, picking up a rather complicated route round the back gardens of houses! The footpath is signposted to the left of 'Weavers', then passes between high fencing and over a stile to the left onto a path between garden fences. Three more stiles follow in quick succession before you escape suburbia, crossing a sleeper bridge into an open field. Turn left along the field edge path.

Just at the end of the hedge/tree belt on your left look out for
a cross-field path on your right; take it. This leads to a
pleasant green lane. Turn left into it and follow it most of the
way back to Castle Camps. So ignore tempting waymarked
paths – first to the right, then left, then right again. Finally,
just before you come to a white house by the lane look out
for a waymarked path again on your right and turn onto it.
This follows the field edge (hedge on left, open field on your
right) back to the village. But just past houses and their
gardens on your left, as you come into an open field, take the
cross field path half right to the pink and white thatched
cottage opposite, Meadow Cottage. Turn left and back to the
road and refreshments.

b South Loop to Camps End 5 miles / 8 km

Castle Camps

Retrace your steps to Meadow Cottage, the pink and white
cottage next to the Bowls Club. Now keep to the path which
passes alongside the cottage and its garden behind; at the
end of the garden turn half left, to follow a cross-field path to
the corner. Here turn left, picking up a good path down to the
Bartlow road.

Turn right along the road, cross it and in just 20 yards turn
left along a footpath by a garage (signposted). There are two
paths; take the **right** fork which passes behind gardens. At
the end of the fence the path keeps left, alongside conifers,
until it crosses an open field towards a large tree in the hedge
on the other side. Go through the hedge by the tree and turn
right to the field corner; here turn left. Now keep on a
headland path, passing though a gap in the hedge after 150
yards. Continue on this field edge path with a hedge on your
right for just under half a mile.

By the field corner you come to a cross track. Turn left onto
the track – then, almost immediately and before you get to a
low bridge with brick parapets, turn right on a field headland
path with a ditch on your left. In 50 yards look out for steps
on your left leading down to a bridge with handrail across the
ditch. Cross it. The OS map shows the right of way crossing
the field beyond, but the path usually used goes round it. So,

on reaching this field turn right onto the headland path. This soon swings left. At the next corner turn right through the hedge, right over a sturdy wooden bridge and across the field to the road beyond **D**.

Camps End

Turn right along the road and, in 120 yards, turn left at the next junction (signposted Camps End and a No Through Road). Opposite Sangsters Farm look out for a 'Public Footpath' sign on your left. Follow it, climbing over a stile next to a gate into a field of pasture. Keep the old tree boundary on your right. The path continues over two more stiles (keeping any fences/hedges on your right) to an open field. There are two cross field paths here, as well as our route, which follows the top field boundary, keeping the field on your left. At the other side of the field the way straight ahead is overgrown, so veer to the **right** of the hedge for 50 yards. Look out for the Cambridgeshire County Council sign requesting walkers to keep dogs on a lead on your left. Turn left here, down the rather narrow path between trees on your left and a fence on your right as far as the road.

Turn right onto the road. Ignore the first 'PF' sign on your right, but take the second, up a track beyond a pink double-fronted farmhouse. The track first passes farm buildings, then swings right (ignore the track forking left). There is an open field on your right and a hedge or ditch on your left. You come to a lane near buildings and then a tarmac road **E**. Turn left here. This road passes by Charlwood Farm (on your right) and then becomes an earthen lane as it swings round to the left and passes alongside the radio mast to the road. On the other side look out for a triangulation point – 126 metres/413 feet!

Turn right along the road for just 50 yards. Cross and pick up a footpath signposted to the left. The route is not always reinstated on the line shown on the map and this route description follows that **commonly** used. After 50 yards the path crosses the end of a ditch; keep straight on until you meet a concrete cross-track. Unless the right of way is clearly marked out ahead through the field, turn left onto the track and follow it, swinging gently right, for almost half a mile as

far as Castle Farm. The track passes between open fields until it approaches Castle Farm; at the first wooden fencing on your left look out for a stile. Cross it. The right of way crosses the pasture field diagonally to the bottom corner, amongst trees. Don't follow the obvious track into the farmyard! Cross the wooden stile and pass the 'FP' sign to join the main drive leading away from the farm towards the church **F**.

The farm is built on the site of the medieval Camps Castle and the remains of the moat are still clear. Follow the drive to pass to the right of the fifteenth century church which has recently been repaired – well worth a detour if open. Just past the church noticeboard look out for a 'PF' signpost on your right. There is an Interpretation Board here providing information on the history of the former castle and later buildings.

Turn right onto the footpath and through a kissing gate. The path crosses a field of pasture to a metal kissing gate on the other side. Continue on a clear path between open fields – the route of villagers attending church services for many generations. After around half a mile the path picks up a fence on the right; just before a stile on the right look out for and take a clear path left, passing over a ditch before crossing an open field towards cottages on the other side. Pass by the houses on your left, and reach the road. Turn left, and almost immediately turn right, passing the village sign, back to the centre of Castle Camps **A**.

26 Horseheath, Balsham

6 miles / 9.5 kilometres

Start: Horseheath, Cambs., West Wickham Road
A [612472].

Maps: Landranger 154. Pathfinder (1004), 1027.

Transport: Car – parking near village green.

Refreshments: Horseheath, The Old Red Lion PH.
Balsham, The Bull PH, The Bell PH.

Points of interest:

This walk can be muddy in winter, but very pleasant at other times of the
year. Good views over undulating countryside.

Horseheath

The walk starts by following the footpath off the West
Wickham Road opposite Cornish Close, signposted 'Streetly
Hall ¾'. This first passes between fences, then when you
reach a green space go ahead, passing lock up garages on
your left. Veer right to a waymarked stile, which you cross.
The path continues alongside a ditch, which you keep on
your right. Pass through trees marking an old field boundary
and look out for a stile on your right, just before the field
corner. Cross it, turning left, soon passing over a sleeper
bridge to pick up a clear field edge path, with the ditch still
on your right. This path swings gently right until it comes to
a T-junction with a grassy track – the Roman Road running
from Cambridge to Haverhill.

Turn left onto the Roman Road. We follow it for just over 1½
miles. Generally it follows a mature hedge on your right and
open fields on your left, although there are a few enclosed
stretches. Ignore cross tracks and field gates. After ¾ mile
you cross a sleeper bridge and then a minor road **B** – pick up
the Roman Road opposite. Eventually the track becomes a
broad, grassy lane enclosed by hedges on both sides. Now
keep a look out for a track on your right; it is waymarked
with a red arrow nailed to a telegraph pole. Turn right up the
track towards Balsham – first earthen, later stony.

When the track turns sharp left (after about ¾ mile), look out
for a signpost 'Balsham ½' **C** by a stile on your right. Cross a

bridge and then the stile. Go over the grassy field and cross the stile opposite. Now turn half right and cross the field diagonally to the corner, where the next stile is on your left. Cross it into an open, cropped field. The right of way goes ahead (direction waymark on the stile) and the route should be reinstated through crops. You are aiming just to the left of the red roofed houses on the other side. The path goes through a gap in a hedge and over a plank bridge; it continues in the same direction. It eventually passes to the left of the houses to reach a lane. Don't cross it, but turn right. You will see a tarmac road ahead and a path forking right, but running alongside the road.

Balsham

If you want to visit Balsham – and possibly a pub – keep to the road and turn left at the junction with Hay Close. This leads into Bartons Close. At the next road T-junction turn left again and in 70 yards you will reach the Bell pub; the village centre is further on. When refreshed retrace your steps to the end of Hay Close and turn left onto a footpath skirting allotments.

If keeping to the main route, take the footpath forking right alongside the tarmac road. When you come to Hay Close, cross it, picking up a footpath opposite. This runs alongside allotments on your right and first a hedge, then gardens, on your left. Keep on the path until you pass a thatched cottage on your right and you meet a road. Turn right. Look out for the 'derestricted' speed sign – you should take the signposted Public Byway which forks right just before it. This track heads towards the Balsham water tower and swings left to pass it **D**. Keep on the track as it changes from hardcore to earth and grass. You soon pass mature trees by on your left, and the path follows an open field downhill; on a clear day there are excellent views to your right to the south. The track goes through a gap in the hedge ahead, still keeping a mature hedge on your left. At the next field boundary the track switches to the north side of the hedge, which is now on your right. This is a good grassy track which takes you to the West Wratting to Bartlow road **E**.

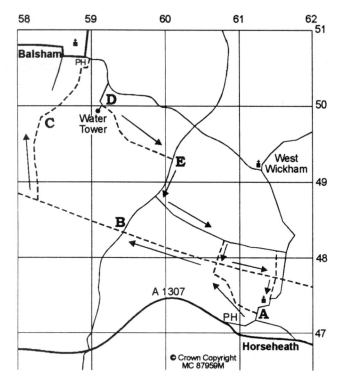

At the road turn right and continue along it for about 600 yards. Take care – there isn't much traffic but it does travel fast! Look out for a lane signposted left 'Streetly End'. Turn left onto it. This lane is much quieter and pleasant to stroll along. Your route passes the extensive buildings of the Streetly Hall Estate on your right. Pass the main drive, then a small pumping station on your left, and continue to the next field boundary on your right. Cross into the field (stile or gate) and follow the field edge track uphill (hedge on your right). This path is not exactly on the line shown on OS maps.

At the field corner you once again meet the Roman Road. Now you turn left onto it and follow it uphill, first with an open field on your right, then more enclosed, as the path passes between hedges on both sides. Continue along the path until you reach a waymarked stile on your right, opposite another on the left. Cross the stile right, into a

rough grass field. Go straight across to another stile with a tall white post beside it. Cross over into a horse-paddock and turn half right over the paddock to yet another stile in the corner by a spinney. Go over the stile, cross a plank bridge and turn left along the edge of a grass field, with the spinney on your left. Emerge onto the road in Horseheath down a short track. At the road turn right and return to your start **A** in 100 yards.

27 Withersfield, West Wickham

7 miles / 11 kilometres

Start: Withersfield, Suffolk, church **A** [652478].

Maps: Landranger 154. Pathfinder 1028.

Transport: Car – some parking by the church.

Refreshments: Withersfield, Fox PH.

                  West Wickham, White Horse PH.

Points of interest:

Withersfield, church, attractive sloping green, village sign; wooded, hilly
countryside. West Wickham, a linear, spring-line village.

Withersfield

Go through Withersfield churchyard **A**, and take the public
footpath north through small fields, with the Stour Brook on
the right. After about 400 yards the track crosses the brook,
to continue for another 300 yards, to the end of a larger field.
Here turn left along a track on a field boundary, with a hedge
to the right. Follow this track to the road (this is common
usage, but the right of way veers off the track). Cross the road
and walk up the drive towards 'Woodhouse' opposite.
Continue forward, crossing a ditch by a bridge, and veer left
following a fence downhill. Cross a stile on your left into a
small meadow. Continue with a hedge on your left, soon
crossing another stile to meet the road. At the road, turn
right for 650 yards, to the start of a signposted headland
footpath on the right.

Follow this path generally north-west, as a good headland
with a hedge on the left. The path (diverted 1988) goes round
several corners, but is well waymarked, towards Over Wood.
The path enters the edge of Over Wood, where you turn left
and walk west for 100 yards, to emerge into an arable field,
over a (rather decrepit) bridge. In the field, the path runs
approximately west, to pick up the field boundary, which
follow towards the corner of Hare Wood. Here the route turns
north, aiming for the west corner of Ash Plantation ahead.
Just beyond Ash Plantation, go through a gap in a tall hedge,
and follow it north on a grassy track with the hedge on the
left. When the hedge ends, continue forward on the grassy
track towards the buildings of Hill Farm. Skirt round to the

left of the farm buildings, to reach and cross the farm access track.

Continue half-right, skirting a conifer hedge, and then walk north-north-west downhill, parallel to the field boundary, towards West Wickham. (If the path is not reinstated in the field, it may be more convenient to use the adjacent field edge.) Cross a bridge over the stream, and continue in the same direction for another 100 yards across the next field. The path enters a paddock where the right of way runs between fences, to emerge through the garden of a former pub at West Wickham **B**.

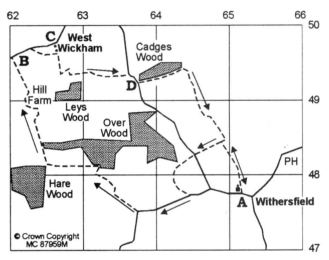

West Wickham

Turn left along the road for 600 yards to visit the White Horse PH. If not visiting the pub, turn right for 200 yards to Burton End. Here turn right beyond the last house, over a stile giving access to an arable field. Walk half-left across the narrow field, to find a plank footbridge in the field boundary opposite; then continue east towards a gap in the hedge bounding the lane opposite. On reaching the lane, cross the bridge over the ditch, enter the lane and turn right, south, along it. (If the lane is overgrown, it may be necessary to use the next track on the right. The field paths described are well waymarked, but if the ground is sticky, users may prefer to

continue along the road from Burton End, and pick up the lane at its start **C**.)

Follow the lane to the end of the hedged section, short of Leys Wood. Turn left along a hedge. Shortly turn right at a crossing hedge, then left, resuming a generally easterly direction, to the road near Cadges Wood. Turn right along the road for 100 yards to **D**, and take the track on the left, running along the southern edge of Cadges Wood. At the east end of the wood, turn right along by the stream. At the end of the field, cross to the eastern side of the stream, the Stour Brook. After two more fields, cross back to the western side and retrace your steps to Withersfield church **A**.

28 Birdbrook, Steeple Bumpstead

9 miles / 14.5 kilometres

Start: Birdbrook, Essex, church **A** [707411].

Maps: Landranger 154. Pathfinder 1028.

Transport: Car – small parking area at church.

Refreshments: Steeple Bumpstead, two pubs.

Points of interest:

Moyn's Park, building, parkland, black swans on lake. Birdbrook, church, village hall, houses with bird motifs, pond with waterbirds. Steeple Bumpstead, church, old guildhall, signed circular walk of 4 miles(part of which is used in this circuit).

Birdbrook

From Birdbrook church **A** go through the churchyard to exit into fields. Turn right, to follow a field boundary, with hedge on right, and arable field on the left. Follow the field boundary round to the left, to pass through a wide grassy gap between the end of a strip of wood on the left, and hedge to the right. The path has become a farm track. Continue along the track west, then turn right after about 100 yards, with a tall hedge on the right. There is a grassy headland around the edge of the field to the corner of Moyn's Wood (but the right of way goes across the corner). Go around the east and north sides of Moyn's Wood, until a waymark post indicates the path turning right (north-west) down the right hand side of a hedge/ditch to the B1054 **B**.

At **B** turn right along the B1054 – take care. After 200 yards, turn left by a signpost. Follow the waymarked nettly path north through a small conifer plantation, across two bridges over streams, then follow the path west as a headland with ditch and rough ground to the left, and an arable field to the right. After 150 yards, at the waymark post, turn right up the arable field towards the right hand side of Upper House Farm, which can be seen ahead. Follow outside the paddock fence to the signpost at the road **C**.

From **C**, turn left, and after 50 yards left again at a minor road junction, to follow a winding lane past Malting House to

---

Lowerhouse Farm. Just before Lowerhouse Farm, a signpost indicates the footpath up the steep roadside bank, then waymarks show the way across an arable field to a ditch, where further waymarks show the footpath turning left along the side of the ditch, with ditch to the right. Shortly cross the ditch on a 2-plank bridge – mind your head on overhanging tree! – and continue in the same direction, now with ditch on left to the buildings on Garlands Farm. Pass through the farmyard on the surfaced drive (note moat, ducks, attractive buildings), to reach Haverhill Road at Wash Bridge **D**.

At **D** cross the road to a signpost indicating a path through a gap beside double green metal gates. Walk down a long thin meadow, with new reservoirs to left. At the end of the meadow, by waymarks, cross a stream by a culvert bridge, and turn right (north) by stream on right, arable field on left. Continue to cross a substantial footbridge. Here turn left (more waymarks) to follow a ditch to Copy Hill Road, emerging by a signpost. Turn left down the road, to find a signpost on the left, just past a house, The Firs **E**, approaching Wiggens Green.

Wiggens Green

At **E**, climb the roadside bank by the sign (which points further to the right than it should), and walk south-east across an arable field to pick up a field boundary, and shortly, a grass track.

When the track meets a crossing ditch, follow the track left for 75 yards, then follow it across the ditch, to continue on a good grass path approximately south across arable fields, not quite as shown on the Pathfinder map. At the next hedge, go through the hedge-gap and turn left, with hedge on left, and arable to right. Continue across a small bridge, across a short cleared track across arable field, and through a further hedge. Waymarks indicate turns right by hedge for 50 yards, left across a field for 100 yards, then right again on a broad grassy ride down towards Steeple Bumpstead, seen ahead. This gives into a narrow passage, where descend steps to the road. Turn right for 50 yards. Cross the ford (footbridge by footpath sign). Continue up a gravel track past gardens to right of the church, and through a kissing gate into a playing

field. Walk up the left hand side of the playing field, to find a gate into the churchyard. Exit from the churchyard **F** to find a main street with two pubs.

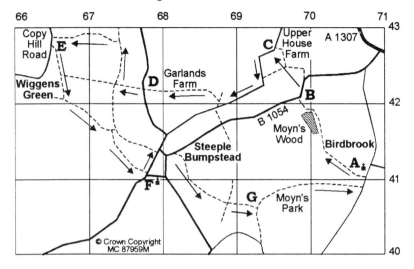

Steeple Bumpstead

Walk down the main street, back towards the ford. Turn right (following waymarks) along a residential passage to a bridge over the river, cross, and turn right alongside the left hand bank of the river (path not shown on map). Emerge onto the B 1057, cross road, turn right to a T-junction, at a sign 'Blois Road'. Immediately ahead is a footpath sign, and a stile up a few steps. Enter a garden, and walk to the back, where exit through a gap at the right hand end of the fence. Follow waymarks ahead, half-left across rough ground to a crossing hedge, then turn right along the hedge. Follow the worn track across a culvert bridge over a ditch, then alongside a ditch on right, then left. The path veers half left, south-east and uphill towards Dock Plantation. On reaching the boundary of the woods, turn right for 75 yards, then left over a stile **G** into a meadow. Walk forward across the meadow, looking for a gap in the wood ahead (waymarked). Go through the gap on a worn path, and follow this into Moyn's Park. On reaching the asphalt drive, turn left along the drive, and follow it to the road at Birdbrook. Turn left to return to the church **A**.

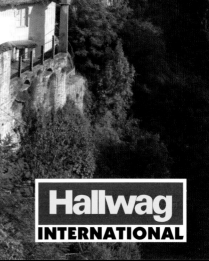

Hallwag
INTERNATIONAL

Foto Titel
© Fotolia.com, Zürich

Foto Innentitel
© Fotalia.com, Madonna del Sasso, Locarno

Fotos Seiten 89 und 95
© Corel Corporation (Ottawa)

Gesamtherstellung:
© Hallwag Kümmerly+Frey AG

ISBN 978-3-8283-0048-4

Hallwag Kümmerly+Frey AG
Grubenstrasse 109
CH-3322 Schönbühl/Bern
www.swisstravelcenter.ch

→ 2017   © 2013 Hallwag Kümmerly + Frey AG, CH-Schönbühl/Bern (2.)

Übersichtskarte · Carte synoptique
Carta sinòttica · Mapa sinóptico

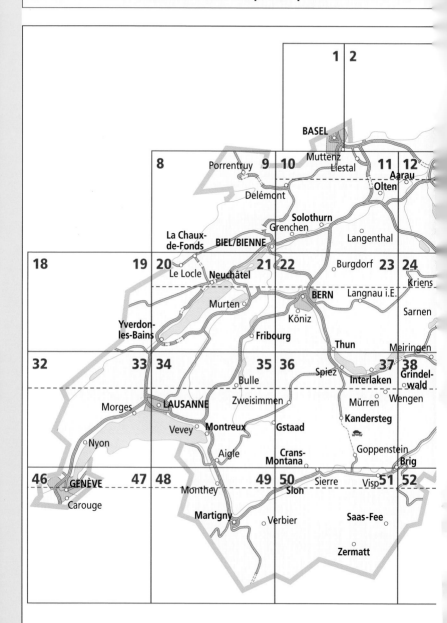

Transitpläne · Plans de transit
Piante di transito · Mapas de tránsito

Map key · Overzichtkaart
Översiktskarta · Oversigtskort

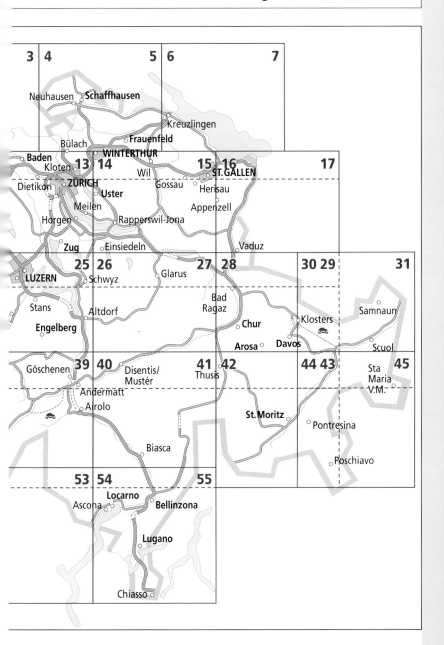

Transit maps · Transitkaarten
Genomfartskartor · Transitkort

Autobahn • Anschluss • Halb-Anschluss Autoroute • Echangeur • Semi-échangeur Autostrada • Svincolo • Semi-svincolo Autopista • Acceso • Semiacceso	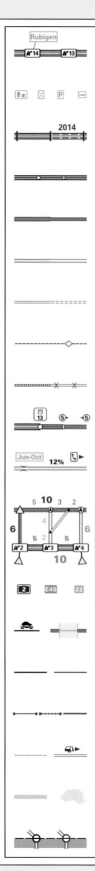	Motorway • Junction • Restricted junction Autosnelweg • Aansluiting • Halve aansluiting Motorväg • Anslutning • Ofullständig anslutning Motorvej • Tilslutningsanlæg • Indskrænket tilslutning
Tankstelle / Bar • Restaurant • Parkplatz • Motel Station-service / bar • Restaurant • Parking • Motel Stazione di servizio / bar • Ristorante • Parcheggio • Motel Estación de servicio / bar • Restaur. • Aparcamiento • Motel		Petrol station / bar • Restaurant • Parking • Motel Benzinestation / bar • Restaurant • Parkeerplaats • Motel Bensinstation / bar • Restaurang • Parkeringsplats • Motell Tankanlæg / bar • Restaurant • Parkeringsplads • Motel
Autobahn im Bau mit Eröffnungsdatum Autoroute en construction avec date d'ouverture Autostrada in costruzione con data d'apertura Autopista en construcción con fecha de apertura	2014	Motorway under construction with opening date Autosnelweg in aanleg met datum van openstelling Motorväg under byggnad med öppningsdatum Motorvej under bygning med åbningsdato
Autostrasse Route rapide Superstrada Autovía		Dual carriageway Autoweg Motortrafikled Motortrafikvej
Hauptstrassen Routes principales Strade principali Carreteras principales		Primary roads Hoofdwegen Huvudvägar Hovedveje
Regionale-, lokale Verbindungsstrasse Route de liaison régionale ou locale Strada di collegamento regionale e locale Carretera de comunicación regional, local		Main-, secondary road Verbindingsweg regionaal, locaal Regional och lokal förbindelseväg Regionale og lokale forbindelsesvej
Nebenstrasse • Fahrweg Autre route • Chemin carrossable Strada secondaria • Strada carrozzabile Carretera secundaria • Ruta		Minor road • Track Secundaire weg • Onverharde weg Övrig väg • Väg Sidevej • Mindre vej
Fussweg • Wanderweg Sentier • Chemin de randonnée Sentiero • Sentiero escursionistico Camino • Sendero		Footpath • Hiking trail Voetpad • Trekroute Gångstig • Vandringsled Gangsti • Vandresti
Zeitlich geregelte Strasse • Gesperrte Strasse Route réglementé suivant un horaire • Route interdite Strada ad ore prefissate • Strada vietata Tráfico regulado temporalmente • Carretera cortada		Road open according to timetable • Closed road Weg met tijdelijk geregeld verkeer • Verboden weg Tillfälligt begränsad framkomlighet • Avstängd väg Tidsbestemt trafik • Spærret vej
Gebührenpflichtige Strassen Routes à péage Strade a pedaggio Carreteras con peaje		Toll-roads Tolwegen Avgiftsbelagd vägar Veje med betalingspligt
Pass • Offene Monate • Steigung • SOS-Tel. Col • Mois d'ouverture • Pente • Tél. SOS Passo • Mesi aperti • Pendenza • Tél. SOS Puerto de mont. • Meses abierto • Pendiente • Tel. SOS	Jun-Oct 12%	Pass • Open months • Gradient • SOS Tel. Pas • Openingsmaanden • Helling • SOS Tel. Pass • Månadsöppen • Backe • SOS-Tel. Pas • Åben måneder • Stigning • SOS-Tel.
Distanzen in Kilometern Distances en kilomètres Distanze in chilometri Distancias en kilómetros		Distances in kilometers Afstanden in kilometers Avstånd i kilometer Afstande i kilometer
Nationalstrasse • Europastrasse • Hauptstrasse Route nationale • Route européenne • Route principale Strada statale • Strada europea • Strada principale Carretera nacional • Carretera europea • Carretera principal		National road • European road • Primary road Nationale weg • Europese weg • Hoofdweg Riksväg • Europaväg • Huvudväg Nationalvej • Europavej • Hovedvej
Autoverlad: Bahn • Fähre Transport des voitures: Voie ferrée • Bac Trasporto automobili: Ferrovia • Traghetto Transporte de automóvil: Ferrocarril • Ferry		Car transportation: Rail • Ferry Transport van auto s: Spoor • Veerdienst Biltransporter: Järnväg • Färja Biltransport: Jernbane • Færge
Eisenbahn: Hauptlinie • Nebenlinie Chemin de fer: Ligne principale • Ligne secondaire Ferrovia: Linea principale • Linea secondaria Ferrocarril: Línea principal • Línea secundaria		Railway: Main line • Branch line Spoorweg: Hoofdspoor • Zijspoor Järnväg: Huvudlinje • Annan linje Jernbane: Hovedstrækning • Sidebane
Luftseilbahn • Sessellift • Bergbahn Téléphérique • Télésiège • Chemin de fer de montagne Funivia • Seggiovia • Ferrovia di montagna Teleférico • Telesilla • Ferrocarril de montaña		Cable car • Chair lift • Mountain railway Kabelbaan • Stoeltjeslift • Bergspoor Linbana • Stollift • Bergbana Tovbane • Stolelift • Bjergbane
Schifffahrtslinie • Für Wohnwagen gesperrt Ligne de navigation • Route interdite aux caravanes Linea di navigazione • Strada vietata alle roulottes Línea marítima • Prohibido para caravanas		Shipping route • Closed to caravans Scheepvaartroute • Verboden voor caravans Färjelinje • Stängd för husvagnar Skibsrute • Lukket for campingvogne
Freizone • Weinbaugebiet Zone franche • Vignoble Zona franca • Viticultura Zona franca • Región vinícola		Tax free zone • Vineyard Belastingvrije zone • Wijnbouwgebied Frizon • Vindistrikt Frihandelszone • Vinavl
Zollabfertigung: 24 Std. • Zeitlich beschränkt Dédouanement: 24 h/24 • Selon horaire Visita doganale: 24 ore/24 • Secondo orario Despacho aduanero: 24/24 horas • Según horario		Customs clearance: 24 hour • Timetabled Inklaring: 24/24 uuren • Naar dienstregeling Tullbehandling: 24/24 timmen • Tidsbegränsad Toldklarering: 24/24 timen • Tidsmæssig begrænse

German/French/Italian/Spanish	Symbols	English/Dutch/Swedish/Danish
Flughafen • Flugplatz • Flugfeld Aéroport • Aérodrome • Terrain d'aviation Aeroporto • Aerodromo • Pista di atterraggio Aeropuerto • Aeródromo • Pista de aterrizaje		Airport • Airfield • Airstrip Luchthaven • Vliegveld • Landingsbaan Trafikflygplats • Flygplats • Flygfält Lufthavn • Flyveplads • Landingsplads
Schloss / Burg • Ruine • Denkmal Château / château fort • Ruine • Monument Castello / rocca • Rudero • Monumento Castillo / fortaleza • Ruina • Monumento		Castle / stately home • Ruin • Monument Kasteel / burcht • Ruine • Gedenkteken Slott / borg • Ruin • Minnesmärke Slot / borg • Ruin • Mindesmærker
Kirche / Kapelle • Kloster • Römische Ruine Eglise / chapelle • Couvent • Ruine romaine Chiesa / cappella • Monastero • Rovina romana Iglesia / capilla • Monasterio • Ruina romana		Church / chapel • Monastery / convent • Roman ruin Kerk / kapel • Klooster • Romeinse ruïne Kyrka / kapell • Kloster • Romersk ruin Kirke / kapel • Kloster • Romersk ruin
Einzelstehendes Hotel / Restaur. • Clubhütte • Jugendherb. Hôtel isolé / restaur. • Cabane de club • Auberge de jeunes. Albergo isolato / ristorante • Capanna • Ostello della gioventù Hotel aislado / restaur. • Ref. de montaña • Albergue juvenil		Secluded hotel / restaurant • Mountain hut • Youth hostel Afgelegen hotel / restaurant • Berghut • Jeugdherberg Ensligt beläget hotell / restaur. • Klubbstugor • Vandrarhem Ensomt beliggende hotel / rest. • Bjerghytte • Vandrehjem
Sendeturm • Aussichtsturm • Höhle Tour d'émission • Tour d'observation • Grotte Torre di trasmissione • Belvedere • Grotta Torre de emisión • Atalaya • Cueva		Transmitter mast • Observation tower • Cave Zendtoren • Uitzichttoren • Grot Telemast • Utsiktstorn • Grotta Teletårn • Udsigtstårn • Hule
Golfplatz • Autodrom • Pferderennbahn Terrain de golf • Circuit automobile • Hippodrome Campo da golf • Circuito automobilistico • Ippodromo Campo de golf • Autódromo • Hipódromo		Golf course • Motor circuit • Racecourse Golfbaan • Autocircuit • Renbaan Golfbana • Motorbana • Kapplöpningsbana Golfbana • Motorsportsbane • Hestesportsbane
Sehenswerter Ort • Sehenswertes Objekt • Schlachtfeld Lieu intéressante • Édifice remarquable • Champ de bataille Luogo d'interesse • Oggetto interes. • Campo di battaglia Loc. de interés • Construcción interes. • Campo de batalla		Place of interest • Object of interest • Battlefield Bezienswaardige plek • Bezienswaardigheid • Slagveld Sevärdhet ort • Sevärdhet objekt • Slagfält Seværdigt sted • Seværdigt objekt • Slagmark
Spital • Feuerstelle (SF) • Freizeitpark Hôpital • Place de grill (SF) • Parc de loisirs Ospedale • Posto per grill (SF) • Parco ricreativo Hospital • Lugar de barbacoa (SF) • Parque recreativo		Hospital • Barbecue site (SF) • Theme park Ziekenhuis • Barbecueplaats (SF) • Recreatiepark Sjukhus • Grillplats (SF) • Nöjespark Sygehus • Grillplads (SF) • Forlystelsespark
Panoramasicht • Schöne Aussicht Vue panoramique • Point de vue Vista panoramica • Veduta Vista panorámica • Bella vista		Panoramic view • Viewpoint Panorama • Mooi uitzicht Panorama • Vacker utsikt Panoramaudsigt • Udsigtspunkt
Naturesehenswürdigkeiten • Thermalbad • Wasserfall Curiosités naturelles • Station thermale • Cascade Curiosità naturali • Stazione termale • Cascata Curiosidades naturales • Balneario • Salto de agua		Natural curiosities • Spa • Waterfall Natuurmonumenten • Kuuroord • Waterval Natursevärdheter • Spa • Vattenfall Natursæverdigheder • Kursted • Vandfald
Camping • Zoo • Tierpark Camping • Jardin zoologique • Parc animalier Campeggio • Zoo • Parco d'animali Camping • Zoo • Parque zoológico		Camp site • Zoo • Wildlife park Camping • Zoo • Dierentuin Camping • Zoo • Djurpark Campingplads • Zoologisk have • Dyrepark
Moto-Cross • Go-Kart • Paragliding Moto-cross • Karting • Parapente Moto-cross • Kart • Paragliding Motocross • Karting • Paravente		Motocross • Karting • Paragliding Motorcross • Karting • Paragliding Moto-Crossbana • Go-Kartbana • Skärmflygning Moto-Cross • Go-Kart • Paragliding
Start: Mountain-Bike • Radwanderweg Départ: Mountain-Bike • Chemin de randonnée cycliste Partenza: Mountain-Bike • Gite in bicicletta Salida: Mountain-Bike • Camino para excursión en bicicleta		Start: Mountain Biking • Cycle track Start: Mountainbiking • Fietsroute Start: Mountain-Bike • Cykelled Start: Mountain-Bike • Cykelrute
Autoreisezug • Jachthafen Service auto-train • Port de plaisance Servizio navetta per auto • Porto per i panfili Servicio auto-tren • Puerto deportivo		Car transporting train • Yacht harbour Autoslaaptrein • Jachthaven Biltåg • Hamn för fritidsbåtar Biltog • Lystbådehavn
Skigebiet: Winter • Sommer Régions de ski: Hiver • Été Regioni di sci: Inverno • Estate Terreno de esquí: Invierno • Verano		Ski resort: Winter • Summer Skigebied: Winter • Zomer Skidområde: Vinter • Sommar Skiområde: Vinter • Sommer
Schlittelweg • Sommerrodeln Piste de luge • Toboggan Sentiero per slitte • Slittino estivo Pista para trineos • Trineo de verano		Sledge run • Summer tobogganing Sleeroute • Zomerrodelen Släde • Sommarrodel Slæde vej • Sommer kælkning
Planetenweg • Naturlehrpfad • Botanischer Garten Chem. «planétaire» • Sentier nat. didactique • Jardin botan. Sentiero «pianeti» • Sent. naturale didattico • Giardino botan. Camino planetario • Senda nat. instructiva • Jardín botánico		Astrology path • Nature-study path • Botanical garden Planetenweg • Natuurpad • Botanische tuin Planetstig • Naturstig • Botansk Trädgård Planet sti • Natursti • Botanisk have

```
0     2     4     6     8     10 km
|—————|—————|—————|—————|—————|
```

1:250 000

Benützung der Landeskarte der Schweiz mit Bewilligung von swisstopo (603B-U/191112)

Distanzentabelle · Tableau des distances
Table of distances · Afstandstabel
Tabella delle distanze · Tabla de distancias · Avståndstabell · Vejlængdetabel

km	Aarau	Altdorf	Baden	Basel	Bellinzona	Bern	Biel/Bienne	Brig	Chiasso	Chur	Delémont	Fribourg	Genève	Glarus	Interlaken	Kandersteg	Kreuzlingen	La Chaux-de-Fonds	Lausanne	Locarno	Lugano	Luzern	Martigny	Neuchâtel	Olten	St. Gallen	St. Margrethen	St. Moritz	Schaffhausen	Scuol/Schuls	Sion	Solothurn	Vevey	Winterthur	Zug	Zürich
Zürich	47	95	23	82	194	125	119	214	244	117	119	157	292	69	178	185	66	193	187	217	219	56	255	170	67	81	108	201	48	223	245	95	211	23	29	—
Zug	57	69	50	124	182	137	131	218	267	131	169	157	307	65	197	204	95	206	214	241	194	30	267	189	79	110	138	267	55	241	294	107	230	65	—	29
Winterthur	66	118	42	101	217	144	138	233	267	138	138	185	311	92	197	204	42	206	210	240	240	79	267	176	86	27	57	245	27	245	301	114	234	—	65	23
Vevey	169	244	192	185	337	90	132	57	390	326	170	52	91	280	149	123	271	113	28	364	362	152	79	96	154	288	315	410	256	402	79	132	—	234	230	211
Solothurn	53	126	76	69	223	41	34	150	274	210	43	66	209	164	108	74	151	60	146	246	248	85	173	38	38	172	199	294	140	326	199	—	132	114	107	95
Sion	240	311	263	256	229	161	200	55	229	397	243	128	162	349	99	44	386	184	99	471	294	214	29	199	225	326	471	481	326	471	—	199	79	301	294	245
Scuol/Schuls	236	207	214	271	186	314	308	376	276	55	310	346	481	144	278	378	216	376	418	380	333	219	471	278	256	178	161	60	240	—	471	326	402	245	241	223
Schaffhausen	92	144	68	127	293	170	164	308	293	104	170	202	337	118	144	151	63	208	274	266	243	105	299	160	112	63	99	266	—	240	326	140	256	27	55	48
St. Moritz	246	222	222	281	151	229	318	324	85	77	318	318	491	152	282	384	218	291	418	67	125	224	454	224	226	188	161	—	266	60	481	294	410	245	267	201
St. Margrethen	151	127	138	186	218	203	207	324	229	77	261	261	396	96	282	384	61	291	333	229	218	137	360	245	171	27	—	161	99	161	471	199	315	57	138	108
St. Gallen	124	100	127	159	270	202	196	346	293	104	234	234	369	118	255	282	63	264	306	378	245	137	360	215	144	—	27	188	63	178	326	172	288	27	110	81
Olten	13	176	100	55	245	68	62	161	245	182	62	100	235	134	121	128	129	130	172	243	220	57	198	113	—	144	171	226	112	256	225	38	154	86	79	67
Neuchâtel	128	199	151	144	348	49	34	144	297	297	79	46	123	237	108	115	321	19	73	321	323	160	140	—	113	215	245	224	160	278	199	38	96	176	189	170
Martigny	213	195	236	256	213	91	115	57	370	370	193	101	135	324	167	72	317	157	72	382	382	219	—	140	198	360	360	454	299	471	29	173	79	267	267	255
Luzern	68	41	91	102	132	91	109	154	190	140	124	102	282	92	66	73	122	177	219	163	165	—	219	160	57	137	137	224	105	219	214	85	152	79	30	56
Lugano	231	132	254	265	27	214	272	151	26	142	272	310	445	190	245	141	209	291	380	42	—	165	382	323	220	245	218	125	243	333	294	248	362	240	194	219
Locarno	229	130	252	263	25	182	270	136	52	140	270	308	443	207	207	140	216	291	291	—	42	163	382	321	243	378	229	67	266	380	471	246	364	240	241	217
Lausanne	187	258	210	203	357	108	105	105	407	344	173	75	62	296	167	132	291	75	—	291	380	219	72	73	172	306	333	418	274	418	99	146	28	210	214	187
La Chaux-de-Fonds	114	216	168	101	284	66	42	161	365	271	60	63	140	254	125	132	249	—	75	291	291	177	157	19	130	264	291	291	208	376	184	60	113	206	206	193
Kreuzlingen	109	161	85	144	246	187	181	276	365	68	140	219	354	140	230	251	—	249	291	216	209	122	317	321	129	63	61	218	63	216	386	151	271	42	95	66
Kandersteg	147	127	166	159	161	57	64	42	234	224	120	102	230	156	43	—	251	132	132	140	141	73	72	115	128	282	384	384	151	378	44	74	123	204	204	185
Interlaken	136	91	159	152	190	57	96	85	240	204	130	95	230	118	—	43	230	125	167	207	245	66	167	108	121	255	282	282	144	278	99	108	149	197	197	178
Glarus	114	85	92	149	171	192	186	201	235	68	180	224	290	—	118	156	140	254	296	207	190	92	324	237	134	118	96	152	118	144	349	164	280	92	65	69
Genève	250	321	273	266	420	161	171	198	470	410	198	138	—	290	230	230	354	140	62	443	445	282	135	123	235	369	396	491	337	481	162	209	91	311	307	292
Fribourg	115	186	138	131	285	36	43	115	335	272	118	—	138	224	95	102	219	63	75	308	310	102	101	46	100	234	261	356	202	346	128	66	52	185	157	157
Delémont	77	150	104	41	240	86	43	173	298	234	—	118	198	180	130	120	140	60	173	270	272	124	193	79	62	234	261	318	170	310	243	43	170	138	169	119
Chur	162	133	138	197	115	234	234	298	167	—	234	272	410	68	204	224	68	271	344	140	142	140	370	297	182	104	77	77	104	55	397	210	326	138	131	117
Chiasso	256	267	267	290	52	298	297	176	—	167	298	335	470	235	240	204	365	365	407	52	26	190	370	297	245	293	229	151	293	276	229	274	390	267	267	244
Brig	172	195	195	188	93	77	83	—	176	298	173	115	198	201	85	42	276	161	105	136	151	154	57	144	161	346	324	324	308	376	55	150	57	233	218	214
Biel/Bienne	77	148	100	93	247	34	—	83	297	234	43	43	171	186	96	64	181	42	105	270	272	109	115	34	62	196	207	318	164	308	200	34	132	138	131	119
Bern	83	154	106	99	253	—	34	77	298	234	86	36	161	192	57	57	187	66	108	182	214	91	91	49	68	202	203	229	170	314	161	41	90	144	137	125
Bellinzona	206	229	229	240	—	253	247	93	52	115	240	285	420	171	190	161	246	284	357	25	27	132	213	348	245	270	218	151	293	186	229	223	337	217	182	194
Basel	70	141	63	—	240	99	93	188	290	197	41	131	266	149	152	159	144	101	203	263	265	102	256	144	55	159	186	281	127	271	256	69	185	101	124	82
Baden	28	119	—	63	229	106	100	195	267	138	104	138	273	92	159	166	85	168	210	252	254	91	236	151	100	127	138	222	68	214	263	76	192	42	50	23
Altdorf	107	—	119	141	229	154	148	195	267	133	150	186	321	85	91	127	161	216	258	130	132	41	195	199	176	100	127	222	144	207	311	126	244	118	69	95
Aarau	—	107	28	70	206	83	77	172	256	162	77	115	250	114	136	147	109	114	187	229	231	68	213	128	13	124	151	246	92	236	240	53	169	66	57	47

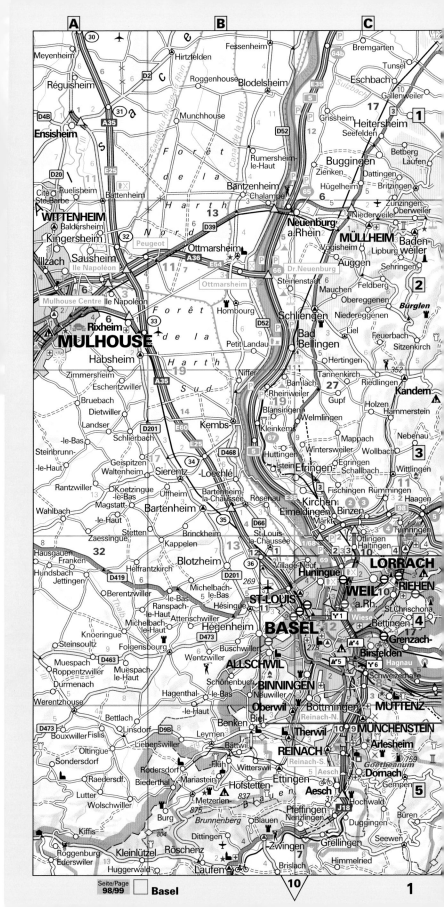

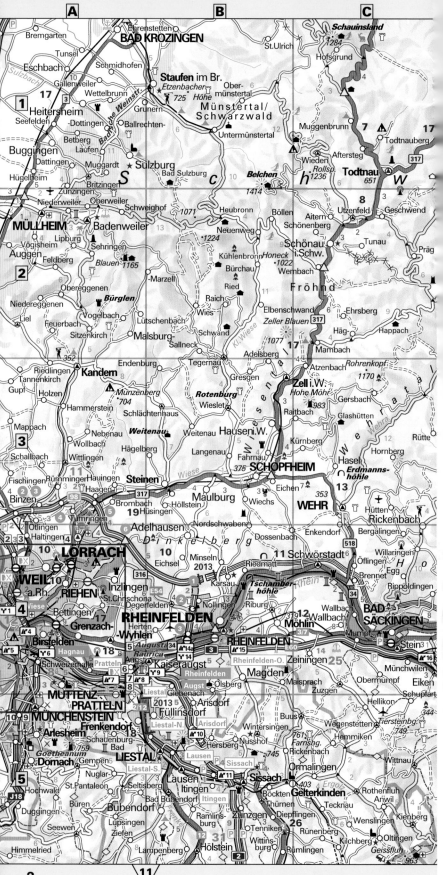

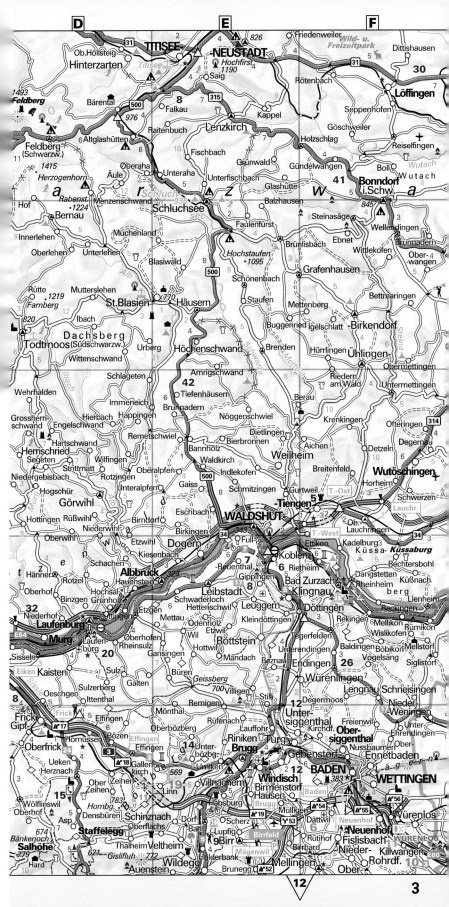

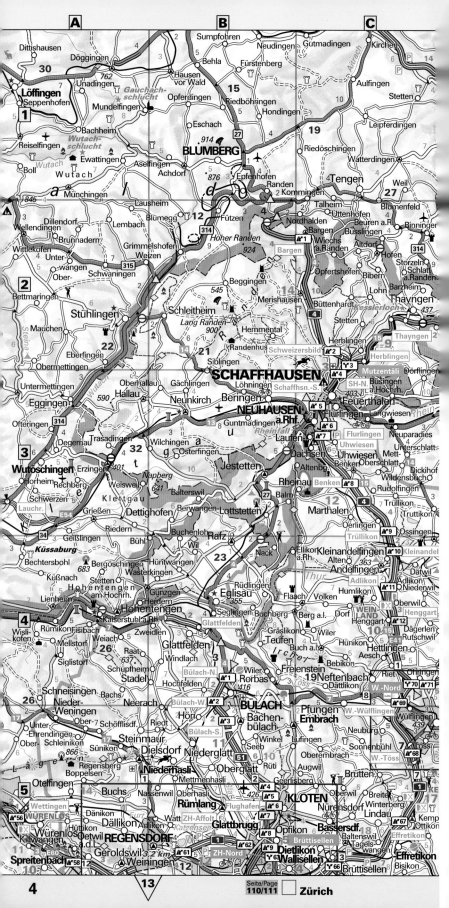

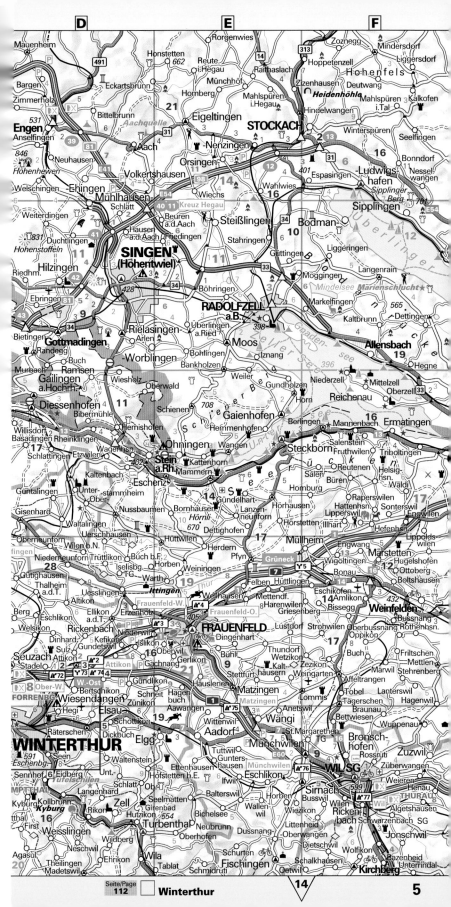

St. Gallen

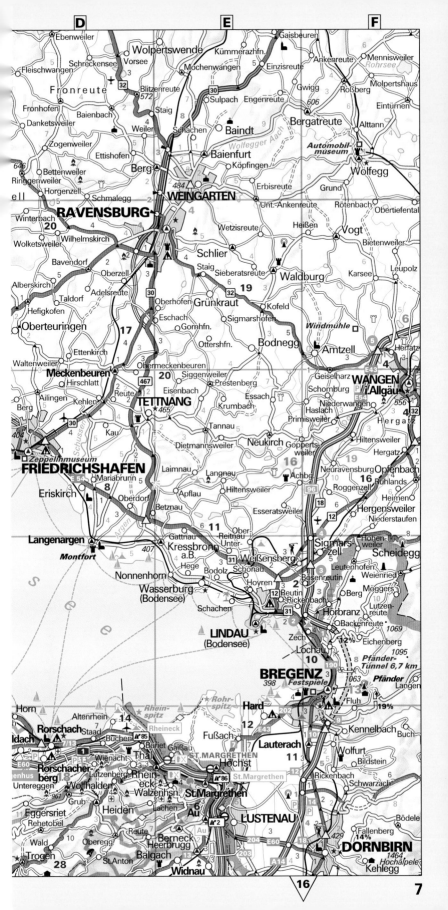

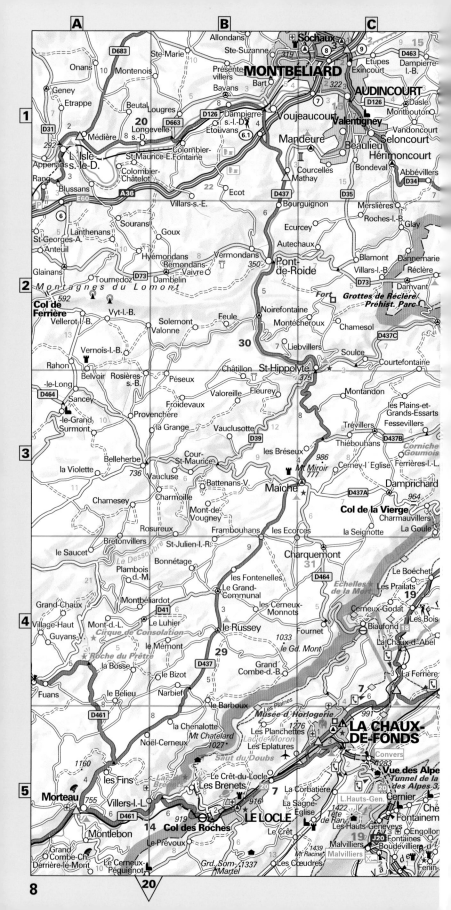

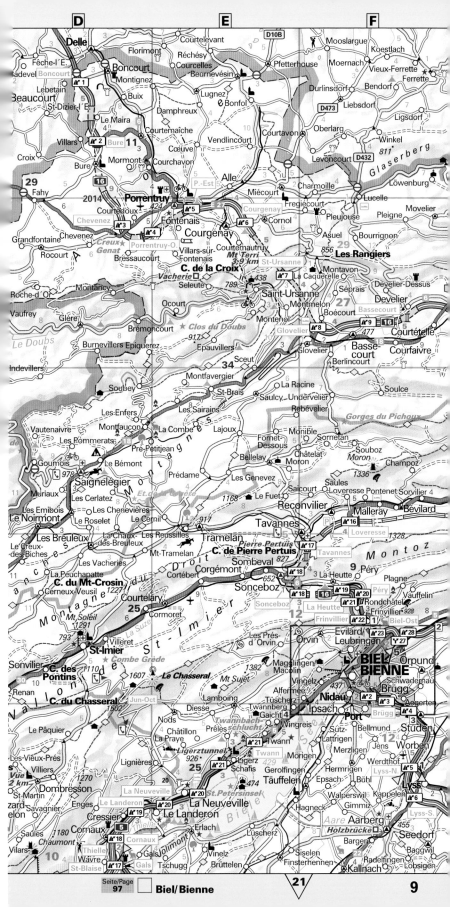

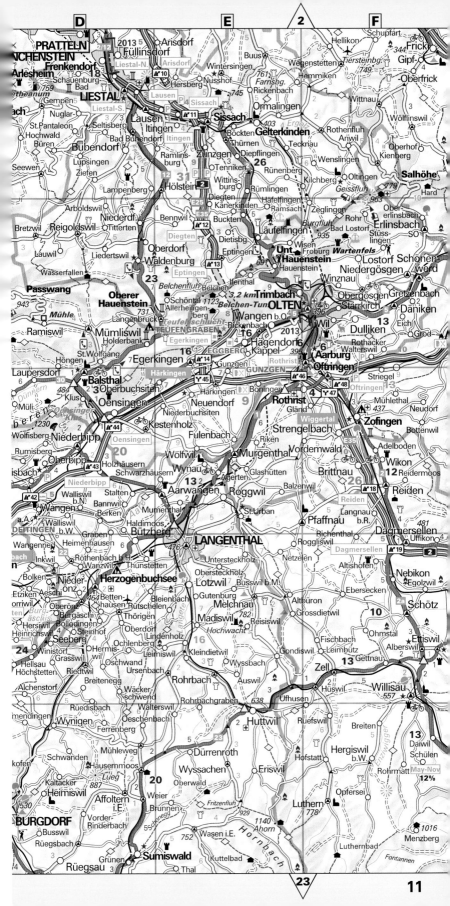

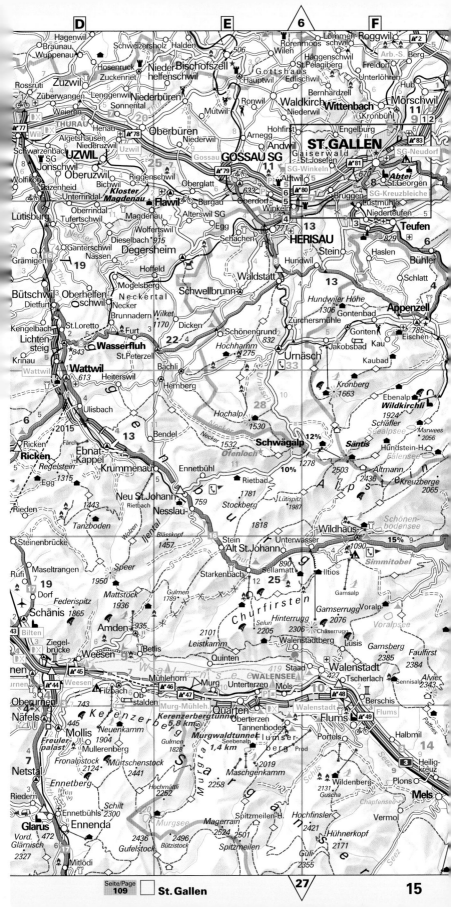

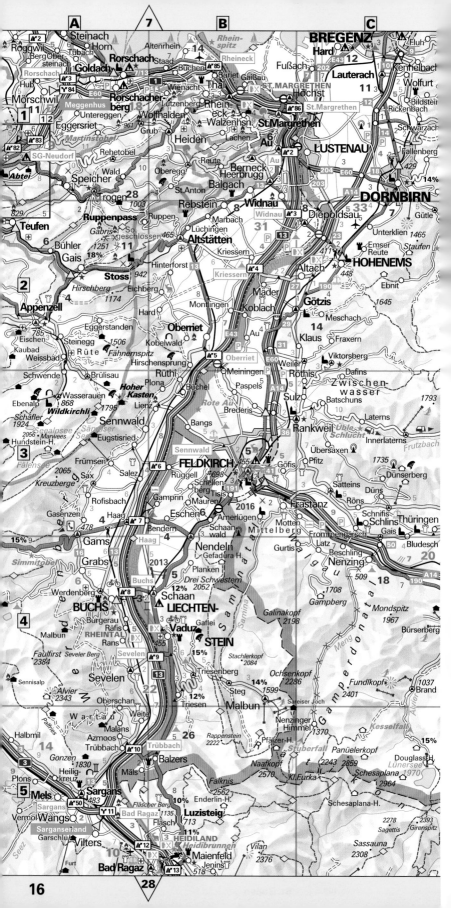

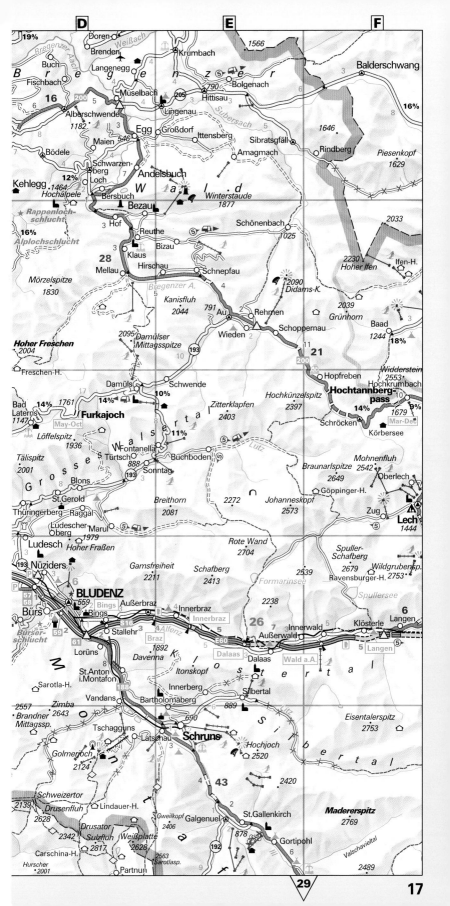

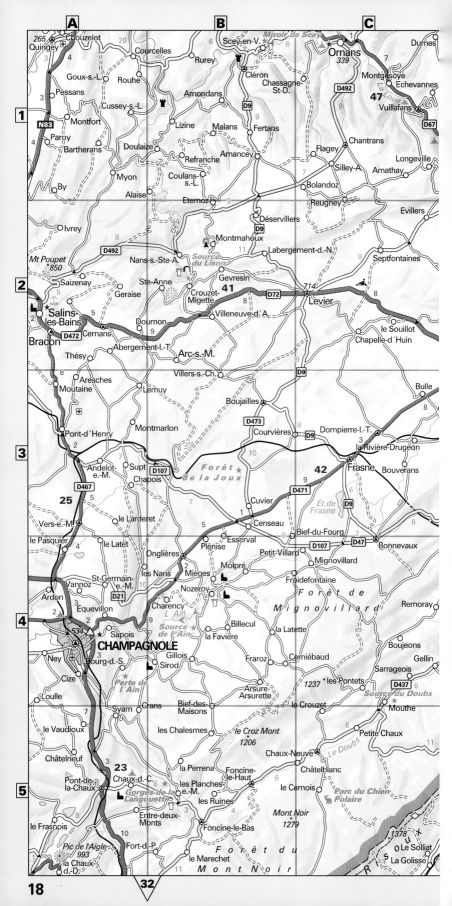

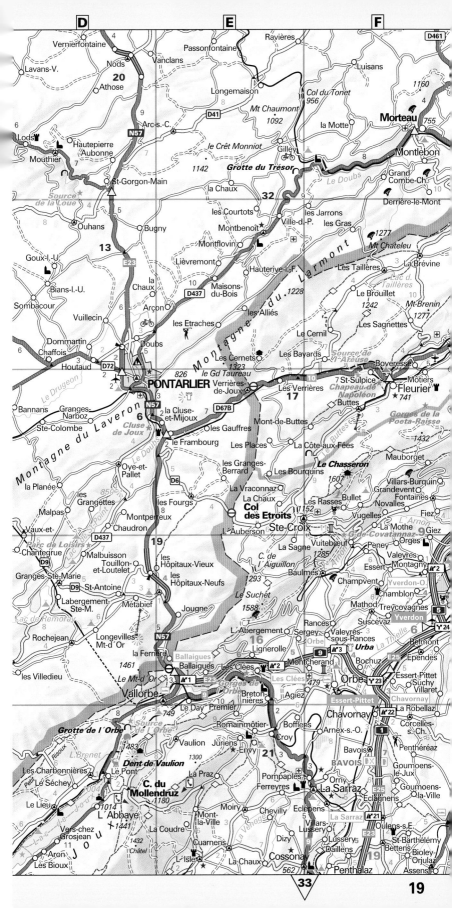

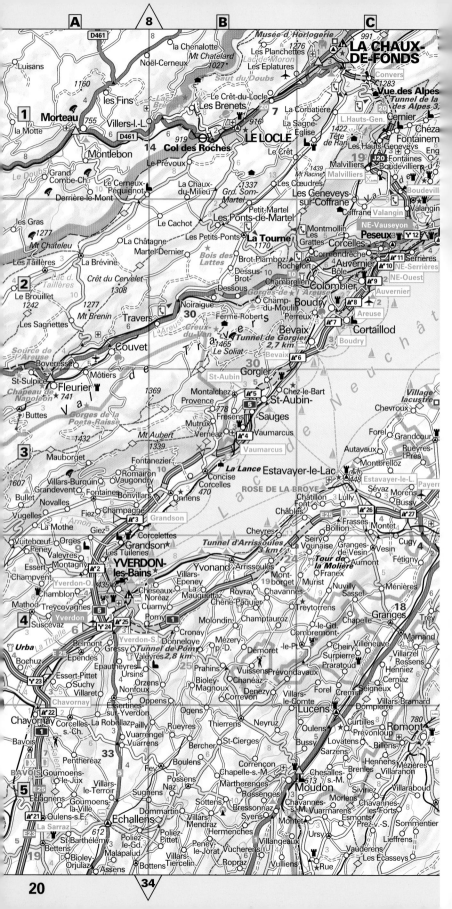

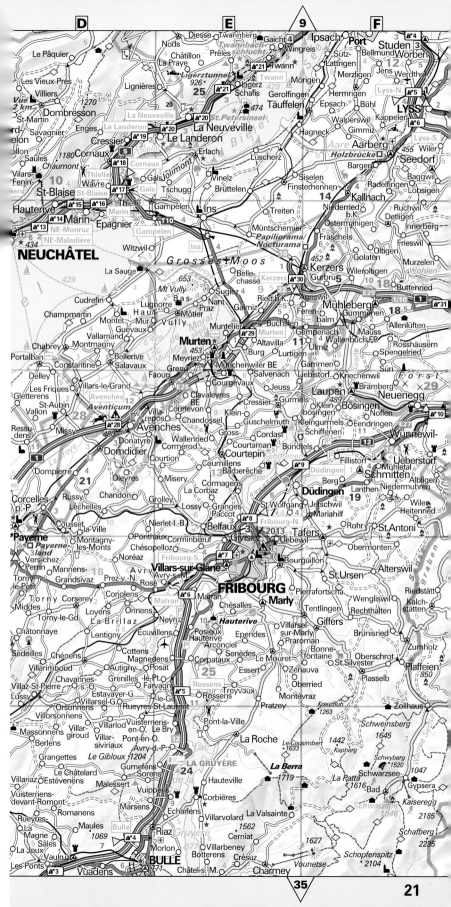

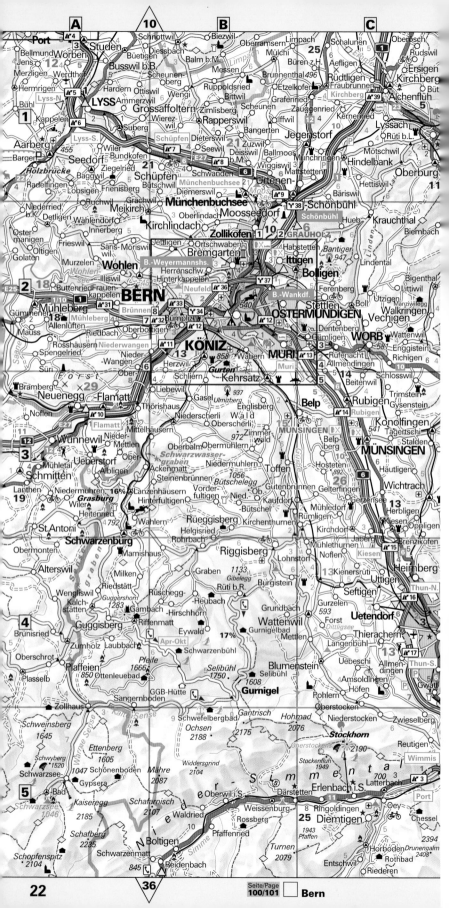

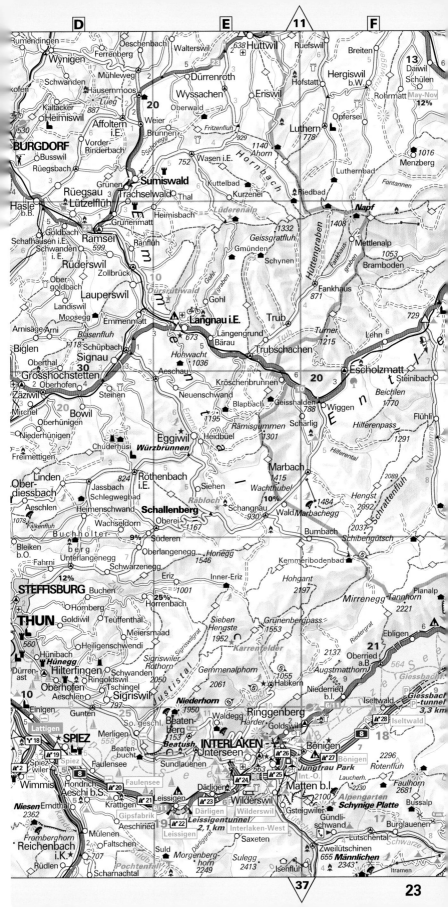

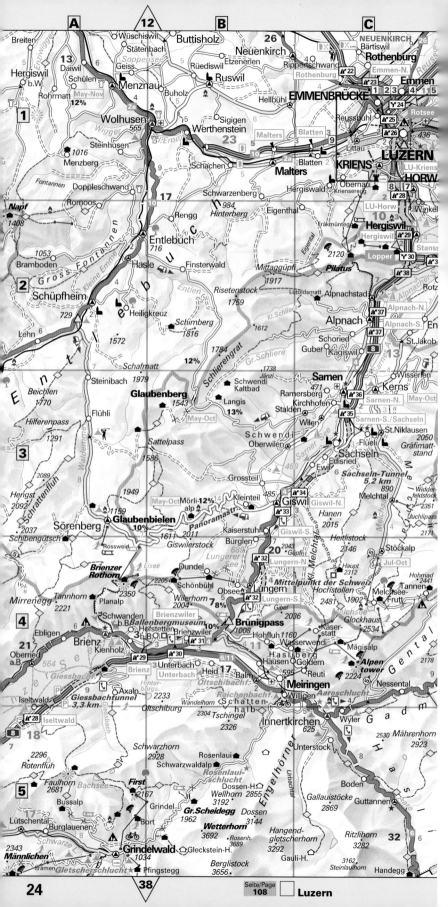

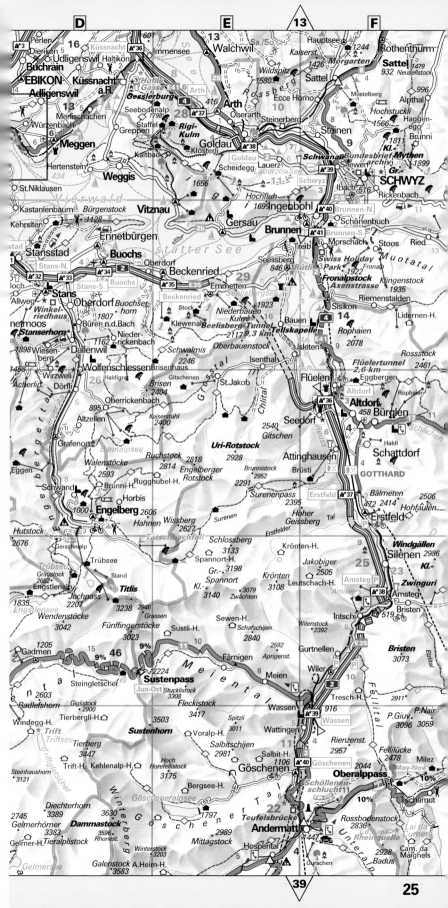

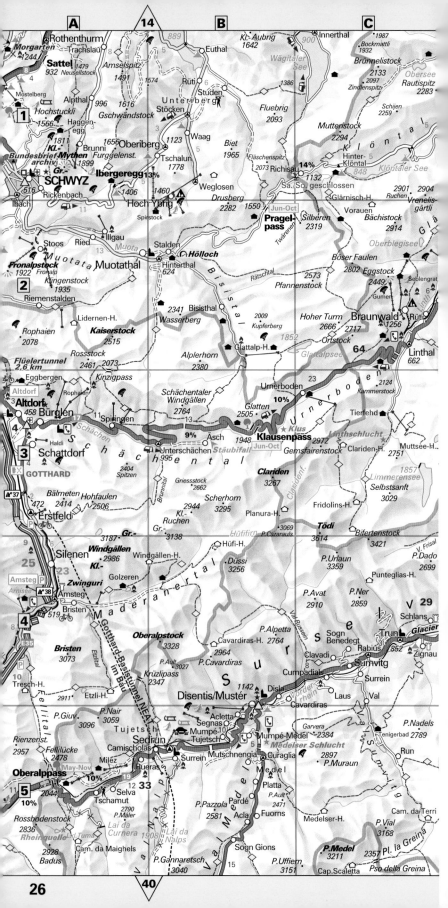

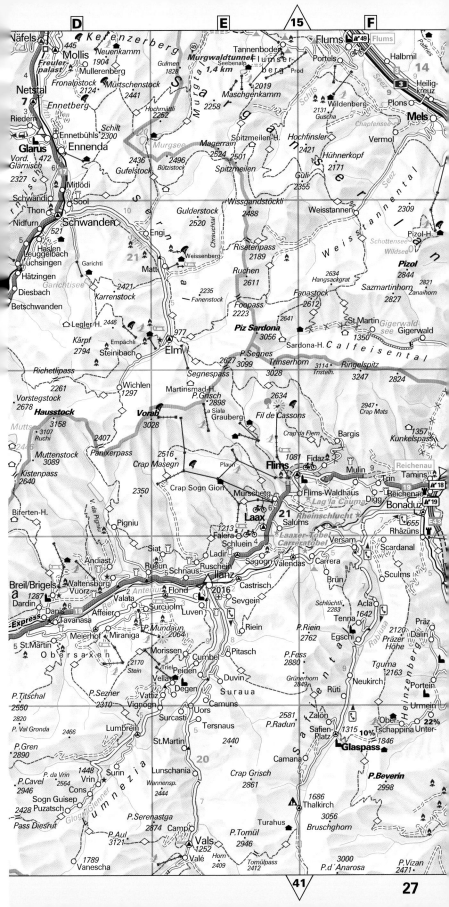

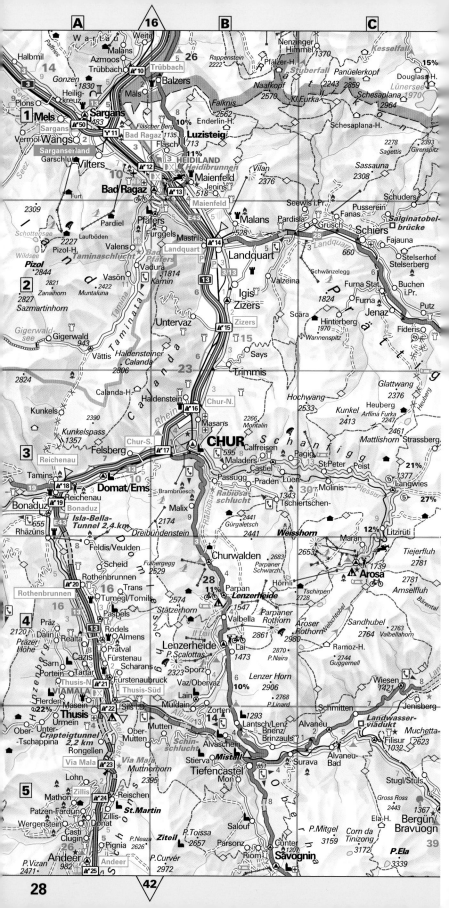

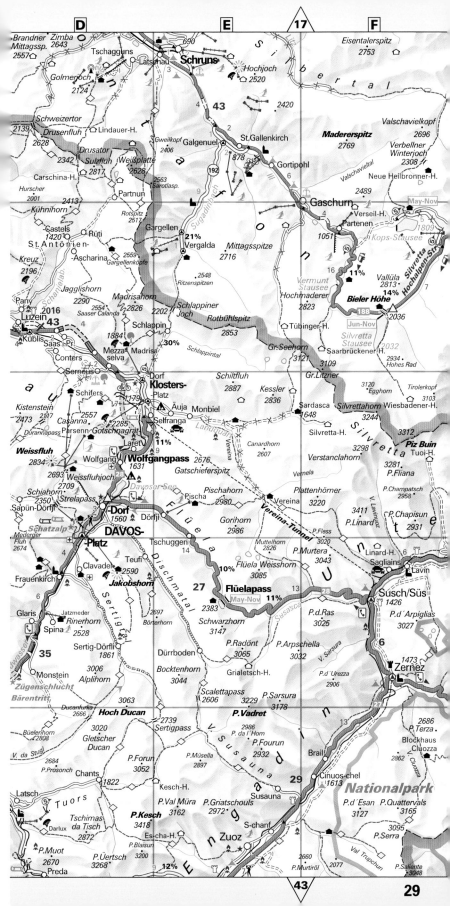

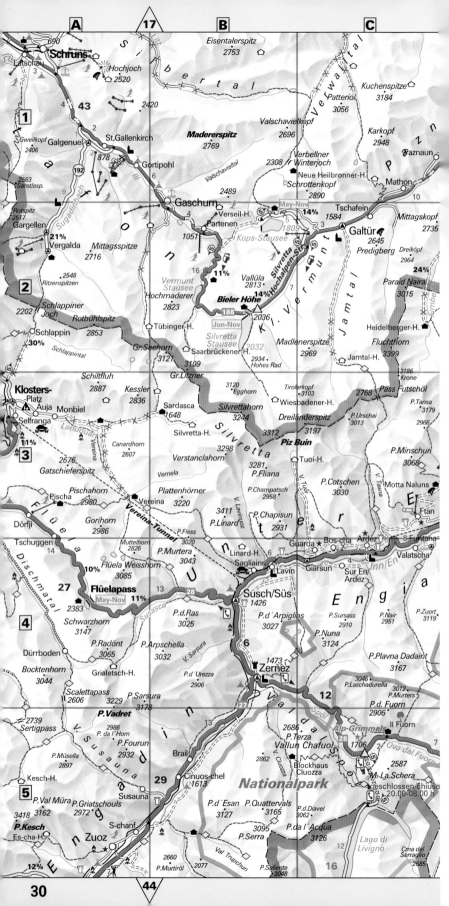

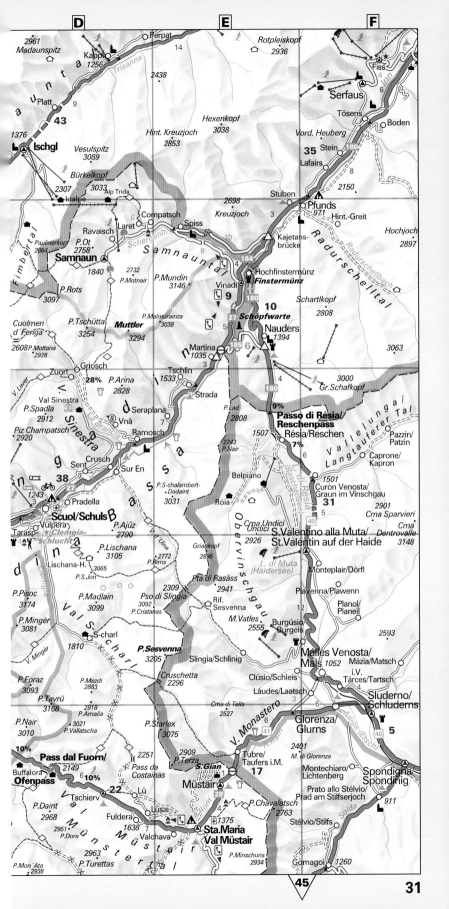

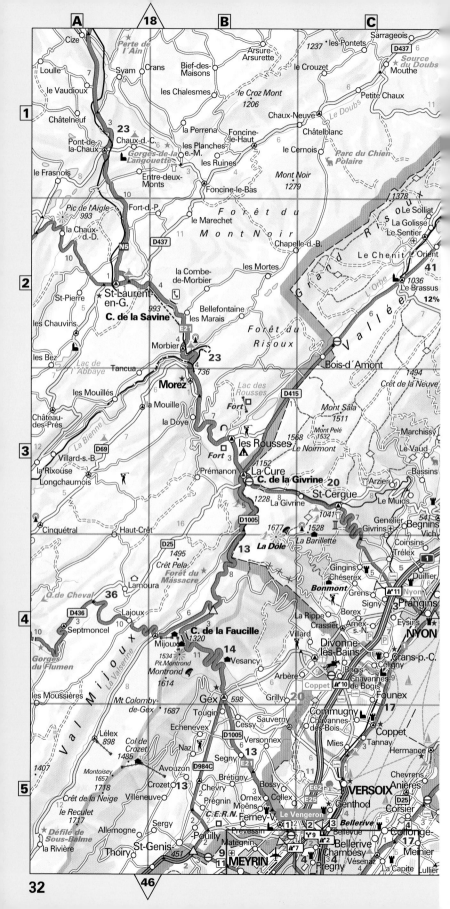

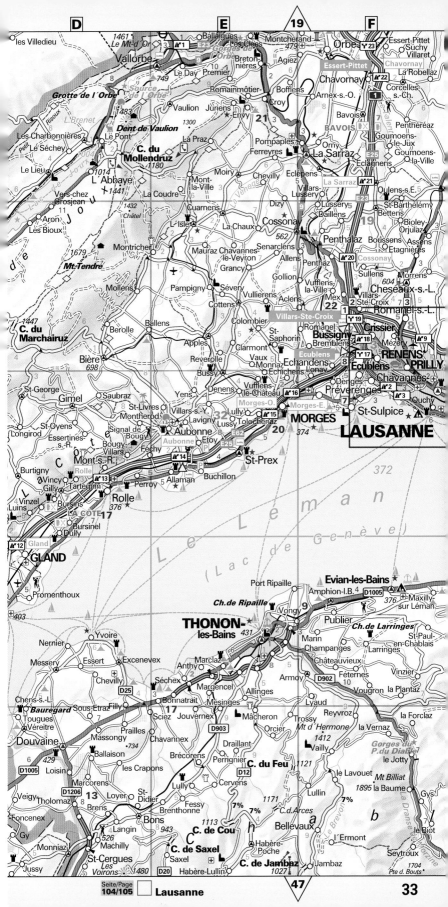

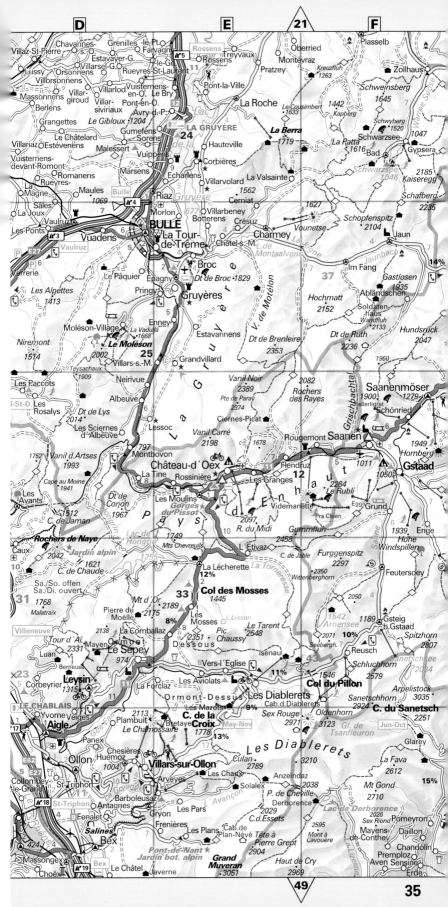

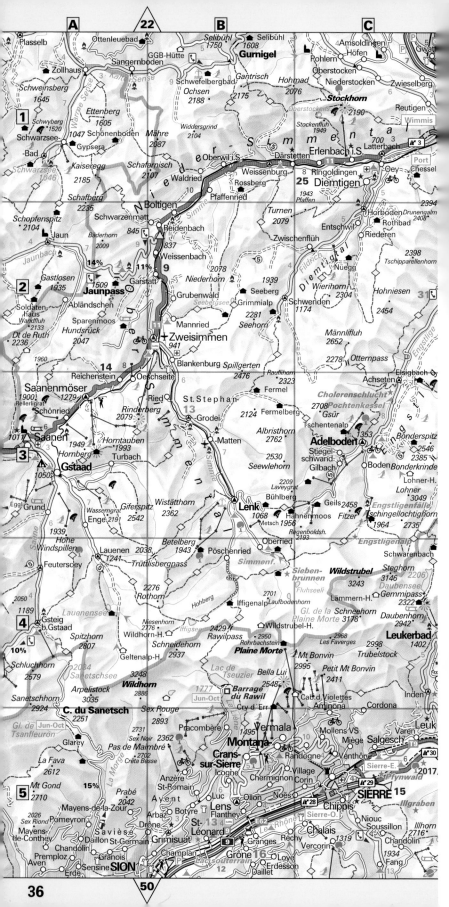

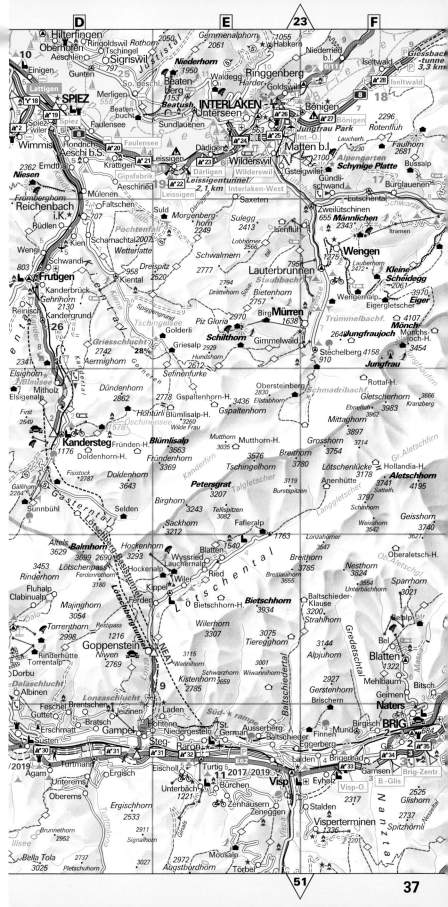

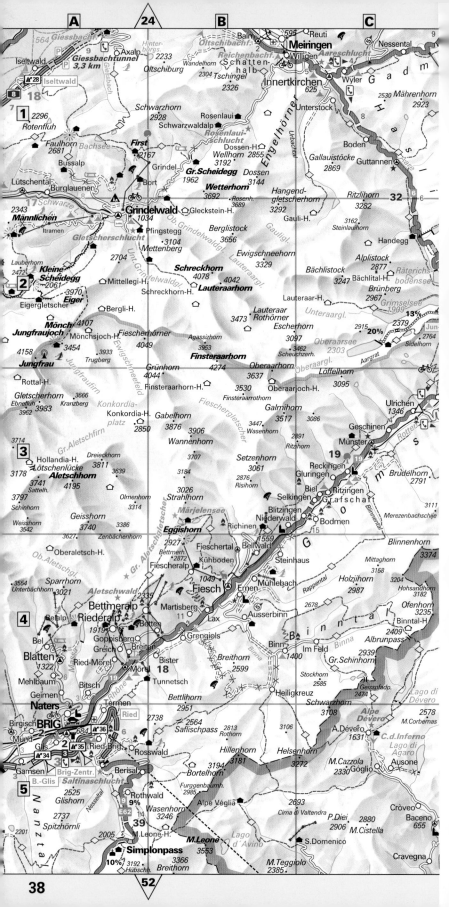

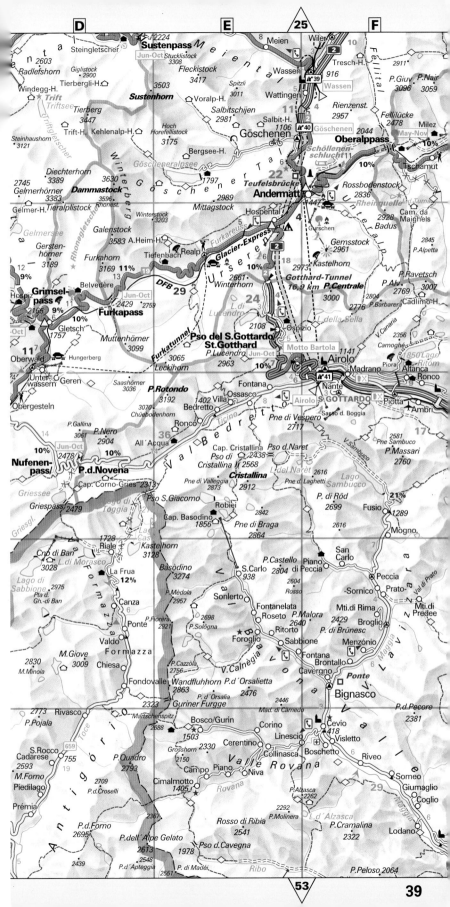

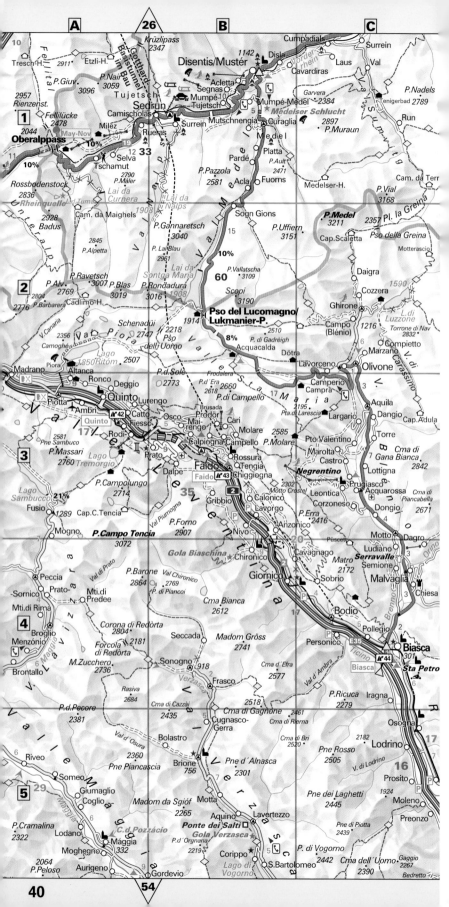

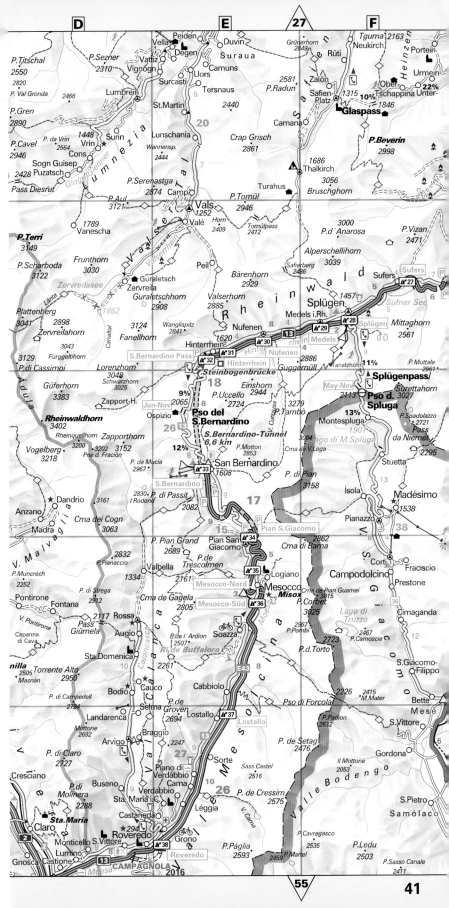

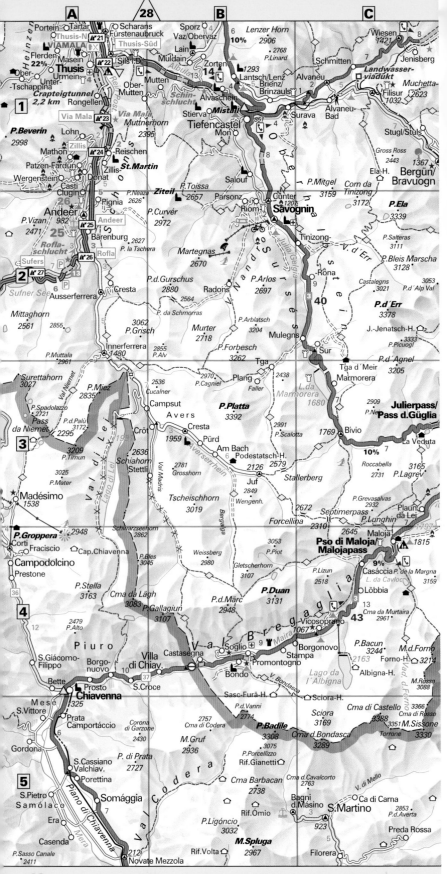

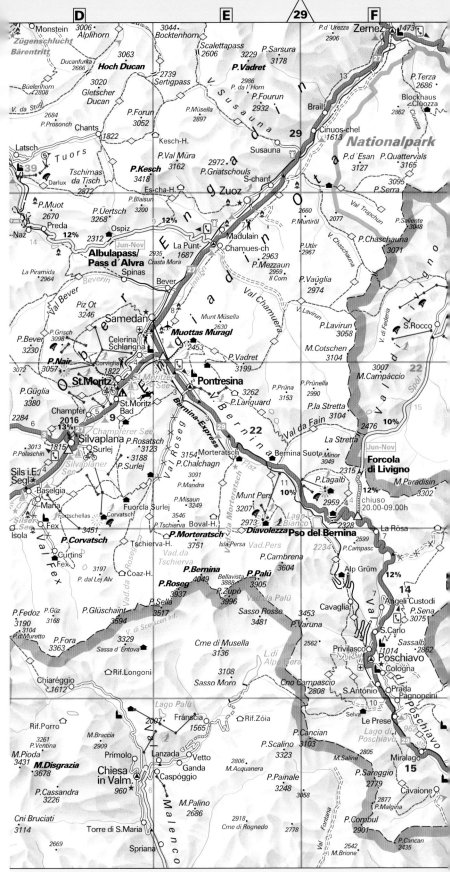

43

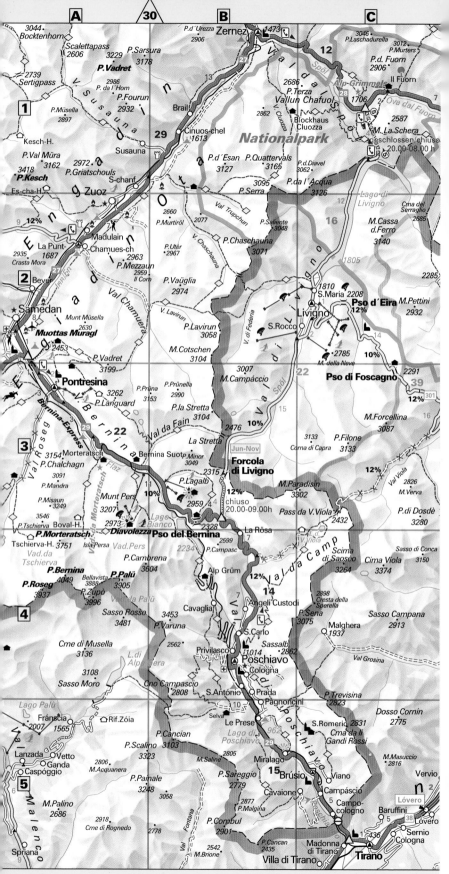

44

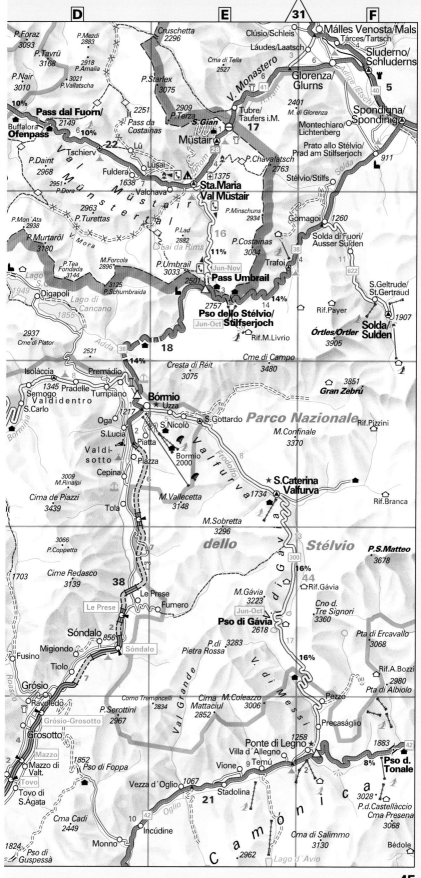

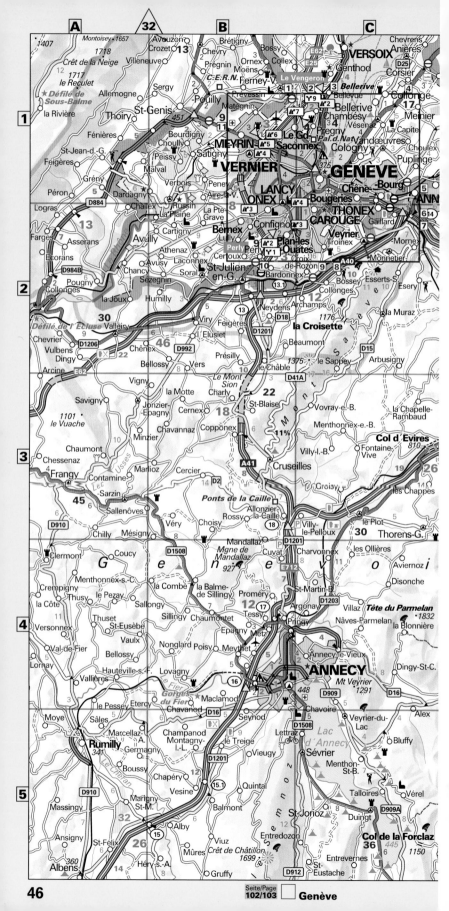

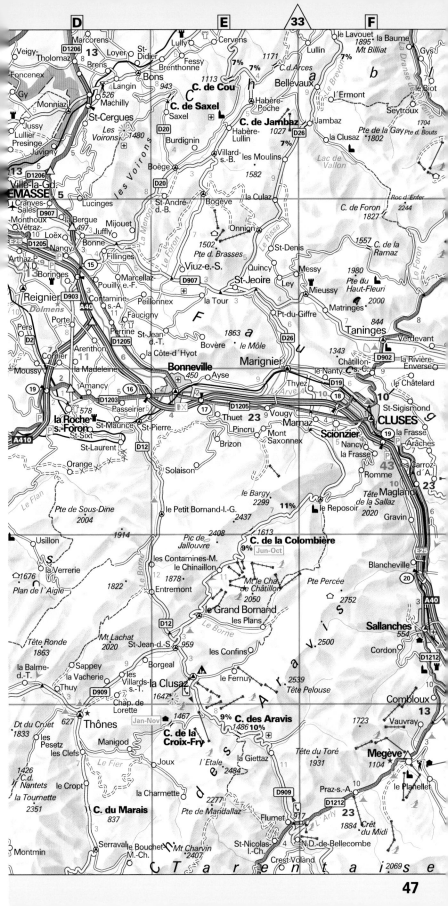

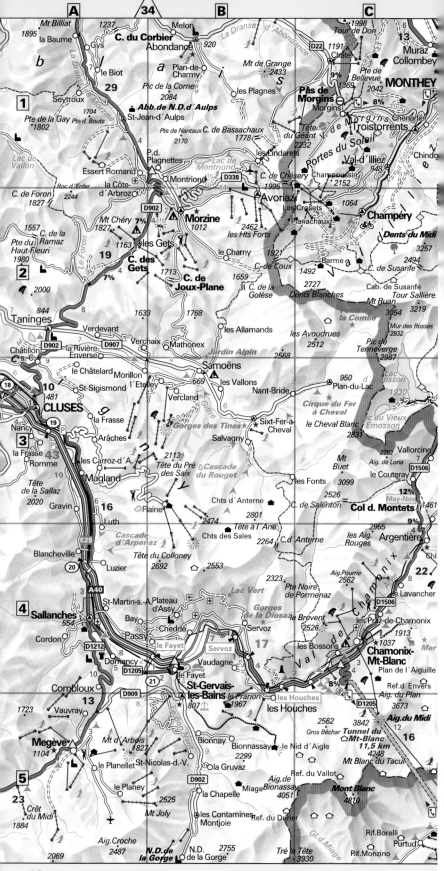

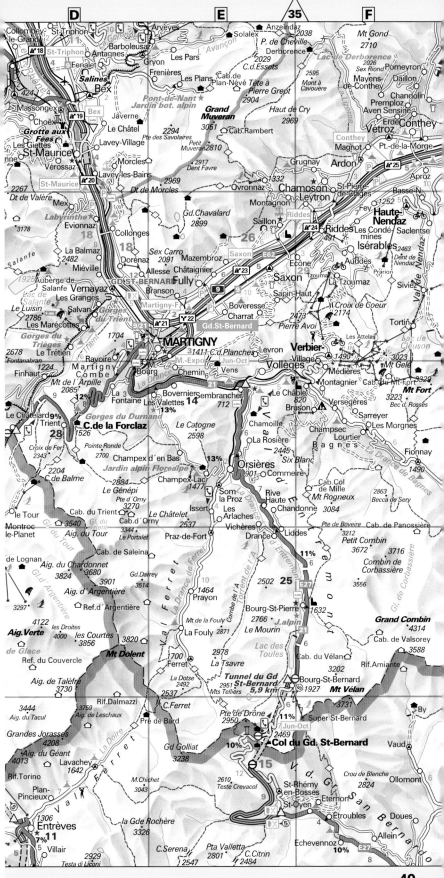

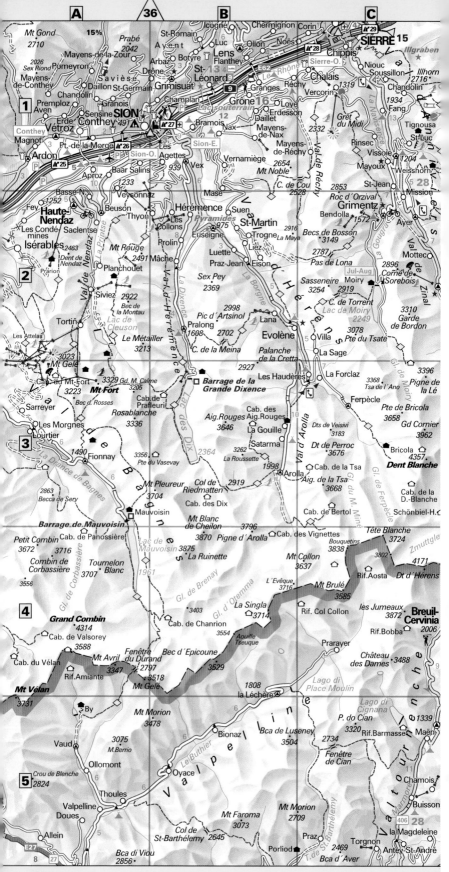

50

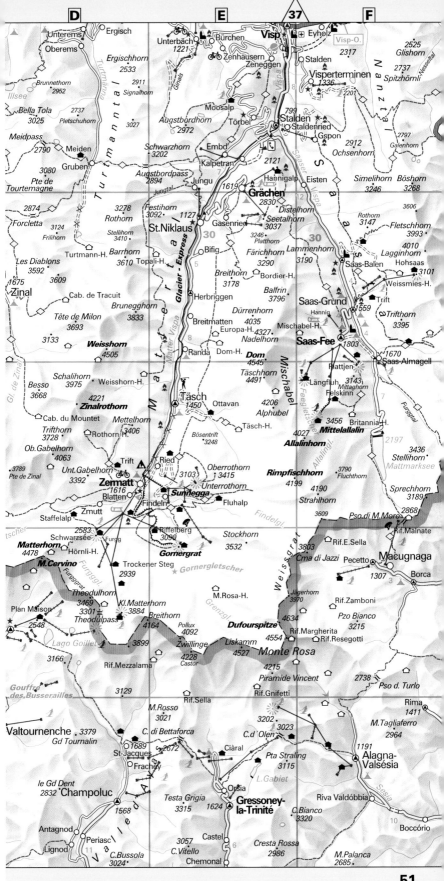

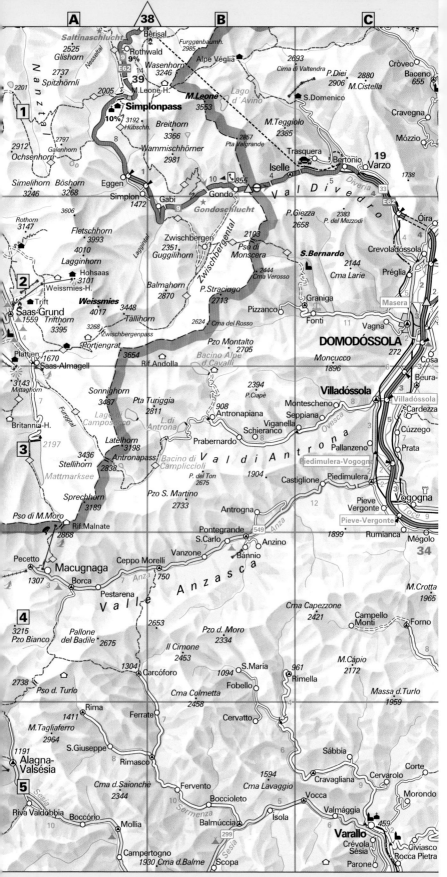

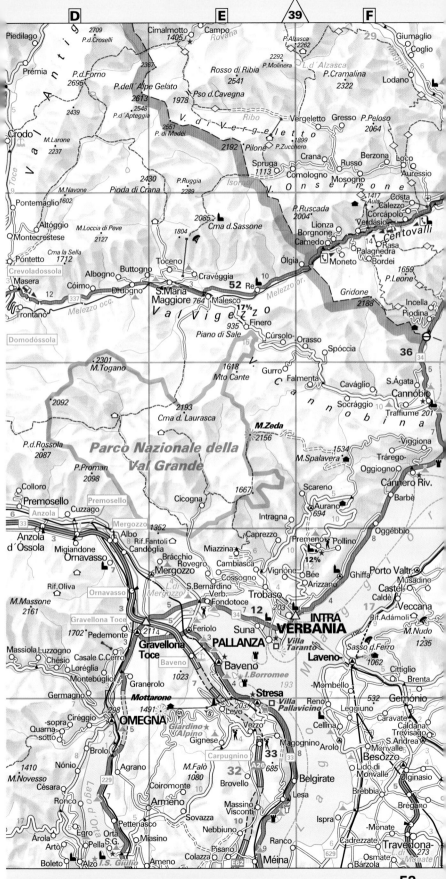

29

Piedilago
Premia
P.d.Croselli 2709
Cimalmotto 1405
Campo
Rovana
P.Alzasca 2262
Giumaglio
Coglio

P.d.Forno 2695
2367
P.dell'Alpe Gelato 2613
1978
Rosso di Ribia 2541
2292
P.Molinera
L.d'Alzasca
P.Cramalina 2322
Lodano

Crodo
2439
2548
P.d'Apteggia
V. d i V e r g e l e t t o
Ribo
Vergeletto
Gresso P.Peloso 2064

M.Larone 2237
2551
P. di Madéi
2192
Pilone
1899
P.Zucchero
Crana
Russo
Berzona
Loco
Auréssio

Pontemaglio 1602
M.Navone
2430
Pioda di Crana
P.Ruggia 2289
Spruga 1113
Isorno
Comologno
Mosogno
V. O n s e r n o n e

Altóggio
Montecrestese
M.Loccia di Peve 2127
2085
Cma d.Sassone
1804
Calezzo
1417
Aula
Corcápolo
Verdásio
Costa

Crevoladóssola
Pontetto 1712
Cma la Sella
Albogno
Buttogno
Toceno
Cravéggia
P.Ruscada 2004
Lionza
Borgnone
Camedo
Centovalli
Rasa
Palagnedra
Bordei

Masera
12
337
Drugno
S.Maria Maggiore 764
Malesco
3
52 Re
10
Ólgia
Moneto
14
Gridone 2188
1659
P.Leone
Incella
Piodina

Trontano
Melezzo occ.
Melezzo or.
V a l V i g e z z o
17%
Finero
935
36
34

Domodóssola
Piano di Sale
15
Cúrsolo
Orasso
Spóccia
S.Ágata

M.Togano 2301
1618
Mto Cante
V.
Gurro
Falmenta
Caváglio
Cannóbio

2092
2193
Cma d. Laurasca
M.Zeda 2156
C a n n o b i n a
Socrággio
Traffiume 201

P.d.Rossola 2087
Parco Nazionale della Val Grande
1667
1534
M.Spalavera
Viggiona
Trárego-
Oggiogno

P.Proman 2098
Cicogna
Scareno
Cánnero Riv.
Barbè

Colloro
Premosello
Premosello
Intragna
Aurano 694
Oggébbio

Premosello
Anzola
Cuzzago
Mergozzo
1352
Caprezzo
Premeno
Pollino
12%
Porto Valtr.
Músadino

Anzola d'Óssola
3
Albo
Rif.Fantoli
Candóglia
Brácchio
Rovegro
Miazzina
Cambiasca
Vignone
Bée
Arizzano
Ghiffa
Castel-
Calde
Veccana
Rif.Adámoli
17

Migiandone
Ornavasso
Mergozzo
Cossogno
S.Bernardino Verb.
Trobaso
203
M.Nudo 1235

Rif.Oliva
Ornavasso
L.di Mergozzo
Fondotoce
34
12
INTRA VERBANIA
Sasso d.Ferro 1062

M.Massone 2161
Gravellona Toce
2114
Feriolo
Suna
Villa Taranto
PALLANZA
Laveno
Cittiglio
Brenta

1702
Pedemonte
Gravellona Toce
Baveno
Baveno
I.Borromee
193
Mombello
532
Gemónio

Massiola
Luzzogno
Casale C.Cerro
Montebúglio
Granerolo
1023
7
Stresa
Villa Pallavicino
Reno
Leggiuno
Caravate
Caldana
Trevisago
S.Andrea

Germagno
-sopra
Ciréggio
298
OMEGNA
Mottarone 1491
Levo
203
Vézzo
Cellina
Arolo
Monvalle
Besozzo

Quarna
-sotto
Brolo
Giardino Alpino
Gignese
Magognino
685
Belgirate
Lido di Monvalle
Olginasio

1410
M.Novesso
Agrano
229
Coiromonte
M.Falò 1080
Carpugnino
Brovello
32
33
33
A26
Lesa
Brébbia
Brégano

Césara
Ronco
Arméno
Sovazza
Massino Visconti
10
Nebbiuno
Ranco
Ispra
-Monate

Árola
Artò
Egro
Pella
Orta S.Giulio
Pettenasco
Miasino
Ameno
Pisano
Colazza
Méina
E62
Cadrezzate
Osmate
Bárzola
Travedona
L.di Monate 273

Boleto
Alzo
I.S. Giulio
Nónio
Chésio
Loréglia
Pedemonte

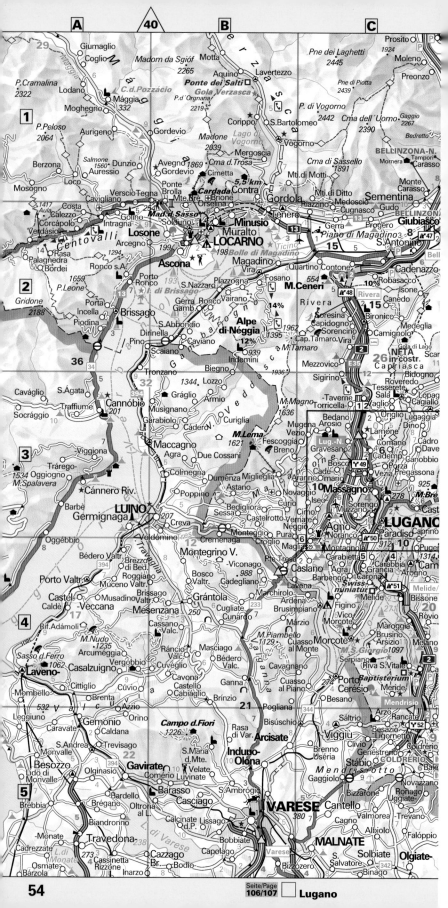

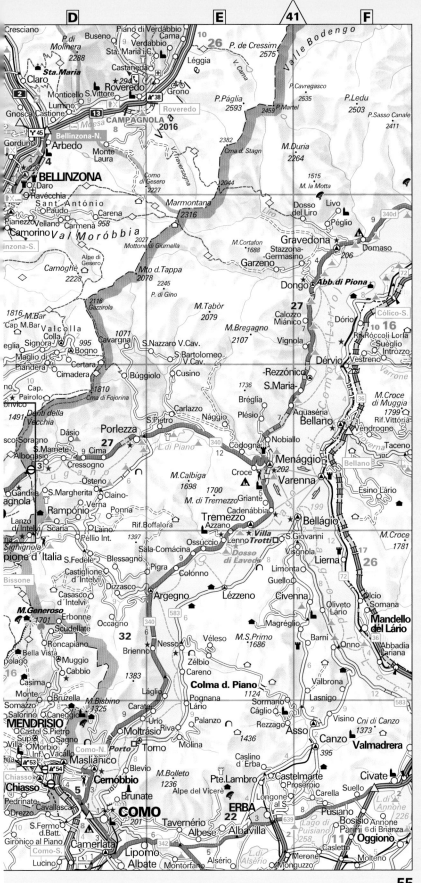

Ortsverzeichnis • Index des lieux
Town index • Plaatsnamenregister
Indice dei luoghi • Indice de lugares
Ortsförteckning • Stedsfortegnelse

Legende · Légende · Legend · Verklaring
Leggenda · Leyenda · Teckenförklaring · Signaturforklaring

8355 Aadorf TG **5** E5

Postleitzahl · Code postal · Postal code · Postcode
Codice postale · Código postal · Postnummer · Postnummer

Ort · Lieu · Town · Plaats · Località · Lugar · Ort · Sted

Kanton · Canton · Canton · Kanton · Cantone · Cantón · Kanton · Kanton

Seite · Page · Page · Pagina · Pagina · Página · Sida · Side

Suchfeld · Grille de recherche · Reference grid · Coördinaten
Quadretto · Area de referencia · Rutnät · Område

AG	Aargau	GE	Genève	OW	Obwalden	UR	Uri
AI	Appenzell-Innerrhoden	GL	Glarus	SG	St. Gallen	VD	Vaud
AR	Appenzell-Ausserrhoden	GR	Graubünden	SH	Schaffhausen	VS	Valais
BE	Bern	JU	Jura	SO	Solothurn	ZG	Zug
BL	Basel-Landschaft	LU	Luzern	SZ	Schwyz	ZH	Zürich
BS	Basel-Stadt	NE	Neuchâtel	TG	Thurgau		
FR	Fribourg	NW	Nidwalden	TI	Ticino	FL	Liechtenstein

Orte mit Stationen der öffentlichen Verkehrsmittel
Lieux avec stations de transports publics
Towns with public transport stations
Plaatsen met stations voor openbaar vervoer
Luoghi con stazione di mezzi pubblici
Lugares con estaciones de medios de transporte
Orter med trafikstationer
Steder med stationer for offentlig transport

Station für · Station pour · Station for · Station voor
Stazione per · Estación para · Station för · Station for

Eisenbahn, Tram, Zahnradbahn, Standseilbahn · Chemin de fer, Tramway, Crémaillère, Funiculaire
Railway, Tramway, Rackrailway, Cable railway · Spoorwag, Tram, Tandradbaan, Kabelbaan
Ferrovia, Tramvai, Cremagliera, Funicolare · Ferrocarril, Tranvia, Cremallera, Funicular
Järnväg, Tram, Kugghjulsbana, Linbana · Jernbane, Sporvogn, Tandhjulsbane, Tovbane

Postauto, Autobus, Trolleybus · Autobus postal, Autobus, Trolleybus
Postal coach, Motor coach, Trolleybus · Postauto, Bus, Trolleybus
Corriera postale, Autobus, Filobus · Autobús postal, Autocar, Trolébus
Postbuss, Buss, Trolleybuss · Postbus, Bus, Trolleybus

Luftseilbahn · Téléphérique · Aerial cable railway · Kabelbaan
Funivia · Teleférico · Linbana · Kabelbane

Schiff · Bateau · Ship · Schip · Batello · Barco · Båt · Skib

Orte mit Sport- und Freizeitmöglichkeiten
Lieux avec possibilités de sport et de loisirs
Towns with sports and free-time possibilities
Plaatsen met sport- en recreatiemogelijkheden
Luoghi con possibilità per sport e tempo di ricambio
Lugares con posibilidades recreativas y de deporte
Orter med möjligheter för sport och fritidsaktiviteter
Steder med sport og fritidsmuligheder

Hallenbad · Piscine couverte · Indoor swimming-pool · Overdekt zwembad
Piscina coperta · Piscina cubierta · Inomhusbad · Indendørs svømmehal

Schwimmbad · Piscine · Swimming-pool · Zwembad · Piscina · Piscina · Simbad · Svømmebad

Eisbahn · Patinoire · Ice rink · Ijsbaan · Pattinaggio · Patinaje · Skridskobana · Skøjtebane

Tennis, offen oder Halle · Tennis, plein air ou couvert
Tennis, open air or indoor · Tennisbaan, openlucht of overdekt
Tennis, aperto o in palestra · Tenis, aire libre o cubierta
Tennis, inom- eller utomhus · Tennis, uden- eller indendørs

Museum · Musée · Museum · Museum · Museo · Museo · Museum · Museum

5330 Bad Zurzach AG **3** F4
5400 Baden AG **3** F5
3267 Baggwil BE **22** A1
1934 Bagnes VS **49** F3
6283 Baldegg LU **12** C4
5333 Baldingen AG **3** F4
6828 Balerna TI **55** D5
9436 Balgach SG **16** B1
1338 Ballaigues VD **19** E4
1144 Ballens VD **33** D2
3303 Ballmoos BE **22** B1
6275 Ballwil LU **12** C4
3860 Balm BE **24** B4
4525 Balm b. G. SO **10** C3
3254 Balm b. M. SO **10** B5
1902 Balmaz, La VS **49** D2
4710 Balsthal SO **11** D3
8303 Baltenswil ZH **4** C5
8362 Balterswil TG **5** E2
3937 Baltschieder (Ausserberg) VS **37** E5
4856 Balzenwil AG **11** E3
9496 Balzers FL **16** B5
3256 Bangerten BE **22** B1
4913 Bannwil BE **11** D3
3552 Bärau BE **23** E2
6917 Barbengo TI **54** C4
1783 Barberêche FR **21** E3
1882 Barboleusaz VD **35** E5
1257 Bardonnex GE **46** B2
7431 Bärenburg GR **42** A2
8344 Bäretswil ZH **14** B2
3282 Bargen BE **21** F1
8233 Bargen SH **4** C2
7019 Bargis GR **27** F3
3323 Bäriswil BE **22** C1
4252 Bärschwil SO **10** B2
6023 Bärtiswil LU **12** C5
8241 Barzheim SH **4** C2
8254 Basadingen TG **5** D3
4000 Basel BS **1** C4
2854 Bassecourt JU **9** F2
8303 Bassersdorf ZH **4** C5
1269 Bassins VD **32** C3
3315 Bätterkinden BE **10** C4
4112 Bättwil SO **1** B5
6466 Bauen UR **25** E2
1446 Baulmes VD **19** F4
8494 Bauma ZH **14** B2
1372 Bavois VD **33** F1
2127 Bayards, Les NE **19** F2
9602 Bazenheid SG **5** F5
3803 Beatenberg BE **37** E1
8413 Bebikon ZH **4** C4
6375 Beckenried NW **25** E2
6930 Bedano TI **54** C3
6981 Bedigliora TI **54** B3
6781 Bedretto TI **39** E3
8228 Beggingen SH **4** B2
1268 Begnins VD **32** C3
5637 Beinwil AG **13** D3
4229 Beinwil SO **11** D4
5712 Beinwil a. S. AG **12** B3
3113 Beitenwil BE **22** C3
3914 Bel VS **37** F4
1782 Belfaux FR **21** E3
4512 Bellach SO **10** C4
1786 Bellechasse FR **21** E2
2713 Bellelay BE **9** E3
1585 Bellerive VD **21** D2
1245 Bellerive, Collonge- GE **46** C1
1293 Bellevue GE **46** C1
5454 Bellikon AG **13** D2
6500 Bellinzona TI **55** D1
2564 Bellmund BE **9** F5
3997 Bellwald VS **38** B4
1432 Belmont VD **20** A4
1092 Belmont VD **34** B3
3123 Belp BE **22** C3
3124 Belpberg BE **22** C3

2744 Belprahon BE **10** B3
2877 Bémont, Le JU **9** D3
9643 Bendel SG **15** D3
9487 Bendern FL **16** A3
8121 Benglen ZH **13** F2
8717 Benken SG **14** C4
8463 Benken ZH **4** C3
4105 Benken, Biel- BL **1** B5
8836 Bennau SZ **14** A4
4431 Bennwil BL **11** E2
5636 Benzenschwil AG **13** D3
1038 Bercher VD **34** B1
3185 Berg FR **21** F3
9305 Berg SG **6** C5
8572 Berg TG **6** A4
8474 Berg ZH **5** D4
8415 Berg a. I. ZH **4** B4
8962 Bergdietikon AG **13** D2
7482 Bergün/Bravuogn GR **28** C5
8965 Berikon AG **13** D2
8222 Beringen SH **4** B3
3900 Berisal VS **38** A5
3376 Berken BE **11** D3
1680 Berlens FR **35** D1
2854 Berlincourt JU **9** F2
8267 Berlingen TG **5** F3
3000 Bern BE **22** B2
9442 Berneck SG **16** B1
1233 Bernex GE **46** B2
9304 Bernhardzell SG **15** F1
1149 Berolle VD **33** D2
6215 Beromünster LU **12** B4
8892 Berschis SG **15** F4
8544 Bertschikon ZH **5** D4
8614 Bertschikon ZH **14** C4
6661 Berzona TI **53** F1
6863 Besazio TI **54** C5
5627 Besenbüren AG **13** D3
8872 Betlis SG **15** D4
8777 Betschwanden GL **27** D2
3991 Betten VS **38** B4
3366 Bettenhausen BE **11** D4
1042 Bettens VD **19** F5
4126 Bettingen BS **2** A4
2544 Bettlach SO **10** B4
3992 Bettmeralp VS **38** A4
8344 Bettswil ZH **14** B2
9553 Bettwiesen TG **5** F5
5618 Bettwil AG **12** C3
2935 Beurnevésin JU **9** E1
1996 Beuson VS **50** A2
2022 Bevaix NE **20** C2
7502 Bever GR **44** A2
2735 Bévilard BE **10** A3
1880 Bex VD **49** D1
5303 Beznau AG **3** E4
6710 Biasca TI **40** C4
2326 Bianzfond BE **22** C2
8836 Biberbrugg SZ **14** A4
4562 Biberist SO **10** C4
8262 Bibermühle SH **5** D3
8242 Bibern SH **4** C2
4578 Bibern SO **10** B4
5023 Biberstein AG **12** B2
8363 Bichelsee TG **5** E5
9248 Bichwil SG **6** A5
6958 Biezikon TI **54** C3
3989 Biel (Grafschaft) VS **38** C3
2500 Biel/Bienne BE **9** F4
4105 Biel-Benken BL **10** C1
3419 Biembach BE **22** C2
2500 Bienne/Biel BE **9** F4
1145 Bière VD **33** D2
4585 Biezwil SO **10** B5
3924 Bifig VS **51** E2
3513 Bigenthal BE **22** C2
3507 Biglen BE **22** C2
6676 Bignasco TI **39** F4
1681 Billens-Hennens FR **34** C1
8865 Bilten GL **14** C4
3996 Binn VS **38** B4

4102 Binningen BL **1** C4
8122 Binz ZH **13** F2
8627 Binzikon ZH **14** A3
1407 Bioley-Magnoux VD **20** B4
1042 Bioley-Orjulaz VD **34** A2
1346 Bioux, Les VD **33** D2
8841 Birchli SZ **14** A4
3903 Birgisch VS **37** F5
8903 Birmensdorf ZH **13** D2
5413 Birmenstorf AG **12** C1
6804 Bironico (Rivera) TI **54** C2
5242 Birr AG **3** E5
5244 Birrhard AG **12** C1
5628 Birri AG **13** D3
5708 Birrwil AG **12** B3
4127 Birsfelden BL **1** C4
8585 Birwinken TG **6** B4
9220 Bischofszell TG **15** E1
8307 Bisikon ZH **14** A2
6436 Bisisthal SZ **26** B2
8514 Bissegg TG **5** F4
6816 Bissone TI **54** C4
3983 Bister VS **38** B4
3982 Bitsch VS **38** A4
3255 Bittwil BE **10** B5
7457 Bivio GR **42** C3
3771 Blankenburg BE **36** B2
6102 Blatten LU **24** C1
3919 Blatten VS **37** E4
3914 Blatten VS **38** A4
3920 Blatten VS **51** D3
4249 Blauen BL **1** B5
5722 Bleien AG **12** B2
3368 Bleienbach BE **11** D4
3674 Bleiken b. O. BE **23** D4
1675 Blessens FR **34** C2
6340 Blickensdorf ZG **13** E4
3989 Blitzingen VS **38** C3
1807 Blonay VD **34** C3
3638 Blumenstein BE **22** C4
5334 Böbikon AG **3** F4
1350 Bochuz VD **19** F4
4461 Böckten BL **11** E1
3864 Boden BE **24** C5
3715 Boden BE **36** C3
6546 Bodio GR **41** D4
6743 Bodio TI **40** C4
3981 Bodmen VS **38** C3
2336 Boécourt JU **9** F2
2856 Boécourt JU **9** F2
1353 Bofflens VD **33** E1
1279 Bogis VD **32** C4
6951 Bogno TI **55** D2
2336 Bois, Les JU **8** C4
6634 Bolastro TI **40** B5
2014 Bôle NE **20** C2
4556 Bolken SO **11** D4
3067 Boll BE **22** C2
3065 Bolligen BE **22** B2
8715 Bollingen SG **14** B3
1474 Bollion FR **20** C3
3366 Bollodingen BE **11** D4
3766 Boltigen BE **22** B5
8561 Boltshausen TG **5** F4
7402 Bonaduz GR **28** A3
8554 Bonau TG **5** F4
2926 Boncourt JU **9** D1
7606 Bondo GR **42** B4
2944 Bonfol JU **9** E1
3806 Bönigen BE **37** F1
4618 Boningen SO **11** E3
5706 Boniswil AG **12** B3
1729 Bonnefontaine FR **21** F4
8906 Bonstetten ZH **13** D2
1427 Bonvillars VD **20** B3
8113 Boppelsen ZH **13** D2
6657 Bordei TI **53** F2
1277 Borex VD **32** C4
6658 Borgnone TI **53** F2
7604 Borgonovo GR **42** B4
8535 Bornhausen TG **5** E3
7545 Bos-cha GR **30** C4
6675 Boschetto TI **39** F5

61

A B C D **E** **F** G H I J K L M N O P Q R S T U V W X Y Z

7104 Egschi GR 27 F4
8321 Ehrikon ZH 5 D5
6205 Eich LU 12 B4
4658 Eich SO 12 A2
9453 Eichberg SG 16 B2
8405 Eidberg ZH 5 D5
6013 Eigenthal LU 24 C2
5074 Eiken AG 2 C4
3646 Einigen BE 37 D1
8840 Einsiedeln SZ 14 A4
3943 Eischoll VS 37 E5
1969 Eison VS 50 B2
3909 Eisten VS 51 F1
5077 Elfingen AG 12 B1
8353 Elgg ZH 14 B1
8566 Ellighausen TG 6 A3
8548 Ellikon a. d. T. ZH 5 D4
8464 Ellikon a. Rh. ZH 4 B4
8767 Elm GL 27 E2
8352 Elsau ZH 5 D5
3926 Embd VS 51 E1
8424 Embrach ZH 13 E1
3711 Emdthal BE 23 D5
2338 Emibois, Les JU 9 D3
6032 Emmen LU 12 C5
6020 Emmenbrücke LU 12 C5
3543 Emmenmatt BE 23 D2
6376 Emmetten NW 25 E2
7013 Ems/Domat GR 28 A3
5304 Endingen AG 3 F4
2875 Enfers, Les JU 9 D3
3780 Enge BE 36 A3
6390 Engelberg OW 25 D3
9032 Engelburg (Gaiserwald) SG 15 F1
2073 Enges NE 21 D1
3077 Enggistein BE 22 C2
8765 Engi GL 27 D2
4208 Engi SO 10 C2
8586 Engishofen TG 6 B4
3086 Englisberg BE 22 B3
2063 Engollon NE 20 C1
8556 Engwang TG 5 F3
8564 Engwilen TG 5 F3
8755 Ennenda GL 27 D1
5408 Ennetbaden AG 3 F5
9651 Ennetbühl SG 15 E3
8755 Ennetbühls GL 27 D1
6373 Ennetbürgen NW 25 D2
6372 Ennetmoos NW 24 C2
1667 Enney FR 35 E2
6162 Entlebuch LU 24 A2
3755 Entschwil BE 36 C2
2829 Envelier JU 10 B3
1323 Envy, Romainmôtier- VD 33 E1
2074 Epagnier NE 21 D2
1663 Epagny FR 35 E2
1066 Epalinges VD 34 A2
1417 Epautheyres VD 20 A4
2885 Epauvillers JU 9 E2
1731 Ependes FR 21 E4
1434 Ependes VD 20 A4
1098 Epesses VD 34 B3
2886 Epiquerez JU 9 D2
2304 Eplatures, Les NE 8 B5
5012 Eppenberg-Wöschnau SO 12 A2
3272 Epsach BE 9 F5
4458 Eptingen BL 11 E2
1976 Erde VS 50 A1
3979 Erdesson VS 50 B1
3947 Ergisch VS 37 D5
4952 Eriswil BE 11 E5
3619 Eriz BE 23 E4
3235 Erlach BE 21 E1
8586 Erlen TG 6 B4
8703 Erlenbach ZH 13 E3
3762 Erlenbach i. S. BE 22 C5
5018 Erlinsbach AG/SO 12 A2
8272 Ermatingen TG 5 F3
6294 Ermensee LU 12 C3
8734 Ermenswil SG 14 B3
3995 Ernen VS 38 B4
8725 Ernetschwil SG 14 C3

3957 Erschmatt VS 37 D5
4228 Erschwil SO 10 C2
3423 Ersigen BE 10 C5
6472 Erstfeld UR 25 F3
8500 Erzenholz TG 5 D4
9492 Eschen FL 16 B3
6274 Eschenbach LU 12 C4
8733 Eschenbach SG 14 C3
8264 Eschenz TG 5 E3
2743 Eschert BE 10 B3
8553 Eschikofen TG 5 F4
8360 Eschlikon TG 14 C1
8474 Eschlikon ZH 5 D4
6182 Escholzmatt LU 23 F2
1670 Esmonts FR 20 C5
1724 Essert FR 21 E4
1442 Essert VD 19 F4
1078 Essertes VD 34 B2
1186 Essertines-s.-R. VD 33 D3
1417 Essertines-sur-Yverdon VD 34 A1
1435 Essert-Pittet VD 19 F4
8133 Esslingen ZH 14 A3
1665 Estavannens FR 35 E2
1695 Estavayer-le-G. FR 35 D1
1470 Estavayer-le-Lac FR 20 C3
1687 Estévenens FR 21 D5
1037 Etagnières VD 34 A2
1660 Etivaz, L' VD 35 E4
1163 Etoy VD 33 E3
8356 Ettenhausen TG 5 E5
8621 Ettenhausen ZH 14 B2
4107 Ettingen BL 10 C1
6218 Ettiswil LU 12 A4
3306 Etzelkofen BE 10 B5
6231 Etzelwil LU 12 B3
6017 Etzenerlen LU 12 B5
5275 Etzgen AG 3 D4
4554 Etziken SO 11 D4
5317 Etzwil AG 3 E4
8259 Etzwilen TG 5 D3
9466 Eugstisried SG 16 A3
1982 Euseigne VS 50 B2
8844 Euthal SZ 14 B5
2533 Evilard/Leubringen BE 9 F4
1902 Evionnaz VS 49 D2
1983 Evolène VS 50 B2
1897 Evouettes, Les VS 34 C4
6072 Ewil OW 24 C3
3931 Eyholz VS 37 F5
1262 Eysins VD 32 C4
3154 Eywald BE 22 B4

F

8630 Fägswil ZH 14 B3
3617 Fahrni BE 23 D4
5615 Fahrwangen AG 12 C3
2916 Fahy JU 9 D2
6760 Faido TI 40 B3
7226 Fajauna GR 28 C2
7153 Falera GR 27 E4
8117 Fällanden ZH 13 F2
3713 Faltschen BE 23 D5
7215 Fanas GR 28 C2
3961 Fang VS 50 C1
3557 Fankhaus BE 23 F2
1595 Faoug VD 21 E3
4539 Farnern BE 10 C3
6484 Farvagnin UR 25 E4
1726 Farvagny-le-Grand FR 35 D1
1726 Farvagny-le-Petit FR 21 E4
3705 Faulensee BE 37 D1
1173 Féchy VD 33 D3
8320 Fehraltorf ZH 14 A2
4232 Fehren SO 10 C2
8552 Felben TG 5 E4
8714 Feldbach ZH 14 B3
4532 Feldbrunnen SO 10 C3
7404 Feldis/Veulden GR 28 A4
8706 Feldmeilen ZH 14 A3
7012 Felsberg GR 28 A3
1880 Fenalet VD 35 D5
3178 Fenedringen FR 21 F3
2063 Fenin NE 20 C1
5645 Fenkrieden AG 13 D4
3916 Ferden VS 37 E4

3206 Ferenbalm BE 21 F2
3066 Ferenberg BE 22 C2
1076 Ferlens VD 34 B2
1984 Ferpècle VS 50 C3
3474 Ferrenberg BE 11 D5
1944 Ferret VS 49 E4
1313 Ferreyres VD 19 E5
2333 Ferrière, La BE 8 C4
3956 Feschel VS 37 D5
6938 Fescoggia TI 54 C3
1532 Fétigny FR 20 C4
8245 Feuerthalen ZH 4 C3
8835 Feusisberg SZ 14 A4
3784 Feutersoey BE 35 F4
7514 Fex GR 43 D3
1044 Fey VD 34 B1
1996 Fey VS 49 F2
1609 Fiaugères FR 34 C2
7019 Fidaz GR 27 F3
7235 Fideris GR 28 C2
3984 Fiersch VS 38 B4
3984 Fiescheralp VS 38 B4
3984 Fieschertal VS 38 B4
6772 Fiesso, Rodi- TI 40 A3
1420 Fiez VD 20 A3
6918 Figino TI 54 C4
7477 Filisur GR 42 C1
3185 Fillistorf FR 21 F3
8757 Filzbach GL 15 D4
3920 Findeln VS 51 E3
1925 Finhaut VS 49 D3
2577 Finsterhennen BE 21 E1
6313 Finstersee ZG 13 F4
6162 Finsterwald LU 24 B2
1948 Fionnay VS 50 A3
8308 First ZH 14 A1
5525 Fischbach AG 12 C2
6145 Fischbach LU 11 F4
8497 Fischenthal ZH 14 C2
8376 Fischingen TG 14 C1
5467 Fisibach AG 4 A4
5442 Fislisbach AG 12 C1
8416 Flaach ZH 4 C4
3175 Flamatt, Wünnewil- FR 22 A3
3978 Flanthey VS 36 B5
7306 Fläsch GR 28 B1
9230 Flawil SG 15 E1
1659 Flendruz VD 35 E3
7426 Flerden GR 42 A1
2114 Fleurier NE 19 F3
7017 Flims GR 27 E3
7018 Flims-Waldhaus GR 27 F3
1896 Flon, Le VS 34 C4
7137 Flond GR 27 E4
6454 Flüeli GR 28 B3
6073 Flüeli OW 24 C3
4112 Flüh, Hofstetten- SO 1 B5
3954 Flühalp VS 37 D4
6173 Flühli LU 24 A3
4534 Flumenthal SO 10 C3
8890 Flums SG 15 F5
8898 Flumserberg SG 15 E5
8247 Flüntigen ZH 4 C3
1473 Font FR 20 C3
1921 Fontaine, La (Martigny-Combe) VS 49 D3
2052 Fontainemelon NE 20 C1
2046 Fontaines NE 20 C1
1421 Fontanes VD 20 A3
6690 Fontana TI 39 E4
6712 Fontana TI 41 D4
6780 Fontana (Bedretto) TI 39 E3
6690 Fontanelata TI 39 E4
1423 Fontanezier VD 20 A3
2902 Fontenais JU 9 E2
8127 Forch ZH 13 F2
1984 Forclaz, La VS 50 C3
1866 Forclaz, La (Ormont-Dessous) VD 35 E4
1475 Forel FR 20 C3
1526 Forel VD 20 C4
1606 Forel (Lavaux) VD 34 B2
2717 Fornet-Dessous BE 9 E3
6690 Foroglio TI 39 E4
3135 Forst BE 22 C4
6574 Fosano TI 54 B2

A B C D E F G H I J K L M N O P Q R S T U V W X Y Z

M

8492 Manzenhueb ZH 14 B2
1613 Maracon VD 34 C2
7050 Maran GR 28 C4
6196 Marbach LU 23 F3
9437 Marbach SG 16 B2
1261 Marchissy VD 32 C3
1923 Marécottes, Les VS 49 D2
3186 Mariahilf FR 21 F3
4115 Mariastein-Metzerlen SO 1 B5
2074 Marin NE 21 D2
1723 Marly FR 21 E4
7456 Marmorera GR 42 C3
1524 Marnand VD 20 C4
6817 Maroggia TI 54 C4
6723 Marolta TI 40 C3
1633 Marsens FR 21 D5
8560 Märstetten TG 5 F4
2316 Martel-Dernier NE 20 B2
8460 Marthalen ZH 4 C3
1063 Martherenges VD 20 B5
1920 Martigny VS 49 E2
1920 Martigny-Bourg VS 49 D3
1921 Martigny-Combe VS 49 D3
7560 Martina GR 31 E2
3994 Martisberg VS 38 B4
9562 Märwil TG 5 F4
6718 Marzano TI 40 C2
7005 Masans GR 28 B3
8933 Maschwanden ZH 13 D3
1968 Mase VS 50 B1
7425 Masein GR 42 A1
8723 Maseltrangen SG 15 D4
6900 Massagno TI 54 C3
1869 Massongex VS 49 D1
1692 Massonnens FR 35 D1
7303 Mastrils GR 28 B2
1217 Mategnin GE 46 B1
1438 Mathod VD 19 F4
7433 Mathon GR 28 A5
1753 Matran FR 21 E4
8766 Matt GL 27 E2
3800 Matten b. Interlaken BE 37 E1
3322 Mattstetten BE 22 C1
8585 Mattwil TG 6 B4
4713 Matzendorf SO 11 D3
9548 Matzingen TG 5 E4
1453 Mauborget VD 20 A3
6216 Mauensee LU 12 A4
1462 Mauguettaz, La VD 20 B4
1625 Maules FR 21 D5
8124 Maur ZH 13 F2
1148 Mauraz VD 33 E2
9493 Mauren FL 16 B3
8576 Mauren TG 6 A4
3205 Mauss BE 21 F2
1976 Mayens-de-Conthey VS 49 F1
1965 Mayens-de-la-Zour VS 36 A5
1961 Mayens-de-Nax VS 50 B1
3979 Mayens-de-Réchy VS 50 C1
3961 Mayoux VS 50 C1
1926 Mazembroz VS 49 E2
6809 Medeglia TI 54 C2
7183 Medel GR 40 B1
7436 Medels i. Rh. GR 41 F2
1936 Médières VS 49 F3
6597 Medoscio TI 54 C2
6045 Meggen LU 25 D1
3904 Mehlbaum VS 38 A4
6485 Mein UR 25 E2
5643 Meienberg AG 13 D4
3294 Meienried BE 10 A4
7134 Meierhof (Obersaxen) GR 27 D4
6344 Meierskappel LU 13 D4
3657 Meiersmaad BE 23 D4
3045 Meikirch BE 22 A2
8706 Meilen ZH 13 F3
1252 Meinier GE 46 C1
2554 Meinisberg BE 10 A4
3860 Meiringen BE 24 B4
5616 Meisterschwanden AG 12 C3

6818 Melano TI 54 C4
4917 Melchnau BE 11 E4
6068 Melchsee-Frutt OW 24 C4
6067 Melchtal OW 24 C3
6815 Melide TI 54 C4
5465 Mellikon AG 3 F4
5507 Mellingen AG 12 C1
8439 Mellstorf AG 4 A4
8887 Mels SG 28 A1
4233 Meltingen SO 10 C2
6850 Mendrisio TI 54 C5
1533 Ménières FR 20 C4
6125 Menzberg LU 24 A1
5737 Menziken AG 12 B3
6313 Menzingen ZG 13 E4
6122 Menznau LU 12 A5
6692 Menzónio TI 39 F4
5634 Merenschwand AG 13 D3
6647 Mergoscia TI 54 B1
6866 Meride TI 54 C4
8232 Merishausen SH 4 C2
3658 Merligen BE 37 D1
6402 Merlischachen SZ 13 D5
2827 Mervelier JU 10 C2
3274 Merzligen BE 9 F5
6563 Mesocco GR 41 E4
3254 Messen SO 10 B5
5274 Mettau AG 3 E4
2806 Mettembert JU 10 A2
8553 Mettendorf TG 5 E4
3135 Mettlen BE 22 C4
6034 Mettlen LU 12 C4
9517 Mettlen TG 6 A4
3557 Mettlenalp BE 24 B3
6288 Mettmen LU 12 C3
8155 Mettmenhasli ZH 4 B5
8932 Mettmenstetten ZH 13 D3
8252 Mett-Oberschlatt TG 4 C3
4116 Metzerlen, Mariastein- SO 1 B5
1031 Mex VD 33 F2
1891 Mex VS 49 D2
3280 Meyriez FR 21 E2
1217 Meyrin GE 46 B1
1008 Mézery VD 34 A2
1407 Mézery-p.-D. VD 20 B4
1684 Mézières FR 34 C1
1083 Mézières VD 34 C1
7248 Mezzaselva GR 29 D2
6805 Mezzovico TI 54 C2
1749 Middes FR 21 D4
2946 Miécourt JU 9 E1
3972 Miège VS 36 C5
1295 Miex VD 32 C5
1904 Miéville VS 49 D2
1896 Miex VS 34 C4
6986 Miglieglia TI 54 B3
6648 Minusio TI 54 B2
7743 Miralago GR 43 F5
7134 Miraniga (Obersaxen) GR 27 D4
3532 Mirchel BE 23 D3
1721 Misery FR 21 E3
3961 Mission VS 50 C2
1565 Missy VD 21 D2
3717 Mitholz BE 37 D3
8756 Mitlödi GL 27 D1
3147 Mittelhäusern BE 22 B3
9122 Mogelsberg SG 15 D2
6677 Moghegno TI 54 A1
6695 Mogno TI 39 F3
4313 Möhlin AG 2 B4
1314 Moiry VD 19 E5
6760 Molare TI 40 B3
6524 Moleno TI 40 C5
1663 Moléson-Village FR 35 D2
7056 Molinis GR 28 C3
1146 Mollens VD 33 D2
3974 Mollens VS 36 C5
1074 Mollie-Margot VD 34 B2
8753 Mollis GL 15 D5

1415 Molondin VD 20 B4
8885 Mols SG 15 E4
7458 Mon GR 28 B5
7251 Monbiel GR 30 A3
8617 Mönchaltorf ZH 14 A2
6659 Moneto TI 53 F2
2715 Monible BE 9 F3
1125 Monnaz VD 33 E3
1254 Monniaz GE 47 D1
7278 Monstein GR 29 D4
1801 Mont Pèlerin VD 34 C3
1934 Montagnier VS 49 F3
6926 Montagnola TI 54 C4
1912 Montagnon VS 49 E2
1442 Montagny VD 20 A4
1776 Montagny-la-Ville FR 21 D3
1774 Montagny-les-Monts FR 21 D4
2027 Montalchez NE 20 B3
3963 Montana-Vermala VS 36 B5
3963 Montana-Village VS 36 B5
2857 Montavon JU 9 F2
1489 Montborget FR 20 B4
1669 Montbovon FR 35 D3
1475 Montbrelloz FR 20 C3
1354 Montcherand VD 19 F4
2116 Mont-de-Buttes NE 19 F3
6875 Monte TI 55 D4
6605 Monte Brè TI 54 B2
6513 Monte Carasso TI 54 C1
6549 Monte Laura GR 55 D1
6998 Monteggio TI 54 B3
2884 Montenol JU 9 E2
1482 Montet FR 20 C3
1674 Montet FR 20 C5
1588 Montet (Haut-Vully) VD 21 D2
1724 Montévraz FR 35 E1
2875 Montfaucon JU 9 D3
2874 Montfavergier JU 9 E3
5237 Mönthal AG 12 B1
1174 Montherod VD 33 D3
1053 Monthenon VD 34 A2
1870 Monthey VS 49 D1
6596 Monti di Ditto TI 54 C1
6596 Monti di Motti TI 54 B1
6694 Monti di Predee TI 40 A4
6693 Monti di Rima TI 39 F4
6533 Monticello GR 55 D1
2924 Montignez JU 9 E1
1328 Mont-la-Ville VD 19 E5
9462 Montlingen SG 16 B2
1587 Montmagny VD 21 D2
2883 Montmelon JU 9 E2
2037 Montmollin NE 20 C2
1081 Montpreveyres VD 34 B2
1820 Montreux VD 34 C4
1147 Montricher VD 33 E2
1052 Mont-s.-Lausanne, Le VD 34 A2
1185 Mont-s.-R. VD 33 D3
2828 Montsevelier JU 10 C2
2723 Mont-Tramelan BE 9 D4
5054 Moosleerau AG 12 A3
3302 Moosseedorf BE 22 B1
6834 Morbio Inferiore TI 55 D5
6835 Morbio Superiore TI 55 D5
1890 Morcles VD 49 D1
6922 Morcote TI 54 C4
3983 Mörel VS 38 A4
1541 Morens FR 20 C3
1110 Morges VD 33 E3
1875 Morgins VS 48 C1
1948 Morgnes, Les VS 49 F3
2572 Morges BE 9 F5
5103 Möriken AG 12 B2
7143 Morissen GR 27 E4
3044 Möriswil BE 22 A2
1674 Morlens FR 20 C5
1638 Morlon FR 21 E5
2922 Mormont JU 9 D1
2712 Moron BE 9 E3
1054 Morrens VD 34 A2
6443 Morschach SZ 25 F2
9402 Mörschwil SG 16 A1
6295 Mosen LU 12 C3

A B C D E F G H I J K L **M** **N** **O** P Q R S T U V W X Y Z

9607 Mosnang SG **15** D2
6611 Mosogno TI **53** F1
1675 Mossel FR **34** C2
1862 Mosses, Les (Ormont-Dessous) VD **35** E4
1431 Mothe, La VD **19** F3
1787 Môtier (Bas-Vully) FR **21** E2
2112 Môtiers NE **20** A3
3324 Môtschwil BE **22** C1
6634 Motta TI **40** B5
3961 Mottec VS **50** C2
6721 Motto TI **40** C3
1510 Moudon VD **20** B5
1660 Moulins, Les VD **35** E3
1724 Mouret, Le FR **21** E4
2740 Moutier BE **10** B3
2812 Movelier JU **10** A2
6939 Mugena TI **54** C3
6838 Muggio TI **55** D4
5037 Muhen AG **12** A2
5642 Mühlau AG **13** D3
3995 Mühleberg BE **21** F2
3203 Mühleberg BE **21** F2
3116 Mühledorf BE **22** C3
4583 Mühledorf SO **10** B4
8874 Mühlehorn GL **15** E4
3185 Mühletal FR **21** F3
4812 Mühlethal AG **11** F3
3127 Mühlethurnen BE **22** C4
3464 Mühleweg BE **11** D5
9613 Mühlrüti SG **14** C2
1273 Muids, Le VD **32** C3
3317 Mülchi BE **10** B5
7082 Muldain (Vaz/Obervaz) GR **42** B1
7455 Mulegns GR **42** C2
3712 Mülenen BE **23** D5
4713 Müli SO **11** D3
7016 Mulin GR **27** F3
8753 Mullerenberg GL **15** D5
8555 Müllheim TG **5** F4
5243 Mülligen AG **12** C1
6221 Mullwil LU **12** B3
4912 Mumenthal BE **11** E3
4717 Mümliswil SO **11** D2
7183 Mumpé-Medel GR **40** B1
7186 Mumpé-Tujetsch GR **40** B1
4322 Mumpf AG **2** C4
3053 Münchenbuchsee BE **22** B1
4142 Münchenstein BL **1** C5
1797 Münchenwiler BE **21** E3
3303 Münchringen BE **22** C1
4333 Münchwilen AG **2** C4
9542 Münchwilen TG **14** C1
3903 Mund VS **37** F5
3110 Münsingen BE **22** C3
3985 Münster VS **38** C3
8596 Münsterlingen TG **6** B3
3286 Muntelier FR **21** E2
3225 Müntschemier BE **21** E2
9313 Muolen SG **6** B4
6436 Muotathal SZ **26** A2
1787 Mur (Bas-Vully) FR/VD **21** D2
6600 Muralto TI **54** B2
1893 Muraz VS **34** C5
8877 Murg SG **15** E4
4853 Murgenthal AG **11** E3
5630 Muri AG **13** D3
3074 Muri BE **22** B2
2338 Muriaux JU **9** D3
1489 Murist FR **20** C4
3825 Mürren BE **37** F2
7032 Murschetg GR **27** E3
3280 Murten FR **21** E2
3034 Murzelen BE **22** A2
9602 Müselbach SG **15** D2
7537 Müstair GR **31** E5
7180 Mustér/Disentis GR **40** B1
6289 Müswangen LU **12** C3
1428 Mutrux VD **20** B3
8968 Mutschellen AG **13** D2
7184 Mutschnengia GR **40** B1

7431 Mutten GR **42** B1
4132 Muttenz BL **2** A4
9246 Mutwil SG **15** E1
6933 Muzzano TI **54** C3

N

8752 Näfels GL **15** D5
8606 Nänikon ZH **14** A2
1786 Nant (Bas-Vully) FR **21** E2
6780 Nant TI **39** F3
6315 Nas ZG **13** F4
9123 Nassen SG **15** D2
8155 Nassenwil AG **4** B5
3904 Naters VS **38** A5
1973 Nax VS **50** B1
7485 Naz GR **43** D2
1041 Naz VD **20** B5
6244 Nebikon LU **11** F4
9126 Necker SG **15** D2
9127 Neckertal SG **15** D2
8173 Neerach ZH **4** B5
8413 Neftenbach ZH **4** C4
6991 Neggio TI **54** C3
1669 Neirivue FR **35** D3
1996 Nendaz, Basse- VS **50** A2
9485 Nendeln FL **16** B4
4574 Nennigkofen SO **10** B4
4224 Nenzlingen BL **10** C1
8484 Neschwil ZH **5** D5
5524 Nesselbach AG **12** C2
3863 Nessental BE **38** C1
9650 Nesslau-Krummenau SG **15** E3
8754 Netstal GL **15** D5
6265 Netzelen LU **11** E4
9652 Neu St. Johann SG **15** E3
6314 Neuägeri ZG **13** E4
8488 Neubrunn ZH **5** E5
8404 Neuburg ZH **13** F1
2000 Neuchâtel NE **20** C2
4813 Neudorf AG **12** A3
6025 Neudorf LU **12** C4
4623 Neuendorf SO **11** E3
3176 Neuenegg BE **22** A3
5432 Neuenhof AG **3** F5
6206 Neuenkirch LU **12** B5
3549 Neuenschwand BE **23** E3
8732 Neuhaus SG **14** C3
8212 Neuhausen a. Rhf. SH **4** C3
6345 Neuheim ZG **13** E4
7107 Neukirch BE **27** F4
9217 Neukirch TG **6** A4
9315 Neukirch TG **6** C4
8213 Neunkirch SH **4** B3
8252 Neuparadies TG **4** C3
8344 Neuthal ZH **14** B2
2520 Neuveville, La BE **21** E1
8566 Neuwilen TG **6** A3
1740 Neyruz FR **21** E4
1515 Neyruz VD **34** B1
2560 Nidau BE **9** F4
8772 Nidfurn GL **27** D2
4704 Niederbipp BE **11** D3
4626 Niederbuchsiten SO **11** E3
9246 Niederbüren SG **15** E1
3085 Niederbütschel BE **22** B3
4435 Niederdorf BL **11** D2
3942 Niedergesteln VS **37** E5
8172 Niederglatt ZH **4** B5
5013 Niedergösgen SO **12** A2
8155 Niederhasli ZH **4** B5
9527 Niederhelfenschwil SG **15** E1
3504 Niederhünigen BE **23** D3
5702 Niederlenz AG **12** B2
3182 Niedermettlen FR **22** A3
3087 Niedermuhlern BE **22** B3
1714 Niedermuhren FR **21** F3
8525 Niederneunforn TG **5** D4
3362 Niederönz BE **11** D4
3424 Niederösch BE **10** C5
6385 Niederrickenbach NW **25** D2
3853 Niederried b. I. BE **37** F1

3283 Niederried b. K. BE **21** F2
5443 Niederrohrdorf AG **3** F5
3145 Niederscherli BE **22** B3
6288 Niederschongau LU **12** C3
3632 Niederstocken BE **36** C1
9052 Niederteufen AR **15** F2
8867 Niederurnen GL **15** D4
9244 Niederuzwil SG **6** A5
3989 Niederwald VS **38** B3
3172 Niederwangen BE **22** B2
8166 Niederweningen ZH **4** A5
5524 Niederwil AG **12** C2
6221 Niederwil LU **12** B3
9205 Niederwil SG **6** B5
9203 Niederwil SG **15** E1
4523 Niederwil SO **10** C3
8500 Niederwil TG **5** D4
6330 Niederwil ZG **13** D4
8452 Niederwil ZH **4** C4
1772 Nierlet-l.-B. FR **21** D3
3960 Niouc VS **36** C5
6671 Niva TI **39** E5
6746 Nivo TI **40** B3
2518 Nods BE **9** E5
3976 Noës VS **36** C5
3116 Noflen BE **22** C4
3178 Noflen FR **21** F3
2103 Noiraigue NE **20** B2
2340 Noirmont, Le JU **9** D3
1417 Nonfoux VD **34** A1
6915 Noranco TI **54** C3
1757 Noréaz FR **21** D4
6207 Nottwil LU **12** B4
6986 Novaggio TI **54** B3
1431 Novalles VD **20** A3
6883 Novazzano TI **54** C5
1845 Noville VD **34** C4
7437 Nufenen GR **41** E2
4412 Nuglar SO **11** D1
4208 Nunningen SO **10** C2
6283 Nunwil LU **12** C4
8855 Nuolen SZ **14** B4
8309 Nürensdorf ZH **4** C5
5415 Nussbaumen AG **12** C1
8537 Nussbaumen TG **5** D3
4453 Nusshof BL **2** B5
1485 Nuvilly FR **20** C4
1260 Nyon VD **32** C4

O

8587 Oberaach TG **6** B4
6315 Oberägeri ZG **13** F4
6414 Oberarth SZ **25** E1
3096 Oberbalm BE **22** B3
4229 Oberbeinwil SO **10** C2
4538 Oberbipp BE **11** D3
3019 Oberbottigen BE **22** A2
5225 Oberbözberg AG **12** B1
4625 Oberbuchsiten SO **11** E3
9245 Oberbüren SG **6** A5
3414 Oberburg BE **22** C1
9565 Oberbussnang TG **5** F4
3085 Oberbütschel BE **22** B3
3672 Oberdiessbach BE **22** C3
3367 Oberdorf BE **11** D4
4436 Oberdorf BL **11** D2
6022 Oberdorf LU **12** A4
6370 Oberdorf NW **25** D2
6375 Oberdorf NW **25** D2
9202 Oberdorf SG **6** B5
4515 Oberdorf SO **10** C3
8635 Oberdürnten ZH **14** B3
9413 Oberegg AI **7** D5
5422 Oberehrendingen AG **3** F5
3618 Oberei BE **23** E3
8425 Oberembrach ZH **4** C5
3948 Oberems VS **37** D5
8102 Oberengstringen ZH **13** D2
5036 Oberentfelden AG **12** A2
5016 Oberentlisbach AG/SO **12** A2
5108 Oberflachs AG **12** B1
5073 Oberfrick, Gipf- AG **12** A1
4564 Obergerlafingen SO **10** C4

68

3981 Obergesteln VS **38** C3
9230 Oberglatt SG **15** E1
8154 Oberglatt ZH **4** B5
3434 Obergoldbach BE **23** D2
4653 Obergösgen SO **11** F2
8216 Oberhallau SH **4** B3
8156 Oberhasli ZH **4** B5
9621 Oberhelfenschwil SG **15** D2
8336 Oberhittnau ZH **14** B2
5062 Oberhof AG **12** A1
5273 Oberhofen AG **3** E4
3533 Oberhofen BE **23** D3
3653 Oberhofen BE **23** D4
8574 Oberhofen TG **6** A3
8361 Oberhofen ZH **21** F2
8636 Oberholz SG **14** C3
3504 Oberhünigen BE **23** D3
8843 Oberiberg SZ **26** B1
6208 Oberkirch LU **12** B4
5727 Oberkulm AG **12** B3
3616 Oberlangenegg BE **23** D4
3038 Oberlindach BE **22** B2
8917 Oberlunkhofen AG **13** D3
3182 Obermettlen FR **22** A3
1713 Obermonten FR **22** A4
3086 Obermuhlern BE **22** B3
4324 Obermumpf AG **2** C4
7431 Obermutten GR **42** A1
6012 Obernau LU **24** C1
8526 Oberneunforn TG **5** D4
3363 Oberönz BE **11** D3
3424 Oberösch BE **10** C5
4589 Oberramsern SO **10** B5
6387 Oberrickenbach NW **25** D3
3775 Oberried BE **36** B4
1724 Oberried FR **21** E4
3854 Oberried a. B. BE **23** F4
8942 Oberrieden ZH **13** E3
9463 Oberriet SG **16** B2
9234 Oberrindal SG **15** D2
5452 Oberrohrdorf AG **3** F5
5647 Oberrüti AG **13** D2
4253 Oberrüti BL **10** B2
7134 Obersaxen GR **27** D4
9479 Oberschan SG **16** A5
3145 Oberscherli BE **22** B3
8418 Oberschlatt ZH **14** B1
1716 Oberschrot FR **21** F4
5415 Obersiggenthal AG **12** C1
8477 Oberstammheim ZH **5** D3
4924 Obersteckholz BE **11** E4
9323 Obersteinach SG **16** A1
3632 Oberstocken BE **36** C1
8884 Oberterzen SG **15** E5
3531 Oberthal BE **23** D2
7428 Obertschappina GR **41** F1
8868 Oberurnen GL **15** D4
9242 Oberuzwil SG **6** A5
7082 Obervaz/Vaz GR **28** B4
8261 Oberwald SH **5** D3
3999 Oberwald VS **39** D2
3173 Oberwangen BE **22** A2
8165 Oberweningen ZH **13** D1
8966 Oberwil AG **13** D2
4104 Oberwil BL **10** C1
8500 Oberwil TG **5** E4
6317 Oberwil ZG **13** E4
8471 Oberwil ZH **4** B4
4309 Oberwil ZH **4** C5
3298 Oberwil b. B. BE **10** B4
3765 Oberwil i. S. BE **22** B5
6062 Oberwilen OW **24** B3
5256 Oberzeihen AG **3** D5
8912 Obfelden ZH **13** D2
6078 Obsee OW **24** B4
8758 Obstalden GL **15** D4
3367 Ochlenberg BE **11** D4
2889 Ocourt JU **9** E2
4347 Ödenholz AG **3** E4
4566 Oekingen SO **10** C4
4702 Oensingen SO **11** D3
8050 Oerlikon ZH **13** E2
8461 Oerlingen ZH **4** C3
4943 Oeschenbach BE **11** D5
5072 Oeschgen AG **3** D4

3776 Oeschseite BE **36** A3
9534 Oetwil SG **14** C1
8955 Oetwil a. d. L. ZH **4** A5
8618 Oetwil a. S. ZH **14** A3
3753 Oey BE **22** C5
4665 Oftringen AG **11** F3
1045 Ogens VD **34** B1
6143 Ohmstal LU **11** F4
8472 Ohringen ZH **4** C4
1580 Oleyres VD **21** D3
6718 Olivone TI **40** C2
1867 Ollon VD **35** D5
3971 Ollon VS **36** B5
4305 Olsberg AG/BL **2** B4
4600 Olten SO **11** F2
3036 Oltigen BE **21** F2
4494 Oltingen BL **2** C5
1213 Onex GE **46** B2
1756 Onnens FR **21** E2
1425 Onnens VD **20** B3
6133 Opfersei LU **23** F1
8584 Opfershofen TG **6** A4
8236 Opfertshofen SH **4** C2
8152 Opfikon ZH **13** E1
1413 Oppens VD **34** B1
9565 Oppikon TG **5** F4
3117 Oppligen BE **22** C3
1350 Orbe VD **19** F4
1430 Orges VD **19** F4
1341 Orient, L' (Le Chenit) VD **32** C2
6945 Origlio TI **54** C3
4466 Ormalingen BL **2** C5
1863 Ormont-Dessous VD **35** D4
1865 Ormont-Dessus VD **35** E4
1317 Orny VD **19** F5
1610 Oron-la-Ville VD **34** C2
1608 Oron-le-Châtel VD **34** C2
2552 Orpund BE **10** A4
6644 Orselina TI **54** B2
1937 Orsières VS **49** E3
1694 Orsonnens FR **35** D1
3042 Ortschwaben BE **22** B2
2534 Orvin BE **9** F4
1413 Orzens VD **34** B1
3476 Oschwand BE **11** D4
6763 Osco TI **40** B3
6703 Osogna TI **40** C5
6781 Ossasco TI **39** E3
8475 Ossingen ZH **4** C4
8218 Osterfingen SH **4** B3
6130 Ostergau LU **12** A5
3036 Ostermanigen BE **21** F2
3072 Ostermundigen BE **22** B2
8112 Otelfingen ZH **4** A5
5504 Othmarsingen AG **12** C2
8913 Ottenbach ZH **13** D3
6275 Ottenhausen LU **12** C4
8307 Ottikon ZH **14** A1
8626 Ottikon ZH **14** B3
3257 Ottiswil BE **10** A5
8561 Ottoberg TG **5** F4
1000 Ouchy VD **34** A3
1522 Oulens VD **34** C1
1377 Oulens-sous-Echallens VD **19** F5
1911 Ovronnaz VS **49** E1

P

1619 Paccots, Les FR **35** D3
7028 Pagig GR **28** B3
7749 Pagnoncini GR **43** F5
1416 Pailly VD **34** B1
6657 Palagnedra TI **53** F2
1607 Palézieux-Gare VD **34** C2
1607 Palézieux-Village VD **34** C2
1142 Pampigny VD **33** E2
1867 Panex VD **35** D5
7243 Pany GR **29** D2
1661 Pâquier, Le FR **35** D2
2058 Pâquier, Le NE **9** D5
6902 Paradiso TI **54** C3
7185 Pardé GR **26** B5
7212 Pardisla GR **28** C2
7076 Parpan GR **28** B4

1882 Pars, Les VD **35** E5
7464 Parsonz GR **28** B5
7246 Partnun GR **29** D1
7417 Paspels GR **28** A4
7062 Passugg GR **28** B3
7433 Patzen-Fardün GR **28** A5
1094 Paudex VD **34** A3
6582 Paudo TI **55** D2
1530 Payerne VD **21** D3
6695 Peccia TI **39** F4
6832 Pedrinate TI **55** D5
7112 Peiden GR **27** E4
7132 Peil GR **41** E2
1242 Peissy GE **46** B1
7029 Peist GR **28** C3
1242 Peney GE **46** B1
1445 Peney VD **19** F4
1059 Peney-le-Jorat VD **20** B5
1305 Penthalaz VD **33** F2
1303 Penthaz VD **33** F2
1375 Penthéréaz VD **34** A1
6035 Perlen LU **13** D5
1258 Perly GE **46** B2
2742 Perrefitte BE **10** A3
2018 Perreux NE **20** C2
1166 Perroy VD **33** D3
6744 Personico TI **40** C4
2603 Péry BE **9** F4
2034 Peseux NE **20** C2
1236 Petite-Grave, La GE **46** B2
2315 Petit-Martel NE **20** B2
2092 Petits-Ponts, Les NE **20** B2
2345 Peuchapatte, La JU **9** D4
7312 Pfäfers SG **28** B5
3765 Pfaffenried BE **22** B5
8122 Pfaffhausen ZH **13** F2
8808 Pfäffikon SZ **14** B4
8330 Pfäffikon ZH **14** B2
6264 Pfaffnau LU **11** E3
5735 Pfeffikon LU **12** B3
4148 Pfeffingen BL **10** C1
8422 Pfungen ZH **4** C4
8505 Pfyn TG **5** E4
6563 Pian San Giacomo GR **41** E4
6959 Piandera TI **55** D2
6582 Pianezzo TI **55** D2
6684 Piano TI **39** E5
6695 Piano di Peccia TI **39** F4
6557 Piano di Verdàbbio GR **41** E5
6579 Piazzogna TI **54** B2
1723 Pierrafortscha FR **21** E4
2542 Pieterlen BE **10** A4
1606 Pigeon, Le VD **34** B3
7443 Pignia GR **28** A5
7156 Pigniu GR **27** D3
3961 Pinsec VS **50** C1
6614 Piodina TI **54** A2
6776 Piotta TI **40** A3
7111 Pitasch GR **27** E4
2117 Places, Les NE **19** E3
1716 Plaffeien FR **22** A4
2536 Plagne BE **10** A4
1283 Plaine, La GE **46** B2
1858 Plambuit VD **35** D5
2325 Planchettes, Les NE **8** B5
1997 Planchouet VS **50** A2
7451 Plang GR **42** B3
9498 Planken FL **16** B4
1228 Plan-les-Ouates GE **46** B2
1888 Plans, Les VD **49** E1
1737 Plasselb FR **21** F4
7185 Platta GR **26** B5
7517 Plaun da Lej GR **42** C3
2807 Pleigne JU **10** A2
2953 Pleujouse JU **9** F2
9464 Plona SG **16** B3
8889 Plons SG **16** A5
3638 Pohlern BE **36** C1
1041 Poliez-le-Grand VD **20** A5
1041 Poliez-Pittet VD **20** B5
6742 Pollegio TI **40** C4
1976 Pomeyron VS **36** A5
2353 Pommerats, Les JU **9** D3
1318 Pompables VD **19** F5
1405 Pomy VD **20** A4
1699 Pont FR **34** C2
1342 Pont, Le VD **19** D5

1852 Roche VD **34** C4
1634 Roche, La FR **35** E1
2913 Roche-d´Or JU **9** D2
2019 Rochefort NE **20** C2
2762 Roches BE **10** B3
2907 Rocourt JU **9** D2
7415 Rodels GR **28** A4
4208 Roderis SO **10** C2
4118 Rodersdorf SO **10** B1
6772 Rodi-Fiesso TI **40** A3
9468 Rofisbach SG **16** A3
2814 Roggenburg BL **1** A5
6265 Roggliswil LU **11** E4
4914 Roggwil BE **11** E3
9325 Roggwil TG **15** F1
1699 Rogivue, La VD **34** C2
5032 Rohr AG **12** B2
1712 Rohr FR **21** F3
4655 Rohr SO **11** F2
4938 Rohrbach BE **11** E4
3155 Rohrbach BE **22** B4
4945 Rohrbachgraben BE **11** E5
8820 Rohrenmoos SG **15** F1
6132 Rohrmatt LU **12** A5
1180 Rolle VD **33** D3
1323 Romainmôtier-Envy VD **33** E1
1423 Romanel VD **20** A3
1122 Romanel VD **33** F2
1032 Romanel-s.-L. VD **34** A2
1626 Romanens FR **21** D5
8590 Romanshorn TG **6** C4
6027 Römerswil LU **12** C4
2538 Romont BE **10** A4
1680 Romont FR **34** C1
6113 Romoos LU **24** A2
7454 Rona GR **42** C2
6576 Rona TI **54** B2
6781 Ronco (Bedretto) TI **39** E3
6776 Ronco (Quinto) TI **40** A3
6622 Ronco s. A. TI **54** A2
2603 Rondchâtel BE **9** F4
7431 Rongellen GR **42** A1
9205 Ronwil SG **6** B5
6037 Root LU **13** D5
1088 Ropraz VD **34** B2
8427 Rorbas ZH **4** B4
9400 Rorschach SG **7** D5
9404 Rorschacherberg SG **16** A1
7742 Rösa, La GR **43** F4
1619 Rosalys, Les FR **35** D3
4244 Röschenz BL **1** B5
1754 Rosé FR **21** E4
2724 Roselet, Le JU **9** D3
1937 Rosière, La VS **49** E3
6548 Rossa GR **41** D4
8932 Rossau ZH **13** E3
2842 Rossemaison JU **10** A2
1513 Rossenges VD **20** B5
1728 Rossens FR **35** E1
1554 Rossens VD **20** C4
3204 Rosshäusern BE **21** F2
1658 Rossinière VD **35** E3
9512 Rossrüti SG **5** F5
6760 Rossura TI **40** B3
3913 Rosswald VS **38** A5
6022 Roth LU **12** A4
5746 Rothacker SO **11** F2
3373 Röthenbach b. H. BE **11** D4
3538 Röthenbach i. E. BE **23** D3
7405 Rothenbrunnen GR **28** A4
6023 Rothenburg LU **12** C5
4467 Rothenfluh BL **2** C5
9565 Rothenhausen TG **6** A4
6418 Rothenthurm SZ **13** F5
4852 Rothrist AG **11** F3
3901 Rothwald VS **38** A5
6343 Rotkreuz ZG **13** D4
8919 Rottenschwil AG **13** D2
9313 Rotzenwil SG **6** B4
6362 Rotzloch NW **24** C2
1659 Rougemont VD **35** F3
6535 Roveredo GR **55** D1
6957 Roveredo TI **54** C3

6821 Rovio TI **54** C4
1463 Rovray VD **20** B4
3113 Rubigen BE **22** C3
3268 Ruchwil BE **22** A2
3437 Rüderswil BE **23** D2
3713 Rüdlen BE **37** D2
8455 Rüdlingen SH **4** B4
8465 Rudolfingen ZH **4** C3
8964 Rudolfstetten AG **13** D2
3423 Rüdtligen BE **10** C5
3422 Rüdtligen BE **10** C5
1673 Rue FR **34** C2
6288 Rüediken LU **12** C3
3474 Rüedisbach BE **11** D4
6017 Rüediswil LU **12** B5
6152 Ruefswil LU **11** F5
3088 Rüeggisberg BE **22** B3
3417 Rüegsau (Hasle b. B.-) BE **23** D1
3418 Rüegsbach BE **23** D1
7189 Rueras (Tujetsch) GR **40** A1
8735 Rüeterswil SG **14** C3
7156 Rueun GR **27** D4
1626 Rueyres FR **21** D5
1414 Rueyres VD **34** B1
1542 Rueyres-les-Prés FR **20** C3
1695 Rueyres-St-Laurent FR **35** D1
5235 Rüfenach AG **3** E5
3075 Rüfenacht BE **22** C2
8723 Rufi SG **15** D4
9491 Ruggell FL **16** B3
3472 Rumendingen BE **11** D5
5464 Rümikon AG **4** A4
4539 Rumisberg BE **11** D3
8153 Rümlang ZH **4** B5
3128 Rümligen BE **22** B3
8332 Rumlikon ZH **14** B2
4444 Rümlingen BL **11** E1
7173 Run GR **40** C1
4497 Rüneberg BL **2** C5
9450 Ruppen SG **16** A2
5102 Rupperswil AG **12** B2
3251 Ruppoldsried BE **10** B5
3153 Rüschegg-Gambach BE **22** B4
3154 Rüschegg-Graben BE **22** B4
3154 Rüschegg-Heubach BE **22** B4
3153 Rüschegg-Hirschhorn BE **22** B4
7154 Ruschein GR **27** E4
8803 Rüschlikon ZH **13** E3
8332 Russikon ZH **14** B2
1281 Russin GE **46** B1
6662 Russo TI **53** F1
1773 Russy FR **21** D3
5644 Rüstenschwil AG **13** D3
6017 Ruswil LU **12** B5
9050 Rüte AI **16** A2
9464 Rüthi GR **41** D3
8782 Rüti GL **26** C2
7246 Rüti GR **29** D2
7107 Rüti GR **41** F1
8185 Rüti ZH **13** E1
8630 Rüti ZH **14** B3
8844 Rüti (Unteriberg) SZ **14** B5
3295 Rüti b. B. BE **10** B4
3421 Rüti b. L. BE **22** C1
3099 Rüti b. R. BE **22** B4
5722 Rütihof AG **12** B2
5406 Rütihof AG **12** C1
4933 Rutschelen BE **11** E4
8471 Rutschwil ZH **5** D4
4522 Rüttenen SO **10** C3

S

6577 S. Abbondio TI **54** B2
6592 S. Antonino TI **54** C2
7745 S. António GR **43** F4
6632 S. Bartolomeo TI **54** B1
7741 S. Carlo GR **43** F4
6690 S. Carlo (Val Bavona) TI **39** E4
6575 S. Nazzaro TI **54** B2
6534 S. Vittore GR **55** D1
3792 Saanen BE **35** F3
3777 Saanenmöser BE **36** A3

7247 Saas i. Pr. GR **29** D2
3905 Saas-Almagell VS **51** F2
3908 Saas-Balen VS **51** F2
3906 Saas-Fee VS **51** F2
3910 Saas-Grund VS **51** F2
6690 Sabbione TI **39** E4
6072 Sachseln OW **24** C3
1996 Saclentse VS **50** A2
5745 Safenwil AG **11** F2
7107 Safien Platz GR **41** F1
2553 Safnern BE **10** A4
1985 Sage, La VS **50** C2
7542 Sagliains GR **29** F4
1451 Sagne, La VD **19** E4
2314 Sagne-Eglise, La NE **20** C1
2149 Sagnettes, Les NE **20** A2
6839 Sagno TI **55** D5
7152 Sagogn GR **27** E4
2732 Saicourt BE **9** F3
2350 Saignelégier JU **9** D3
1913 Saillon VS **49** E2
2875 Sairains, Les JU **9** E3
6954 Sala TI **54** C3
8493 Saland ZH **14** B2
1585 Salavaux VD **21** D2
8507 Salen TG **5** F3
8268 Salenstein TG **5** F3
1625 Sâles FR **21** D5
9465 Salez SG **16** A3
3970 Salgesch VS **36** C5
1991 Salins VS **50** A1
8599 Salmsach TG **6** C4
6872 Salorino TI **55** D5
7462 Salouf GR **28** B5
7031 Salums GR **27** E3
1922 Salvan VS **49** D2
1794 Salvenach FR **21** E3
7503 Samedan GR **44** A2
7563 Samnaun GR **31** D2
8833 Samstagern ZH **13** F4
6565 San Bernardino GR **41** E3
6695 San Carlo (Val Peccia) TI **39** F4
6026 Sandplatten LU **12** C4
1738 Sangernboden BE **36** A1
6583 Sant´António TI **55** D2
1907 Sapin-Haut VS **49** E2
7057 Sapün-Dörfji GR **29** D3
7320 Sargans SG **28** A1
3044 Säriswil BE **22** A2
5614 Sarmenstorf AG **12** C3
7423 Sarn GR **28** A4
6060 Sarnen OW **24** C3
1315 Sarraz, La VD **19** F5
1948 Sarreyer VS **49** F3
1683 Sarzens VD **34** C1
1534 Sassel VD **20** C4
1984 Satarma VS **50** B3
1242 Satigny GE **46** B1
6417 Sattel SZ **13** F5
1189 Saubraz VD **33** D3
2026 Sauges, St-Aubin- NE **20** B3
2873 Saulcy JU **9** E3
2732 Saules BE **9** F3
2063 Saules NE **21** D1
2065 Savagnier NE **21** D1
1965 Savièse VS **50** A1
1073 Savigny VD **34** B2
7460 Savognin GR **42** B2
9468 Sax SG **16** A3
3813 Saxeten BE **23** E5
1907 Saxon VS **49** E2
7202 Says GR **28** B2
6578 Scaiano TI **54** B2
7402 Scardanal GR **27** F4
6951 Scareglia (Valcolla) TI **55** D2
2883 Sceut JU **9** E3
9494 Schaan FL **16** B4
9486 Schaanwald FL **16** B3
9112 Schachen AR **15** E2
6105 Schachen LU **24** B1
8200 Schaffhausen SH **4** C3

2748 Souboz BE 9 F3
2864 Soulce JU 9 F3
3961 Soussillon VS 50 C1
2805 Soyhières JU 10 B2
9042 Speicher AR 16 A1
3204 Spengelried BE 21 F2
3700 Spiez BE 37 D1
3700 Spiezwiler BE 37 D1
7277 Spina GR 29 D4
7502 Spinas GR 43 D2
6464 Spiringen UR 26 A3
8816 Spitzen ZH 13 F4
7435 Splügen GR 41 F2
7078 Sporz GR 28 B4
8957 Spreitenbach AG 4 A5
6663 Spruga TI 53 E1
9413 St. Anton AI 7 D5
1713 St. Antoni FR 21 F3
7246 St. Antönien-Ascharina GR 29 D2
7241 St. Antönien-Castels GR 29 D2
4126 St. Chrischona BS 2 A4
6212 St. Erhard LU 12 B4
9000 St. Gallen SG 6 C5
8735 St. Gallenkappel SG 14 C3
9011 St. Georgen SG 6 C5
3936 St. German VS 37 E5
6372 St. Jakob NW 24 C2
6461 St. Jakob UR 25 E3
9030 St. Josefen (Gaiserwald) SG 15 F1
9620 St. Loretto SG 15 D2
9543 St. Margarethen TG 14 C1
9430 St. Margrethen SG 7 E5
7114 St. Martin GR 41 E1
7315 St. Martin SG 27 F2
7134 St. Martin, Obersaxen GR 27 D4
7500 St. Moritz GR 43 D3
7500 St. Moritz Bad GR 43 D3
3425 St. Niklaus BE 10 C4
4532 St. Niklaus SO 10 C3
3924 St. Niklaus VS 51 E2
6000 St. Niklausen LU 25 D1
6066 St. Niklausen OW 24 C2
4421 St. Pantaleon SO 11 D1
9225 St. Pelagiberg (Gottshaus) TG 6 B5
7028 St. Peter GR 28 C3
9127 St. Peterzell SG 15 E2
1736 St. Silvester FR 21 F4
3772 St. Stephan-Grodei BE 36 B3
3773 St. Stephan-Matten BE 36 B3
3772 St. Stephan-Ried BE 36 B3
4915 St. Urban LU 11 E3
1717 St. Ursen FR 21 F4
3186 St. Wolfgang FR 21 E3
4710 St. Wolfgang SO 11 D2
6546 Sta. Domenica GR 41 D4
6541 Sta. Maria in Calanca GR 41 E5
7536 Sta. Maria Val Müstair GR 31 E5
9422 Staad SG 7 D5
8880 Staad SZ 15 F4
2540 Staad SO 10 B4
6855 Stábio TI 54 C5
8174 Stadel AG 7 D4
8404 Stadel ZH 5 D4
8712 Stäfa ZH 14 A3
5053 Staffelbach AG 12 A3
3510 Stalden BE 22 C3
6436 Stalden SZ 26 B2
3922 Stalden VS 51 E1
6063 Stalden (Schwendi) OW 24 C3
3932 Stalden (Visperterminen) VS 37 F5
3933 Stalderried VS 51 E1
8143 Stallikon ZH 13 E2
4913 Stalten BE 11 D3
7605 Stampa GR 42 B4

6370 Stans NW 25 D2
6362 Stansstad NW 25 D2
9656 Starkenbach SG 15 E4
8717 Starrberg SG 14 C4
4656 Starrkirch SO 11 F2
6022 Stätenbach LU 12 A5
1566 St-Aubin FR 21 D3
2024 St-Aubin-Sauges NE 20 B3
5603 Staufen AG 12 B2
1040 St-Barthélémy VD 20 A5
2072 St-Blaise NE 21 D2
2874 St-Brais JU 9 E3
1264 St-Cergue VD 32 C3
1064 St-Cierges VD 34 B1
3824 Stechelberg BE 37 F2
8266 Steckborn TG 5 E3
1450 Ste-Croix VD 19 E3
3612 Steffisburg BE 23 D4
9497 Steg FL 16 B4
8496 Steg ZH 14 C2
3945 Steg-Hohtenn VS 37 D5
9503 Stehrenberg TG 5 F4
4332 Stein AG 2 C4
9063 Stein AR 15 F2
9655 Stein SG 15 D4
8260 Stein a. Rh. SH 5 D3
9323 Steinach SG 16 A1
9314 Steinebrunn TG 6 C4
9050 Steinegg (Rüte) AI 16 A2
9320 Steinenloh TG 6 C4
3534 Steinen BE 23 D3
6422 Steinen SZ 25 F1
8492 Stennen ZH 14 B2
8722 Steinenbrücke SG 15 D4
3148 Steinenbrünnen BE 22 B3
6416 Steinerberg SZ 25 E1
3995 Steinhaus VS 38 B4
6312 Steinhausen ZG 13 E4
4556 Steinhof SO 11 D4
6114 Steinhusen LU 24 A1
8767 Steinibach GL 27 D2
6173 Steinibach LU 24 A3
8162 Steinmaur ZH 13 D1
7226 Stelserberg GR 28 C2
8499 Sternenberg ZH 14 C2
5608 Stetten AG 12 C2
8234 Stetten SH 4 C2
9507 Stettfurt TG 5 E4
3066 Stettlen BE 22 C2
7446 Stettli GR 42 B3
1188 St-George VD 33 D3
1965 St-Germain (Savièse) VS 50 A1
1898 St-Gingolph VS 34 B4
3715 Stiegelschwand BE 36 C3
7459 Stierva GR 42 B1
5233 Stilli AG 3 E4
2610 St-Imier BE 9 D4
3961 St-Jean VS 50 C1
1806 St-Légier-La Chiésaz VD 34 C3
1958 St-Léonard VS 50 B1
1176 St-Livres VD 33 E3
3961 St-Luc VS 50 C1
1609 St-Martin FR 34 C2
2054 St-Martin NE 21 D1
1969 St-Martin VS 49 D1
1890 St-Maurice VS 49 D1
6067 Stöckalp OW 24 C4
8842 Stöcken (Unteriberg) SZ 26 B1
6433 Stoos SZ 25 F2
1187 St-Oyens VD 33 D3
1955 St-Pierre-de-Clages VS 49 F1
1162 St-Prex VD 33 E3
7558 Strada GR 31 E3
7057 Strassberg GR 28 C3
4802 Strengelbach AG 11 F3
5745 Striegel AG 11 F3
8514 Strohwilen TG 5 F4
1966 St-Romain (Ayent) VS 36 B5
1113 St-Saphorin VD 33 E2

1071 St-Saphorin (Lavaux) VD 34 B3
2123 St-Sulpice NE 19 F3
1025 St-Sulpice VD 33 F3
1867 St-Triphon VD 35 D5
2557 Studen BE 10 A5
8845 Studen (Unteriberg) SZ 14 B5
7482 Stugl/Stuls GR 28 C5
7482 Stuls/Stugl GR 28 C5
2882 St-Ursanne JU 9 E2
4655 Stüsslingen SO 11 F2
3262 Suberg BE 22 A1
4553 Subingen SO 10 C4
1433 Suchy VD 20 A4
3618 Süderen BE 23 D3
1969 Suen VS 50 B2
7434 Sufers GR 41 F2
1786 Sugiez (Bas-Vully) FR 21 E2
1043 Sugnens VD 20 B5
5034 Suhr AG 12 B2
8583 Sulgen TG 6 A4
1036 Sullens VD 33 F2
5085 Sulz AG 3 D4
6284 Sulz LU 12 C3
8544 Sulz ZH 5 D4
8614 Sulzbach ZH 14 A2
4339 Sulzerberg AG 3 D4
3454 Sumiswald BE 23 D1
7175 Sumvitg GR 26 C4
3800 Sundlauenen BE 37 E1
8162 Sünikon ZH 13 D1
7456 Sur GR 42 C2
7554 Sur En GR 31 D3
7546 Sur En/Ardez GR 30 C4
7114 Suraua GR 41 E1
7472 Surava GR 42 B1
7115 Surcasti GR 41 E1
7138 Surcuolm GR 27 D4
3204 Süri BE 21 F2
7148 Surin GR 41 D1
7513 Surlej GR 43 D3
1528 Surpierre FR 20 C4
7188 Surrein (Sedrun) GR 40 B1
7173 Surrein (Sumvitg) GR 26 C4
6210 Sursee LU 12 B4
7542 Süs/Susch GR 29 F4
7526 Susauna GR 29 E5
1437 Suscévaz VD 19 F4
7542 Susch/Süs GR 29 F4
3952 Susten VS 37 D5
2572 Sutz BE 9 F5
1510 Syens VD 20 B5

T

8492 Tablat ZH 14 B1
1712 Tafers FR 21 F4
8317 Tagelswangen ZH 4 C5
5522 Tägerig AG 12 C2
9554 Tägerschen TG 5 F4
3111 Tägertschi BE 22 C2
8274 Tägerwilen TG 6 A3
2406 Taillères, Les NE 19 F2
7015 Tamins GR 28 A3
1896 Tanay VS 34 C4
6214 Tann LU 12 B4
1295 Tannay VD 32 C5
6068 Tannen OW 24 C4
8898 Tannenboden SG 15 E5
7553 Tarasp-Vulpera GR 31 D3
7422 Tartar GR 28 A4
1180 Tartegnin VD 33 D3
3929 Täsch VS 51 E3
2575 Täuffelen BE 9 F5
7162 Tavanasa GR 27 D4
2710 Tavannes BE 9 F3
6807 Taverne TI 54 C3
1607 Tavernes, Les VD 34 C2
4492 Tecknau BL 2 C5
5306 Tegerfelden AG 3 F4
6652 Tegna TI 54 B1
6598 Tenero TI 54 B2
6760 Tengia TI 40 B3
7106 Tenna GR 27 F4
4456 Tenniken BL 11 E1
5617 Tennwil AG 12 C3

W

A
B
C
D
E
F
G
H
I
J
K
L
M
N
O
P
Q
R
S
T
U
V
W
X
Y
Z

8620 Wetzikon ZH **14** B2
6231 Wetzwil LU **12** B4
8704 Wetzwil ZH **13** F3
8767 Wichlen GL **27** D3
3114 Wichtrach BE **22** C3
8967 Widen AG **13** D2
9443 Widnau SG **7** E5
8036 Wiedikon ZH **13** E2
4537 Wiedlisbach BE **11** D3
9405 Wienacht AR **7** D5
3255 Wierezwil BE **22** B1
7494 Wiesen GR **28** C4
6383 Wiesenberg NW **25** D2
8542 Wiesendangen ZH **5** D4
8262 Wiesholz SH **5** D3
8372 Wiezikon TG **14** C1
6192 Wiggen LU **23** F3
3053 Wiggiswil BE **22** B1
5637 Wiggwil AG **13** D3
8556 Wigoltingen TG **5** F4
4806 Wikon LU **11** F3
5276 Wil AG **3** E4
9500 Wil SG **5** F5
4656 Wil SO **11** F2
8196 Wil ZH **4** B4
8492 Wila ZH **14** B1
8217 Wilchingen SH **4** B3
8489 Wildberg ZH **5** D5
5103 Wildegg AG **3** E5
8465 Wildensbuch ZH **4** C3
3812 Wilderswil BE **23** E5
9658 Wildhaus-Alt St. Johann SG **15** F4
6062 Wilen OW **24** C3
9225 Wilen (Gottshaus) TG **6** B5
8525 Wilen b. N. TG **5** D4
9535 Wilen b. W. TG **5** F5
3266 Wiler BE **22** A1
1714 Wiler FR **22** A3
6482 Wiler UR **25** F4
3918 Wiler VS **37** E4
8427 Wiler ZH **4** B4
8414 Wiler ZH **4** C4
3428 Wiler b. U. BE **10** C4
3207 Wileroltigen BE **21** F2
5058 Wiliberg AG **12** A3
6236 Wilihof LU **12** A3
3425 Willadingen BE **10** C4
8846 Willerzell SZ **14** B4
3860 Willigen BE **38** B1
6130 Willisau LU **12** A4
8253 Willisdorf TG **5** D3
3752 Wimmis BE **23** D5
9315 Winden TG **6** C4
5210 Windisch AG **3** E5
8175 Windlach ZH **4** B4
2513 Wingreis BE **9** E5
6235 Winikon LU **12** A3
4558 Winistorf SO **11** D4
6048 Winkel LU **24** C2
8185 Winkel ZH **13** E1
9015 Winkeln SG **15** E2
8312 Winterberg ZH **13** F1

4451 Wintersingen BL **11** E1
8400 Winterthur ZH **14** A1
4652 Winznau SO **11** F2
6383 Wirzweli NW **25** D2
4634 Wisen SO **11** E2
5463 Wislikofen AG **3** F4
5632 Wissenbach AG **12** C3
6064 Wisserlen OW **24** C3
8053 Witikon ZH **13** E2
9303 Wittenbach SG **15** F1
9547 Wittenwil TG **5** E5
4108 Witterswil SO **1** B5
4443 Wittinsburg BL **11** E1
5064 Wittnau AG **11** F1
5053 Wittwil AG **12** A3
3236 Witzwil BE **21** D2
5610 Wohlen AG **12** C2
3033 Wohlen BE **22** A2
5512 Wohlenschwil AG **12** C2
6386 Wolfenschiessen NW **25** D2
9116 Wolfertswil SG **15** E2
7265 Wolfgang GR **29** D3
9427 Wolfhalden AR **7** D5
8633 Wolfhausen ZH **14** B3
9533 Wolfikon SG **5** F5
4704 Wolfisberg BE **11** D3
5063 Wölflinswil AG **12** A1
4628 Wolfwil SO **11** E3
6110 Wolhusen LU **24** B1
8832 Wollerau SZ **14** A4
8038 Wollishofen ZH **13** E2
3076 Worb BE **22** C2
3252 Worben BE **10** A5
8408 Wülflingen ZH **14** A1
3184 Wünnewil-Flamatt FR **21** F3
9514 Wuppenau TG **15** D1
5303 Würenlingen AG **3** F4
5436 Würenlos AG **4** A5
6006 Würzenbach LU **25** D1
6022 Wüschiswil LU **12** A5
3862 Wyler BE **38** C1
4923 Wynau BE **11** E3
3472 Wynigen BE **11** D5
4954 Wyssachen BE **11** E5
4934 Wyssbach BE **11** E4
3919 Wyssried VS **37** E4

Y

1137 Yens VD **33** E3
1400 Yverdon-les-Bains VD **20** A4
1462 Yvonand VD **20** B4
1853 Yvorne VD **35** D5

Z

7107 Zalön GR **41** F1
3309 Zauggenried BE **10** C5

3532 Zäziwil BE **23** D3
4495 Zeglingen BL **11** F2
5079 Zeihen AG **3** D5
4314 Zeiningen AG **2** C4
6144 Zell LU **11** F4
8487 Zell ZH **14** B1
1724 Zenauva FR **21** E4
3934 Zeneggen VS **37** E5
3931 Zenhäusern VS **37** E5
3920 Zermatt VS **51** D3
7530 Zernez GR **29** F4
7132 Zervreila GR **41** D2
5732 Zetzwil AG **12** B3
9556 Zezikon TG **5** F4
4417 Ziefen BL **11** D1
8866 Ziegelbrücke SG **15** D4
3054 Ziegelried BE **22** A1
4564 Zielebach BE **10** C4
7167 Zignau GR **26** C4
8588 Zihlschlacht TG **6** B4
7432 Zillis GR **28** A5
3255 Zimlisberg BE **10** B5
3086 Zimmerwald BE **22** B3
3961 Zinal VS **50** C2
7205 Zizers GR **28** B2
3920 Zmutt VS **51** D3
4800 Zofingen AG **11** F3
3436 Zollbrück BE **23** D2
1711 Zollhaus FR **36** A1
3052 Zollikofen BE **22** B2
8702 Zollikon ZH **13** E2
7082 Zorten (Vaz/Obervaz) GR **42** B1
8585 Zuben TG **6** B3
9523 Züberwangen SG **5** F5
4528 Zuchwil SO **10** C4
9526 Zuckenriet SG **6** A5
5621 Zufikon AG **13** D2
6300 Zug ZG **13** E4
4234 Zullwil SO **10** C2
1719 Zumholz FR **22** A4
8126 Zumikon ZH **13** F2
8353 Zünikon ZH **5** D4
4455 Zunzgen BL **2** B5
7556 Zuort GR **31** D3
7524 Zuoz GR **29** E5
9106 Zürchersmühle AR **15** E2
8000 Zürich ZH **13** E2
4315 Zuzgen AG **2** C4
3303 Zuzwil BE **22** B1
9524 Zuzwil SG **15** D1
8192 Zweidlen ZH **4** B4
3815 Zweilütschinen BE **23** F5
3770 Zweisimmen BE **36** B2
3645 Zwieselberg BE **36** C1
8909 Zwillikon ZH **13** D3
4222 Zwingen BL **1** B5
3901 Zwischbergen VS **52** B2
3756 Zwischenflüh BE **36** C2

Seen • Lacs • Lakes • Meren
Laghi • Lagos • Sjöar • Søer

Name/Meter ü. Meer
Nom/Altitude m
Name/Height in m
Naam/Hoogte in m

A

Ägerisee 724	**13** F4
Albigna, Lago da l´* 2163	**42** C4
Alpnacher See 434	**24** C2
Alzasca, Lago d´ 1855	**39** F5
Arnensee 1542	**35** F4
Arnisee 1368	**25** F4

B

Bachsee 2265	**24** A5
Baldegger See 463	**12** C4
Bannalpsee* 1587	**25** D3
Bianco, Lago* 2234	**44** B3
Bieler See 429	**9** F5
Blausee 887	**37** D3
Bodensee (CH, A, D) 396	**6** B3
Brenet, Lac 1002	**33** D1
Brenets, Lac des (CH, F) 750	**8** B5
Bret, Lac de* 674	**34** B3
Brienzer See 564	**24** A4
Burgäschisee 465	**11** D4

C

Cauma, Lag la 997	**27** F3
Cavloc, La da 1907	**42** C4
Champfèrer See 1791	**43** D3
Chapfensee 1030	**27** F1
Cleuson, Lac de* 2186	**50** A2
Curnera, Lai da* 1956	**26** A5

D

Daubensee 2206	**36** C4
Davoser See* 1559	**29** D3
Derborence, Lac de 1449	**35** F5
Dittligsee 652	**22** C4
Dix, Lac des* 2364	**50** B3

E

Eisee 1896	**24** B4
Emosson, Lac d´* 1930	**48** C3
Engstlensee 1850	**25** D4

F

Fälensee 1452	**16** A3
Flachsee 380	**13** D2
Fluhseeli 2045	**36** C4

G

Garichtisee 1629	**27** D2
Gelmersee* 1849	**39** D2
Genève, Lac de/ Léman, Le (CH, F) 372	**33** E4
Gigerwaldsee* 1335	**27** F2
Glattalpsee 1852	**26** C2
Göscheneralpsee* 1797	**25** E5
Greifensee 435	**13** F2
Griessee* 2386	**39** D3
Grimselsee* 1909	**38** C2
Gruère, Etang de la 998	**9** D3
Gruyère, Lac de la* 677	**35** E1

H

Hallwiler See 449	**12** B3
Hinterburgseeli 1514	**24** A4
Hongrin, Lac de l´* 1255	**35** D3

I

Iffigsee 2065	**36** B4
Illsee 2360	**51** D1

J

Joux, Lac de 1004	**19** D5

K

Katzensee 439	**4** B5
Klöntaler See* 848	**26** C1

L

Lai, Il 1481	**28** B4
Lauenensee 1381	**36** A4
Lauerzer See 447	**25** F1
Lei, Lago di (CH, I)* 1931	**42** A3
Léman, Le/Genève, Lac de (CH, F) 372	**33** D4
Limmernsee* 1857	**26** C3
Lioson, Lac 1848	**35** E4
Lucendro, Lago di* 2134	**39** E2
Lugano, Lago di (CH, I) 271	**55** D3
Lungerer See* 689	**24** B4
Luzzone, Lago di* 1590	**40** C2

M

Maggiore, Lago/ Verbano (CH/I) 193	**53** F4
Märjelensee 2300	**38** B3
Marmorera, Lai da* 1680	**42** C3
Mattmarksee* 2197	**51** F3
Mauensee 504	**12** A4
Mauvoisin, Lac de* 1961	**50** A4
Melchsee* 1891	**24** C4
Moiry, Lac de* 2249	**50** C2
Montsalvens, Lac de* 801	**35** E2
Moossee 521	**22** B1
Morat, Lac de/Murtensee 429	**21** E2
Moron, Lac de (CH, F)* 716	**8** B5
Murgsee 1820	**27** D1
Murtensee/Morat, Lac de 429	**21** E2
Muttsee 2446	**27** D3

N

Nalps, Lai da* 1908	**26** B5
Narèt, Lago del* 2310	**39** E3
Neuchâtel, Lac de 429	**21** D2

O

Oberaarsee* 2303	**38** C2
Oberblegisee 1422	**26** C2
Obersee GL 989	**14** C5
Obersee SZ/SG 406	**14** B4
Oberstockensee 1665	**36** C1
Öschinensee 1578	**37** D3

P

Pfäffiker See 537	**14** B2
Poschiavo, Lago di* 962	**43** F5

R

Räterichsbodensee* 1767	**38** C2
Rims, Lai da 2396	**45** E2
Ritóm, Lago* 1850	**40** A2
Rotsee 419	**12** C5

S

Salanfe, Lac de* 1925	**49** D2
Sambucco, Lago* 1461	**39** F3
Sämtiser See 1209	**16** A3
Sanetschsee* 2034	**36** A4
Sarner See 469	**24** B3
Schiffenensee* 532	**21** E3

Schönenbodensee 1097	**15** F3
Schottensee 2335	**27** F2
Schwarzsee 1046	**22** A5
Seealpsee 1141	**16** A3
Seebergsee 1831	**36** B2
Seelisbergsee 738	**25** E2
Sella, Lago della 2256	**39** F2
Sempacher See 504	**12** B4
Sihlsee* 889	**14** B4
Silser See 1797	**43** D3
Silvaplaner See 1791	**43** D3
Sontga Maria, Lai da* 1908	**40** B2
Soppensee 596	**12** B5
St. Moritzer See* 1768	**43** E3
Sufner See* 1401	**41** F2

T

Taillères, Lac des 1036	**19** F2
Thuner See 558	**37** D1
Toules, Lac des* 1810	**49** E4
Tremorgio, Lago 1830	**40** A3
Triftsee 1660	**39** D1
Trübsee 1764	**25** D4
Tschingelsee 1150	**37** D2
Tseuzier, Lac de* 1777	**36** B4
Tuma, Lai da 2345	**25** F5
Türler See 643	**13** E3

U

Untersee 396	**5** E3
Urner See 434	**25** F2

V

Val Viola, Lagh da	**44** C4
Verbano/Maggiore, Lago (CH/I) 193	**54** B2
Vierwaldstätter See 434	**25** D1
Vieux Emosson, Lac du* 2205	**48** C3
Vogorno, Lago di* 470	**54** B1
Voralpsee 1123	**15** F4

W

Wägitaler See* 900	**14** C5
Walensee 419	**15** D4
Wildsee 2438	**27** F2
Wohlensee* 481	**22** A2

Z

Zervreilasee* 1862	**41** D2
Zuger See 413	**13** E4
Zürichsee 406	**13** E3

* Stauseen oder gestaute Naturseen
  Lacs artificiels ou lacs naturels avec retenue
  Artificial lakes or natural lakes which are dammed up
  Kunstmatige meren of natuurlijke meren die worden ingedijkt

Flüsse • Rivières • Rivers • Rivieren
Fiumi • Ríos • Floder • Floder

Passstrassen
Cols accessibles en véhicule
Accessible for vehicles
Berijdbare passen
Accessibile ai veicoli
Accesibles por vehículos
Bergspassvägar · Pasveje

Name/Meter ü. Meer/%
Nom/Altitude m/%
Name/Height in m/%
Naam/Hoogte in m/%

Name	Grid
Ächerlipass 1458 15%	25 D3
Aiguillon, Col de l´ 1293	19 E4
Albispass 791 8%	13 E3
Albulapass/ Alvra, Pass d´ 2312 12%	43 D2
Alvra, Pass d´/ Albulapass 2312 12%	43 D2
Bänkerjoch 674	3 D5
Bernina, Passo del 2328 12%	44 B3
Bözberg 569	12 B1
Brünigpass 1008 10%	24 B4
Chalet-à-Gobet, Le 872	34 B2
Chasseral, Col du 1502 11%	9 D4
Croix, Col de la JU 789	9 E2
Croix, Col de la VD 1778 13%	35 E5
Etroits, Col des 1152 8%	19 E3
Etzelpass 950 20%	14 B4
Flüelapass 2383 11%	29 E4
Forclaz, Col de la 1526 12%	49 D3
Fuorn, Pass dal/ Ofenpass 2149 10%	45 D1
Furkapass 2429 11%	39 D2
Givrine, Col de la 1228 8%	32 B3
Glaubenberg 1543 13%	24 B3
Glaubenbielen 1611 12%	24 B3
Grand St-Bernard, Col du (CH, I) 2469 11%	49 E5
Grimselpass 2165 9%	39 D2
Güglia, Pass dal/ Julierpass 2284 13%	42 C3
Gurnigel 1608 17%	22 B4
Hulftegg 953 10%	14 C2
Ibergeregg 1406 13%	26 A1
Jaunpass 1509 14%	36 A2
Julierpass/ Güglia, Pass dal 2284 13%	42 C3
Katzenstrick 1053	14 A4
Kerenzerberg 743 9%	15 D4
Klausenpass 1948 10%	26 B3
Lenzerheide 1547 11%	28 B4
Livigno, Forcola di (CH, I) 2315 12%	44 B3
Lucomagno, Passo del/ Lukmanier-Pass 1914 10%	40 B2
Lukmanier-Pass/Lucomagno, Passo del 1914 10%	40 B2
Luzisteig 713 10%	28 B1
Maloja, Passo di/ Malojapass 1815 9%	42 C4
Malojapass/ Maloja, Passo di 1815 9%	42 C4
Marchairuz, Col du 1447 12%	33 D2
Mollendruz, Col du 1180 8%	19 D5
Mont-Crosin, Col du 1227 12%	9 D4
Monte Ceneri 554 10%	54 C2
Morgins, Pas de (CH, F) 1369 9%	48 C1
Mosses, Col des 1445 12%	35 E4
Néggia, Alpe di 1395 12%	54 B2
Novena, Passo di/ Nufenenpass 2478 10%	39 D3
Nufenenpass/ Novena, Passo di 2478 10%	39 D3
Oberalppass 2044 10%	25 F5
Oberer Hauenstein 731 6%	11 E2
Ofenpass/ Fuorn, Pass dal 2149 10%	45 D1
Passwang 943 11%	11 D2
Pierre Pertuis, Col de 827 9%	9 E4
Pillon, Col du 1546 11%	35 F4
Planches, Col des 1411 15%	49 E2
Pontins, Col des 1110 9%	9 D4
Pragelpass 1550 14%	26 B2
Rangiers, Les 856 12%	9 F2
Raten 1077	13 F4
Ricken 794 9%	15 D3
Roches, Col des (CH, F) 919	20 B1
Ruppenpass 1003 9%	16 A2
Saanenmöser 1279 9%	36 A3
Salhöhe 779 9%	12 A1
San Bernardino, Passo del 2065 12%	41 E3
San Gottardo, Passo del/ St. Gotthard 2108 10%	39 E2
Sattel 932	13 F5
Sattelegg 1190 14%	14 B4
Schallenberg 1167 12%	23 E3
Scheltenpass 1051 12%	10 C2
Schwägalp 1278 12%	15 F3
Simplonpass 2005 10%	52 A1
Spluga, Passo della/Splügen- pass (CH, I) 2113 13%	41 F3
Splügenpass/Spluga, Passo della (CH, I) 2113 13%	41 F3
St. Gotthard/San Gottardo, Passo del 2108 10%	39 E2
Staffelegg 621 10%	3 D5
Stoss 932	16 A2
Sustenpass 2224 9%	25 D4
Tourne, La 1170 10%	20 B2
Umbrail, Pass (CH, I) 2501 11%	45 E2
Unterer Hauenstein 691 6%	11 E2
Vue des Alpes 1283 10%	8 C5
Wasserfluh 843 10%	15 D2
Weissenstein 1279 22%	10 C3
Wildhaus 1090 15%	15 F4
Wolfgangpass 1631 11%	29 D3

Fusspässe
Cols accessibles à pied
Accessible on foot
Bewandelbare passen
Accessibile a piedi · Accesibles a pie
Gångväg · Tilgængelig for gående

Name/Meter ü. Meer
Nom/Altitude m
Name/Height in m
Naam/Hoogte in m

Name	Grid
Albrunpass (CH, I) 2409	38 C4
Antronapass (CH, I) 2838	52 A3
Arflina Furka 2247	28 C3
Augstbordpass 2894	51 D1
Balme, Col de (CH, F) 2204	49 D3
Bonderkrinde 2385	36 C3
Cavegna, Passo di 1978	53 E1
Chaude, Col de 1621	35 D4
Chésery, Col de (CH, F) 1995	48 B1
Cheville, Pas de 2038	35 E5
Costainas, Passo da 2251	45 D1
Cou, Col de 2528	50 C1
Coux, Col de (CH, F) 1921	48 B2
Cristallina, Passo di 2568	39 E3
Croix de Coeur 2174	49 F2
Cruschetta (CH, I) 2296	31 E4
Diesrut, Pass 2428	27 D5
Drusator (CH, A) 2342	29 D1
Ducanfurka 2666	43 D1
Durannapass 2117	29 D3
Essets, Col des 2029	35 E5
Fellilücke 2478	39 F1
Fenêtre du Durand (CH, I) 2797	50 A4
Fenga, Cuolmen d´ 2608	31 D2
Ferret, Col (CH, I) 2537	49 E5
Foopass 2223	27 E2
Forcellina 2672	42 C3
Forcletta 2874	51 D2
Forcola, Passo di (CH, I) 2226	41 F4
Futschöl, Pass (CH, A) 2768	30 C3
Geisspfadpass (CH, I) 2474	38 C4
Gemmipass 2322	36 C4
Giümela, Pass 2117	41 D4
Glaspass 1846	41 F1
Greina, Passo della 2357	40 C2
Griespass (CH, I) 2479	39 D3
Grosse Scheidegg 1962	24 B5
Grünenbergpass 1553	23 E4
Guriner Furgge 2323	39 E4
Hilferenpass 1291	23 F3
Hohtürli 2778	37 E3
Jable, Col de 1884	35 E4
Jaman, Col de 1512	35 D3
Jochpass 2207	25 D4
Juchlipass 2171	24 C3
Kinzigpass 2073	26 A3
Kistenpass 2640	27 D3
Kleine Furka (CH, A) 2243	16 C5
Kleine Scheidegg 2061	37 F2
Krüzlipass 2347	26 A4
Kunkelspass 1357	28 A3
Lona, Pas de 2787	50 C2
Lötschenlücke 3178	37 F3
Lötschenpass 2690	37 D4
Meidpass 2790	51 D1
Meina, Col de la 2702	50 B2
Monscera, Passo di (CH, I) 2103	52 B2
Monte Moro, Passo di (CH, I) 2868	52 A3
Naret, Passo di 2438	39 E3
Niemet, Pass da (CH, I) 2295	42 A3
Otterpass 2278	36 C2
Panixerpass 2407	27 D3
Passit, Passo di 2082	41 E3
Piz Lunghin 2645	42 C3
Rawilpass 2429	36 B4
Redòrta, Forcola di 2181	40 A4
Restipass 1216	37 D4
Richetlipass 2261	27 D3
Riedmatten, Col de 2919	50 B3
Risetenpass 2189	27 E2
Safierberg 2486	41 E2
Saflischpass 2564	38 B5
San Giacomo, Passo (CH, I) 2313	39 D3
Sanetsch, Col du 2251	36 A5
Sattelpass 1586	24 B3
Scalettapass 2606	44 A1
Schlappiner Joch (CH, A) 2202	30 A2
Schmorras, Pass da 2564	42 B2
Schweizertor (CH, A) 2139	29 D1
Sefinenfurke 2612	37 E2
Segnespass 2627	27 E2
Septimerpass 2310	42 C3
Sertigpass 2739	44 A1
Slingia, Passo di (CH, I) 2309	31 E4
Stallerberg 2579	42 B3
Strelapass 2350	29 D3
Stretta, La (CH, I) 2476	44 B3
Surenenpass 2291	25 E3
Sunsafe, Col de 2494	48 C2
Theodulpass (CH, I) 3301	51 D4
Tomülpass 2412	27 E5
Torrent, Col de 2919	50 C2
Trescolmen, Passo de 2161	41 E4
Trüttlisbergpass 2038	36 B4
Uomo, Passo dell´ 2218	40 B2
Val Viola, Pass da (CH, I) 2432	44 C3
Verne, Col de (CH, F) 1814	34 B5
Zwischbergenpass 3268	52 A2

79

Berge • Montagnes • Mountains • Bergen
Monti • Montañas • Berg • Bjerge

Name/Meter ü. Meer
Nom/Altitude m
Name/Height in m
Naam/Hoogte in m

A

Aargrat 38 C2
Ádula 41 D3
Aermighorn 2742 37 D2
Agassizhorn 3953 38 B2
Ahorn 1140 23 E1
Aiguille d´Argentière (CH, F) 3901 49 D4
Aiguille de la Tsa 3668 50 C3
Aiguille du Chardonnet (CH, F) 3680 49 D4
Aiguille du Tour (CH, F) 3540 49 D4
Aiguilles Rouges 3646 50 B3
Albis 915 13 E3
Albristhorn 2762 36 B3
Aletschhorn 4195 38 A3
Allalinhorn 4027 51 F3
Alperschellihorn 3039 41 F2
Alpettes, Les 1413 35 D2
Alphubel 4206 51 E3
Alpjuhorn 3144 37 F4
Alplerhorn 2380 26 B2
Alplihorn 3006 29 D4
Alplistock 2877 38 C2
Alpstein 15 E3
Altels 3629 37 D4
Altmann 2436 15 F3
Alvier 2343 16 A4
Amselfluh 2781 28 C4
Amselspitz 1491 14 A5
Aouille Tseuque (CH, I) 3554 50 B4
Aprigenstock 2592 25 E4
Aroser Rothorn 2980 28 B4
Arpelistock 3035 36 A4
Augstbordhorn 2972 51 E1
Augstmatthorn 2137 23 F4
Aula 1417 53 F2

B

Bächistock 2914 26 C2
Bächlistock 3247 38 C2
Bachtel 1115 14 B3
Bäderhorn 2009 36 A2
Badus 2928 25 F5
Balfrin 3796 51 E2
Balmahorn 2870 52 B2
Bälmeten 2414 26 A3
Balmhorn 3699 37 D4
Bantiger 947 22 C2
Bärenhorn 2929 41 E2
Barillette, La 1528 32 C3
Barrhorn 3610 51 D2
Basòdino (CH, I) 3274 39 E4
Bec d´Epicoune (CH, I) 3529 50 B4
Bec de la Montau 2922 50 A2
Bec des Rosses 3223 50 A3
Becca de Sery 2863 49 F3
Becs de Bosson 3149 50 C2
Beichlen 1770 23 F3
Belchenfluh 1123 11 E2
Bella Lui 2548 36 B4
Bella Tola 3025 51 D1
Bellavista (CH, I) 3888 43 E4
Berglistock 3656 38 B2
Berra, La 1719 35 E1
Besso 3668 51 D3
Betelberg 1943 36 B4
Bettlihorn 2951 38 B4
Bettmerhorn 2872 38 B4
Biet 1965 26 B1
Bietenhorn 2757 37 E2

Bietschhorn 3934 37 E4
Bifertenstock 3421 26 C4
Birghorn 3243 37 E3
Blasenfluh 1118 23 D2
Blässkopf 1457 15 E4
Blauen 837 1 B5
Blinnenhorn (CH, I) 3374 38 C4
Blümlisalp 3663 37 E3
Bockmattli 1932 14 C5
Bocktenhorn 3044 30 A4
Bonderspitz 2546 36 C3
Bortelhorn (CH, I) 3194 38 B5
Börterhorn 2697 29 E4
Bösentrift 3248 51 E3
Böser Faulen 2802 26 C2
Böshorn 3268 52 A1
Bouquetins 3838 50 C4
Bözberg 12 B1
Breithorn BE/VS 3780 37 E3
Breithorn VS (CH, I) 4164 51 D4
Breithorn VS 2599 38 B4
Breithorn VS 3178 51 E2
Breithorn VS 3366 52 B1
Breithorn VS 3785 37 F4
Breitlauihorn 3655 37 E4
Brienzer Rothorn 2350 24 A4
Brisen 2404 25 D3
Bristen 3073 26 A4
Brudelhorn 2791 38 C3
Brünberg 2967 38 C2
Brunegghorn 3833 51 D2
Brünnelistock 2133 14 C5
Brunnenberg 875 1 B5
Brunnethorn 2952 51 D1
Brunnistock 2952 25 E3
Bruschghorn 3056 27 F5
Bucheggberg 10 B4
Bueberg 633 10 B2
Büelenhorn 2808 43 D1
Buochserhorn 1807 25 D2
Bürgenstock 1128 25 D2
Burgfluh 935 11 F2
Bürkelkopf (CH, A) 3033 31 D1
Burstspitzen 3119 37 E3
Bütschelegg 1056 22 B3
Bützistock 2496 27 E1

C

Camoghè 2228 55 D2
Camoghé 2356 40 A2
Canardhorn 2607 29 E3
Cape au Moine 1941 35 D3
Casanna 2557 29 D3
Castalegns 3021 42 C2
Catogne, Le 2598 49 E3
Chamossaire, Le 2113 35 D5
Chasseral, Le 1607 9 E4
Chasseron, Le 1607 19 F3
Châtel 1432 19 D5
Châtelet, Le 2537 49 E3
Chaumont 1180 21 D1
Cheval Blanc, le (CH, F) 2831 48 C3
Chreuzegg 1314 14 C3
Chüebodenhorn 3070 39 E3
Churfirsten 2205 15 E4
Cima Bianca 2612 40 B4
Cima d´Efra 2577 40 B4
Cima da Lägh (CH, I) 3083 42 A4
Cima da li Gandi Rossi (CH, I) 2831 44 C5
Cima da Murtaira 2961 42 C4

Cima de Gagela 2805 41 E4
Cima de Pian Guamei (CH, I) 3015 41 F4
Cima de Val Loga (CH, I) 3004 41 F3
Cima dei Cogn 3063 41 D3
Cima del Rosso (CH, I) 2624 52 B2
Cima del Serraglio (CH, I) 2685 44 C2
Cima dell´Uomo 2390 54 C1
Cima della Bondasca (CH, I) 3289 42 C5
Cima della Trosa 1869 54 B1
Cima dello Stagn (CH, I) 2382 55 E1
Cima di Barna (CH, I) 2862 41 F4
Cima di Bri 2520 40 C5
Cima di Castello (CH, I) 3388 42 C5
Cima di Cazzài 2435 40 B5
Cima di Fojorina (CH, I) 1810 55 D3
Cima di Gagnone 2518 40 B4
Cima di Gana Bianca 2842 40 C3
Cima di Jazzi (CH, I) 3803 51 F4
Cima di Piancabella 2671 40 C3
Cima di Rierna 2461 40 B5
Cima di Rosso 3366 42 C5
Cima di Sassello 1891 54 C1
Cima Verosso 2444 52 B2
Clariden 3267 26 B3
Combin de Corbassière 3716 49 F4
Corbetta 1400 34 C3
Corn da Tinizong 3172 28 C5
Corne de Sorebois 2896 50 C2
Cornettes de Bise (CH, F) 2432 34 B5
Corno Campascio (CH, I) 2808 44 B4
Corno di Gesero 2227 55 D1
Corona di Redòrta 2804 40 A4
Cousimbert, Le 1633 35 E1
Crap da Flem 27 F3
Crap Grisch 2861 27 E5
Crap Masegn 2516 27 E3
Crap Mats 2947 27 F3
Crasta Mora 2935 44 A2
Cresta della Sperella (CH, I) 2898 44 C4
Crêt de la Neuve 1494 32 C3
Crêt du Cervelet 1308 20 A2
Crêta Besse 2702 36 A5
Cristallina 2912 39 E3
Croix de Fer 2343 49 D3
Cucalner 2536 42 B3
Culan 2789 35 E5

D

Dammastock 3630 25 D5
Därliggrat 23 E5
Daubenhorn 2942 36 C4
Dent Blanche 4357 50 C3
Dent d´Hérens (CH, I) 4171 50 C4
Dent de Brenleire 2353 35 E2
Dent de Broc 1829 35 E2
Dent de Corjon 1967 35 D3
Dent de Lys 2014 35 D3
Dent de Morcles 2969 49 E1
Dent de Nendaz 2463 50 A2

Dent de Perroc 3676 50 C3
Dent de Ruth 2236 35 F2
Dent de Valère 2267 49 D2
Dent de Vaulion 1483 33 D1
Dent Favre 2917 49 E1
Denti della Vecchia (CH, I) 1491 55 D3
Dents Blanches (CH, F) 2727 48 C2
Dents de Veisivi 3183 50 C3
Dents du Midi 3257 48 C2
Diablerets, Les 3210 35 E5
Diablons, Les 3592 51 D2
Diavolezza 2973 43 E3
Diechterhorn 3389 25 D5
Distelhorn 2830 51 E2
Doldenhorn 3643 37 D3
Dôle, La 1677 32 B4
Dom 4545 51 E2
Dossen 3144 24 B5
Dotse, La 2492 49 E4
Drättehorn 2794 37 E2
Drei Schwestern (A, FL) 2052 16 B4
Dreieckhorn 3811 38 A3
Dreiländerspitz (CH, A) 3197 30 C3
Dreispitz 2520 37 E2
Drunengalm 2408 22 C5
Drusberg 2282 26 B2
Drusenfluh (CH, A) 2628 29 D1
Dufourspitze 4634 51 E4
Dündenhorn 2862 37 D3
Dürrenhorn 4035 51 E2
Düssi 3256 26 B4

E

Ebnefluh 3962 37 F3
Eggishorn 2927 38 B4
Eggstock 2449 26 C2
Eiger 3970 38 A2
Einshorn 2944 41 E3
Ellstabhorn 2830 37 E3
Elsighorn 2341 37 D3
Engelberger Rotstock 2818 25 E3
Engelhörner 2855 24 B5
Ergischhorn 2533 37 D5
Eschenberg 591 14 A1
Escherhorn 3097 38 B2
Ettenberg 1605 36 A1
Etzel 1098 14 A4
Evêque, L´ 3716 50 B4
Ewigschneehorn 3329 38 B2

F

Fähnernspitz 1506 16 A2
Falkenfluh 1078 23 D3
Falknis (CH, FL) 2562 16 B5
Fanastock 2612 27 F2
Fanellhorn 3124 41 D2
Fanenstock 2235 27 E2
Färichhorn 3290 51 E2
Farnsberg 761 11 E1
Faulfirst 2384 15 F4
Faulhorn 2681 24 A5
Fava, La 2612 35 F5
Faverges, Les 2968 36 C4
Federispitz 1865 15 D4
Ferdenrothorn 3180 37 D4
Festihorn 3092 51 E2
Fiescherhörner 4049 38 A2
Fil de Cassons 2634 27 E3
Finsteraarhorn 4274 38 B2

80

Andere Verkehrswege · Autres voies de communications
Other means of communication · Andere verbindingen
Altre vie di comunicazione · Otras vías de comunicación
Övriga trafikvägar · Andre tilkørselsveje

Alpen- und Strassentunnels · Tunnels routiers alpins
Alpin road tunnels · Berg- en verkeerstunnels
Gallerie alpino stradale · Túneles alpinos y de carretera
Alp- og vägtunneller · Alpe- og vejtunneller

Flugplätze, Flugfelder · Aérodromes, Terrains d'aviation
Airfields, Landing fields · Vliegvelden, Landingsbaan
Aerodromi, Campi d'aviazione
Aérodromos, Campos de aviación
Flyplatser, Flygfält · Flyveplads, Landingsplads

Name/Länge
Nom/Longueur
Name/Length
Naam/Lengte

		Altenrhein	**16** B1
		Ambri	**40** A3
		Amlikon	**5** F4
		Bad Ragaz	**28** A1
Arrissoules, Tunnel d' 3 km	**20** B4	Bellechasse	**21** E2
Belchen-Tunnel 3,2 km	**11** E2	Bex	**49** D1
Gotthard-Tunnel 16,9 km	**39** E2	Biel-Kappelen	**10** A5
Grand St-Bernard, Tunnel du (CH, I) 5,9 km	**49** E4	Birrfeld	**3** E5
Kerenzerbergtunnel 5,8 km	**15** E5	Buochs	**25** D2
San Bernardino-Tunnel 6,6 km	**41** E3	Buttwil	**12** C3
Sachseln-Tunnel 5,2 km	**24** C3	Chaux-de-Fondx, La - Les Eplatures	**8** B5
Seelisberg-Tunnel 9,3 km	**25** E2	Côte, La (Prangins)	**33** D4
		Courtelary	**9** E4
		Dittingen	**1** B5
		Ecuvillens	**21** E4

Autotransport per Bahn
Transport des autos (voie ferrée)
Car transportation (rail) · Autotransport (Spoor)
Trasporto automobili (ferrovia)
Transporte de coches (ferrocarril)
Biltransport (järnväg) · Transport (bane)

		Fricktal-Schupfart	**11** F1
		Grenchen	**10** B4
		Gruyères	**35** E2
		Hasenstrick (Oberdürnten)	**14** B3
		Hausen am Albis	**13** E3
		Interlaken	**37** E1
Furka Oberwald-Realp	**39** D2	Langenthal (Bleichenbach)	**11** D4
Furka Realp-Oberwald	**39** E2	Lausanne-Blécherette	**34** A2
Lötschberg Goppenstein-Kandersteg	**37** D4	Locarno	**54** C2
Lötschberg Kandersteg-Goppenstein	**37** D3	Lommis	**5** F4
Oberalp (XI-IV) Andermatt-Sedrun	**25** F5	Lugano-Agno	**54** C3
Oberalp (XI-IV) Sedrun-Andermatt	**40** B1	Luzern-Beromünster	**12** B4
Simplon Brig-Iselle (I)	**38** A5	Montricher	**33** E2
Simplon Iselle (I)-Brig	**52** C1	Môtiers	**20** A2
Vereina Klosters (Selfranga)-Lavin (Sagliains)	**30** A3	Münster	**38** C3
Vereina Lavin (Sagliains)-Klosters (Selfranga)	**29** F4	Neuchâtel	**20** C2
		Porrentruy	**9** D2
		Raron	**37** E5

Autofähren · Bacs pour autos
Car ferries · Veerboten voor auto's
Traghetti per automobili · Transbordadores
Bilfärjor · Autofærge

		Reichenbach	**37** D2
		Saanen	**35** F3
		Samedan	**44** A2
		Schaffhausen	**4** B3
Bodensee: Romanshorn-Friedrichshafen (D)	**6** C3	Schänis	**15** D4
Vierwaldstättersee: Gersau-Beckenried	**25** E2	Sion	**50** A1
Zürichsee: Meilen-Horgen	**13** F3	Sitterdorf	**6** B4
		Speck-Fehraltorf	**14** A2
		St. Stephan	**36** B3
		Thun	**22** C4

Flughäfen · Aéroports · Airports · Luchthavens
Aeroporti · Aeropuertos
Trafikflygplatser · Lufthavn

		Triengen	**12** B3
		Wangen-Lachen	**14** B4
		Winterthur	**5** D5
Basel-Mulhouse (CH, F)	**1** B4	Yverdon	**20** A4
Bern-Belp	**22** B3	Zweisimmen	**36** B2
Genève-Cointrin	**46** B1		
Zürich-Kloten	**13** E1		

Ausflugsstationen · Buts d'excursion
Excursion points · Vertrekpunten voor excursies
Punti di escursione · Puntos de excursión
Hållplats för utflykter · Udflugtssteder

Bergstationen, Hotels, Restaurants · Stations alpines, Hôtels, Restaurants
Mountain stations, Hotels, Restaurants · Bergstations, Hôtels, Restaurants
Stazioni alpine, Alberghi, Ristoranti · Estaciones de montaña, Hoteles, Restaurantes
Bergstationer, Hotell, Restauranger · Bjergstationer, Hoteller, Restauranter

Acquacalda **40** B2	Allerheiligenberg	Alpen tower **24** C4	Balmberg **10** C3	Bella Vista **55** D4
Ahorn **23** E1	**11** E2	Anzeindaz **35** E5	Barme **48** C2	Belvedère **39** D2
Albula Ospiz **43** D2	Alliaz, L' **34** C3	Attelas, Les **49** F2	Beatenbucht **37** D1	Bendolla **50** C2
All´Acqua **39** E3	Alp Grüm **44** B4	Atzmännig **14** C3	Belalp **38** A4	Berneuse **35** D4
Allenwinden **14** C2	Alp Trida **31** D1	Bad Lostorf **11** F2	Belchen **11** E2	Bernina Suot **43** E3

Binzberg **10** B3
Birg **37** E2
Blapbach **23** E3
Blockhaus Cluozza **43** F1
Bort **24** A5
Brambrüesch **28** B3
Bretaye **35** E5
Bricola **50** C3
Brischern **37** F5
Brisenhaus **25** E2
Brusada **40** B3
Brüsti **25** F3
Buchenegg **13** E3
Buffalora **45** D1
Bühlberg **36** B3
Bussalp **24** A5
Campra **40** C3
Caquerelle, La **9** F2
Cardada **54** B1
Chamoille **49** E3
Champoussin **48** C1
Chäserrugg **15** F4
Chaux, Les **35** E5
Chessel **22** C5
Chuderhüsi **23** D3
Ciernes-Picat **35** E3
Cimetta **54** B1
Corvatsch **43** D3
Corviglia **43** D3
Crap Sogn Gion **27** E3
Crosets Les **48** C2
Cry d´Err **36** B4
Darlux **29** D5
Derborence **35** F5
Diavolezza **43** E3
Dötra **40** B2
Ebenalp **15** F3
Egg **15** D3
Eggbergen **25** F3
Eggen **25** D3
Eggli **35** F3
Eigergletscher **37** F2
Eischen **15** F2
Elsigbach **36** C3
Elsigenalp **37** D3
Empächli **27** D2
Engstlenalp **25** D4
Engstligenalp **36** C3
Fafleralp **37** E3
Färch **15** D3
Felskinn **51** F2
Fermel **36** B3
Fermelberg **36** B3
Ferme-Robert **20** B2
Fex **43** D4
Finnen **37** F5

First, Grindelwald **24** A5
Fluhalp **51** E3
Fräkmüntegg **24** C2
Froburg **11** E2
Fuorcla Surlej **43** D3
Fuorn, Il **44** C1
Furgg **51** D4
Furt **28** A1
Furtschellas **43** D3
Gaflei (FL) **16** B4
Gamsalp **15** F4
Garichti **27** D2
Garschlu **28** A1
Geils **36** C3
Geisshalden **23** E3
Gerschnialp **25** D4
Girenbad **14** B3
Gitschenen **25** E3
Glarey **36** A5
Glattalp-Hütte **26** B2
Gmünden **23** E2
Gola di Lago **54** C2
Golderli **37** E2
Golzeren **26** A4
Gornergrat **51** E4
Gottschalkenberg **13** F4
Grauberg **27** E3
Griesalp **37** E2
Grimmialp **36** B2
Grimsel Hospiz **39** D2
Grindel **24** B5
Gumen **26** C2
Guraletsch **41** D2
Gurnigelbad **22** B4
Gurschen **39** F2
Gypsera **22** A5
Haggenegg **26** A1
Hahnenmoos **36** B3
Haldi **25** F3
Haldigrat **25** D3
Handegg **38** C2
Hannig **51** F2
Hannigalp **51** E1
Hard **12** A1
Hasenstrick **14** B3
Heidelberger-Hütte **30** C2
Heuberg **28** C3
Hinter Klöntal **26** C1
Hockenalp **37** E4
Hohsaas **52** A2
Hörnli **28** B4
Hungerberg **39** D2
Iffigenalp **36** B4
Iltios **15** F4
Inner-Eriz **23** D3

Isenau **35** E4
Itramen **37** F2
Jatzmeder **29** D4
Javerne **49** D1
Jungfraujoch **38** A2
Kaubad **15** F3
Kemmeribodenbad **23** F4
Klewenalp **25** E2
Klösterli **25** E1
Krienseregg **24** C1
Kühboden **38** B4
Kuttelbad **23** E1
Längfluh **51** F3
Langis **24** B3
Lauchernalp **37** E4
Laufböden **28** A2
Lothenbach **13** E4
Luan **35** D4
Lüderenalp **23** E2
Luthernbad **23** F1
Lütoldsmatt **24** C2
Madrisa **29** D2
Mägisalp **24** C4
Malbun **16** A4
Mänziwilegg **22** C2
Mauvoisin **50** A3
Mayen **35** D4
Mazots, Les **35** E4
Meiden **51** D4
Melchsee-Frutt **24** C4
Metsch **36** B3
Milez **40** A1
Mittelallalin **51** F3
Moiry **50** C2
Moosalp **51** E1
Moosegg **23** D2
Mörlialp **24** B3
Mornera **54** C1
Morteratsch **43** E3
Mostelberg **13** F5
Motta Naluns **30** C3
Muottas Muragl **44** A2
Nüegg **36** C2
Oberesitenberg **37** E3
Oberwald **23** E1
Ottavan **51** E3
Ottenleuebad **22** A4
Pardiel **28** A2
Parsenn **29** D3
Pfingstegg **38** A2
Pierre du Moëllé **35** D4
Piora **40** A2
Pischa **30** A3
Pizol-Hütte **28** A2
Plaine Morte **36** B4
Planachaux **48** C2
Planalp **24** A4

Plattjen **51** F3
Plaun **27** E3
Podestatsch-Haus **42** B3
Pra Cluen **35** F3
Prarion **49** F2
Prod **15** E5
Ramsach **11** E2
Randenhus **4** B2
Rellerligrat **35** F3
Richinen **38** B3
Riedbad **23** E1
Rietbach **15** D3
Rietbad **15** E3
Riffelberg **51** E4
Rigi-Kaltbad **25** E1
Rigi-Kulm **25** E1
Rigi-Scheidegg **25** E1
Rigi-Staffel **25** E1
Rinderhütte **37** D4
Ring **10** B2
Robiei **39** E3
Rophaien **26** A3
Rosenlaui **38** B3
Rossberg **22** B5
Rossweid **24** A4
Rothbad **22** E1
Salanfe, Auberge de **49** D2
San Bernardino Ospizio **41** E3
San Gottardo Ospizio **39** E2
Säntis **15** F3
Sardasca **30** B3
Sareiser Joch (A, FL) **16** B5
Sasso della Boggia **39** F3
Sauge, La **21** D2
Scära **28** C2
Schifers **29** D3
Schlegwegbad **23** D3
Schönbühl **24** B4
Schönenboden **22** A5
Schwägalp **15** F3
Schwänzelegg **28** C2
Schwarenbach **36** C4
Schwarzenbühl **22** B4
Schwarzsee **51** D4
Schwarzwaldalp **38** B1
Schwefelbergbad **36** B1
Schwendi Kaltbad **24** B3
Schynen **23** E2
Schynige Platte **23** F5
Seblengrat **26** C2

Seebenalp **15** E5
Seeberg **36** B2
Seebodenalp **13** E5
Selden **37** D3
Selibühl **22** B4
Sellamatt **15** E4
Selva **44** B5
Sennisalp **15** F4
Serpiano **54** C4
Siala, La **27** E3
Signal de Bougy **33** D3
Solalex **35** E5
Soldatenhaus **35** F2
Sparenmoos **36** A2
Spirstock **26** B2
Staffelalp **51** D3
Stand **25** D4
Steingletscher **25** D4
Stock **25** F2
Suld **23** E5
Sunnbühl **37** D3
Sunnegga **51** E3
Super St-Bernard **49** E4
Tampori **54** C1
Tanatzhöhi **41** F2
Tenigerbad **40** C1
Tga d´Meir **42** C2
Tiefenbach **39** E2
Tierfehd **26** C3
Tignousa **50** C1
Torrentalp **37** D4
Treib **25** E2
Triel **27** E4
Trift VS **51** D3
Trift VS **51** F2
Trockener Steg **51** D4
Trübsee **25** D4
Tschentenalp **36** C3
Tunnetsch **38** A4
Turahaus **27** E5
Twannberg **9** E5
Tzoumaz **49** F2
Val Sinestra **31** D3
Veduta, La **42** C3
Vens **49** E3
Vereina **29** E3
Videmanette **35** F3
Voralp **15** F4
Vorauen **26** C2
Wasserfallen **11** D2
Weissenberg **27** E2
Weisshorn **50** C1
Wengernalp **37** F2
Wildenberg **15** F5
Zugerberg **13** E4

Berghäuser, Clubhütten · Auberges de montagne, Cabanes Mountain inns, Mountain huts · Bergherbergen, Berghutten
Alberghi di montagna, Capanne · Albergues de montaña, Refugios Fjällbyggnader, Klubbstugor · Bjerkroer, Bjerghytter

Adula, Capanna **40** C3
Aiguilles Rouges, Cabane des **50** B3
Albert Heim-Hütte **39** E2
Albigna-Hütte **42** C4
Alpe di Gesero **55** D2
Anen-Hütte **37** F3
Bächlital-Hütte **38** C2
Baltschieder-Klause **37** F4
Basodino, Capanna **39** E3
Bergli-Hütte **38** A2
Bergsee-Hütte **25** E5
Bertol, Cabane de **50** C3
Bietschhorn-Hütte **37** E4
Biferten-Hütte **27** D3
Binntal-Hütte **38** C4
Blümlisalp-Hütte **37** E3
Bordier-Hütte **51** E2

Boval-Hütte **44** A3
Britannia-Hütte **51** F3
Brunni-Hütte **25** D3
Cadlimo-Hütte **40** A2
Calanda-Hütte **28** A3
Campo Tencia, Capanna **40** A3
Carschina-Hütte **29** D1
Cava, Capanna di **41** D4
Cavardiras-Hütte **26** B4
Chanrion, Cabane de **50** B4
Clariden-Hütte **26** C3
Coaz-Hütte **43** D4
Col de Mille, Cabane du **49** F3
Corno-Gries, Capanna **39** D3
Cristallina, Capanna **39** E3
Dent-Blanche, Cabane de la **50** C3

Diablerets, Cabane des **35** F4
Dix, Cabane des **50** B3
Doldenhorn-Hütte **37** D3
Dom-Hütte **51** E2
Dossen-Hütte **24** B5
Ela-Hütte **28** C5
Enderlin-Hütte **28** B1
Es-cha-Hütte **30** A5
Etzli-Hütte **40** A1
Europa-Hütte **51** E2
Finsteraarhorn-Hütte **38** B3
Forno-Hütte **42** C4
Fridolins-Hütte **26** C3
Fründen-Hütte **37** D3
Gauli-Hütte **24** C5
Gefadura-Hütte **16** B4
Gelmer-Hütte **25** D5
Geltenalp-Hütte **36** A4
GGB-Hütte **22** B4
Glärnisch-Hütte **26** C2

Gleckstein-Hütte **24** B5
Grialetsch-Hütte **29** E4
Gspaltenhorn-Hütte **37** E3
Hollandia-Hütte **37** F3
Hörnli-Hütte **51** D4
Hüfi-Hütte **26** B4
Hundstein-Hütte **16** A3
Jürg-Jenatsch-Hütte **42** C2
Kehlenalp-Hütte **39** D1
Kesch-Hütte **30** A5
Konkordia-Hütte **38** A3
Krönten-Hütte **25** E4
Lämmern-Hütte **36** C4
Lauteraar-Hütte **38** C2
Legler-Hütte **27** D2
Leutschach-Hütte **25** F4
Lidernen-Hütte **26** A2
Linard-Hütte **29** F4
Lischana-Hütte **31** D4
Lohner-Hütte **36** C3

Maighels, Camona da **26** A5
Malnate, Rifugio **52** A2
Martinsmad-Hütte **27** E3
Medelser-Hütte **26** C5
Mischabel-Hütte **51** F2
Mittellegi-Hütte **38** A2
Mönchsjoch-Hütte **38** A2
Monte Leone-Hütte **52** B1
Monte Rosa-Hütte **51** E4
Mont-Fort, Cabane du **49** F3
Motterascio **40** C2
Mountet, Cabane du **51** D3
Mutthorn-Hütte **37** E3
Muttsee-Hütte **27** D3
Oberaarjoch-Hütte **38** B3

86

Oberaletsch-Hütte **37** F4
Orny, Cabane d´ **49** D3
Pairolo, Capanna **55** D3
Panossière, Cabane de **50** A4
Plan-Névé, Cabane de **49** E1
Planura-Hütte **26** B3
Prafleuri, Cabane de **50** B3
Punteglias-Hütte **26** C4
Püscett **40** C4
Rambert, Cabane **49** E1
Ramoz-Hütte **28** C4

Rothorn-Hütte **51** D3
Rottal-Hütte **37** F3
Rugghubel-Hütte **25** E3
Salbit-Hütte **39** E1
Saleina, Cabane de **49** E4
Sardona-Hütte **27** E2
Sasc-Furä-Hütte **42** B4
Scaletta, Capanna **40** C2
Schesaplana-Hütte **28** C1
Schönbiel-Hütte **51** D3
Schreckhorn-Hütte **38** B2

Sciora-Hütte **42** C5
Sewen-Hütte **25** E4
Silvretta-Hütte **30** B3
Singla, La **50** B4
Spannort-Hütte **25** E4
Spitzmeilen-Hütte **27** E1
Stelserhof **28** C2
Susanfe, Cabane de **48** C2
Sustli-Hütte **25** E4
Tamaro, Capanna **54** C2
Täsch-Hütte **51** E3
Terri, Camona da **26** C5
Tierbergli-Hütte **39** D1

Topali-Hütte **51** E2
Tracuit, Cabane de **51** D2
Tresch-Hütte **39** F1
Trient, Cabane du **49** D3
Trift-Hütte **39** D1
Tsa, Cabane de la **50** C3
Tschierva-Hütte **44** A4
Tuoi-Hütte **29** F3
Turtmann-Hütte **51** D2
Valsorey, Cabane de **49** F4
Vélan, Cabane du **49** F4

Vignettes, Cabane des **50** B4
Violettes, Cabane des **36** C4
Voralp-Hütte **39** E1
Weisshorn-Hütte **51** D3
Weissmies-Hütte **52** A2
Wildhorn-Hütte **36** B4
Wildstrubel-Hütte **36** B4
Windegg-Hütte **39** D1
Windgällen-Hütte **26** B4
Zapport-Hütte **41** D3

Landschaftsnamen · Noms régionaux
Regional names · Streeknamen
Nomi regionali · Nombres regionales
Landskampsnamn · Regionale navne

Ajoie **9** E1
Ambra, Val d´ **40** C4
Anniviers, Val d´ **50** C1
Arolla, Val d´ **50** C3
Bagnes, Val de **50** A3
Baltschiedertal **37** E5
Bärental **28** C4
Bavona, Val **39** E4
Bedretto **54** C1
Bedretto, Val **39** E3
Bergalga **42** B3
Bernina, Val **44** A3
Bever, Val **43** D2
Binntal **38** C4
Bisistal **26** B2
Blénio, Val **40** C3
Blinnental **38** C3
Bondasca, Val **42** B4
Bregaglia, Val (CH, I) **42** C4
Brunnital **26** B3
Bucheggberg **10** B4
Calanca, Val **41** E4
Calanda **28** B2
Calfeisental **27** F2
Calnègia, Val **39** E4
Cama, Valle da **41** E5
Camp, Val da **44** B4
Canaltal **41** D2
Canaria, Valle **39** F2
Carassino, Val di **40** C2
Centovalli **54** A2
Chamuera, Val **43** E2
Chaschauna, Val **44** B2
Chironico, Val **40** B4
Chlital **25** E3
Chrauchtal **27** E2
Cluozza, Val **43** F1
Combe de l´A **49** E3
Côte, La **33** D3
Curciusa, Val **41** E3
Diemtigtal **36** C2
Dischmatal **30** A4
Domleschg **28** A3
Eigental **24** C2
Emmental **23** D2
Engelbergertal **25** D3
Engiadin´Ota/Ober Engadin **44** A2

Engiadina Bassa/Unter Engadin **31** D4
Engstligental **37** D2
Ennetberg **15** D5
Entlebuch **24** B2
Entremont, Val d´ **49** E3
Err, Val d´ **42** C2
Erstfelder Tal **25** E3
Etzlital **26** A4
Fain, Val da **43** E3
Faller **42** B3
Fankhausgraben **23** F2
Fellital **25** F4
Ferret, Val **49** E4
Fex, Val **43** D4
Fimbertal (CH, A) **31** D2
Flüela **30** A3
Fontannen **23** F1
Forst **22** A3
Frisal, Val **26** C4
Frodalera **40** B3
Fronalp **25** F2
Furggtal **52** A3
Gadmental **25** D4
Gambarogno (CH, I) **54** B2
Gasterntal **37** D3
Gental **24** C4
Ginals **51** E1
Gohlgraben **23** E2
Goms **38** C3
Gorneren **37** D2
Göschener Tal **25** E5
Gredetschtal **37** F4
Grischbachtal **35** F3
Gross Fontannen **24** A2
Grosses Moos **21** E2
Grosstal **25** E3
Gruyère, La **35** E2
Gulden **10** C2
Haslital **38** C1
Hérémence, Val d´ **50** B2
Hérens, Val d´ **50** B2
Heuberg **28** C3
Hilferental **23** F3
Hornbach **23** E1

Hüttengraben **23** F2
Ijental **15** D4
Illiez, Val d´ **48** C1
Isla Persa **43** E4
Joux, Vallée de **19** D5
Jungtal **51** E2
Justistal **37** D1
Kandertal **37** D2
Kiental **37** D2
Klein Melchtal **24** C4
Klettgau (CH, D) **4** B3
Klöntal **26** C1
Laggintal **52** A2
Länta **41** D2
Lavaux **34** B3
Laver, Val **31** D3
Lavinuoz, Val **29** F3
Lavirun, Val **43** E2
Lavizzara, Val **40** A4
Leventina, Valle **40** A3
Lindental **25** E4
Lodrino, V. di **40** C5
Lötschental **37** E4
Lumnezia **27** D5
Maderanertal **26** B4
Madris, Val **42** B3
Mággia, Valle **39** F4
Malcantone **54** B3
Malvaglia, Val **41** D3
Mattertal **51** E2
Medel, Val **40** B1
Meiental **25** E4
Melchtal **24** C3
Mendrisiotto (CH, I) **54** C5
Mesolcina, Valle **41** E4
Mingèr, Val **31** D4
Mirrenegg **23** F4
Mora, Val **45** D2
Morgins, Val de **48** C1
Moróbbia, Val **55** D2
Motélon, Vallée de **35** E2
Münstertal/Müstair, Val **31** D5
Muotatal **25** F2
Müstair, Val/Münstertal **31** D5
Nalps, Val **26** B5

Nandro, Val **42** B2
Nanztal **37** F5
Necker **15** E3
Nendaz, Val de **50** A2
Nessetlal **38** A5
Nieder-Simmental **22** B5
Niemet, Val **42** A3
Ober Engadin/ Engiadin´Ota **30** A5
Oberhalbstein **28** B5
Ober-Simmental **36** B3
Onsernone, Valle (CH, I) **53** F1
Osura, Val d´ **40** A5
Palfries **16** A5
Pays d´Enhaut **35** F3
Piano di Magadino **54** C2
Pigniu, Val da **27** D3
Piora, Val **40** A2
Piumogna, Val **40** A3
Plaines, Les **8** B5
Plaun la Greina **26** C5
Pontirone, Val **41** D4
Poschiavo, Val di **43** F4
Prato, Val di **40** A4
Prättigau **28** C2
Rappental **38** C4
Rätschtal **26** B2
Réchy, Val de **50** C1
Rheinwald **41** F2
Riviera **40** C4
Roseg, Val **44** A3
Russein, Val **26** B4
Ruz, Val de **20** C1
Saastal **51** F1
Safiental **27** F4
Salanfe **48** C2
Sambuco, Valle **39** F3
Saminatal (A, FL) **16** B3
Samnauntal **31** D2
Santa Maria, Valle **40** B2
Sarganserland **15** E5
Sarsura, Val **30** B4
Schächental **26** A3
Schanfigg **28** B3
S-charl, Val **31** D4

Schlappintal **30** A2
Schons **28** A5
Seerücken **5** F3
Sernftal **27** D1
Sertigtal **29** D4
Sihltal **13** E3
Sinestra, Val **31** D3
Soustal **37** E2
Spiggengrund **37** D2
Spöl, Val dal **44** B1
St-Imier, Vallon de **9** E4
Stugl, Val da **42** C1
Sumvitg, Val **40** C1
Surenen **25** E3
Surselva **27** D4
Sursés **42** B2
Susauna, Val **44** A1
Taminatal **28** A2
Tasna, Val **30** C3
Toggenburg **15** D2
Travers, Val de **20** B2
Traversagna, Valle **55** E1
Trupchun, Val **30** B5
Tuoi, Val **30** C3
Tuors, Val **29** D5
Turtmanntal **51** E2
Uina, Val d´ **31** D3
Unter Engadin/Engia-dina Bassa **31** D3
Unteralp **25** F5
Urbachtal **38** B1
Urnerboden **26** C3
Urseren **39** E2
Valser Tal **41** E1
Veddasca, Val (CH, I) **54** B2
Vereina **29** E3
Vergeletto, Val di **53** E1
Vernela **29** E3
Verzasca, Val **40** B4
Wägital **14** C4
Weisstannental **27** F2
Welschtobel **28** C4
Werdenberg **16** A3
Zinal, Val de **50** C2
Zwischbergental **52** B2

Sehenswürdigkeiten · Curiosités
Places of interest · Bezienswaardigheden
Attrazioni turistiche · Atracciones turísticas
Sevärdheter · Seværdigheder

Sehenswerte Bauwerke · Constructions
Constructions · Gebouwen
Attrazioni costruite · Monumentos
Sevärda byggnader · Seværdige bygninger

Abtei, St. Gallen **6** C5
Alpamare **14** B4
Aquaparc **34** C4
Augusta Raurica **2** A4
Aventicum **21** D3
Axenstrasse **25** F2
Ballenbergmuseum **24** B4
Baptisterium, Riva San Vitale **54** C4
Bauregard **33** D5
Bellerive **46** C1
Bonmont **32** C4
Bundesbriefarchiv **25** F1
Chillon, Château de **34** C4
Dixence, Barrage de la Grande **50** B3
Frauental **13** D4
Freulerpalast **15** D5
Gesslerburg **13** D5
Glérolles **34** B3
Gnadental **12** C2
Goetheanum **1** C5
Grasburg **22** A3

Habsburg **3** E5
Hauterive **21** E4
Heidegg **12** C3
Holzbrücke, Aarberg **21** F1
„Horlogerie, Musée d`; La Chaux-de-Fonds» **8** C5
Hünegg **23** D4
Ittingen, Kartause **5** D4
Kapelle, Sempach **12** C4
Kloster, Einsiedeln **14** A4
Kloster, Magdenau **6** A5
Klosterkirche, St. Urban **11** E3
Kyburg **14** A1
Lance, La **20** B3
Landwasserviadukt **42** C1
Madonna del Sasso **54** B2
Mauvoisin, Barrage de **50** A3
Misox **41** E4
Mistail **42** B1
Mittelpunkt der Schweiz **24** C4

Morgarten **13** F5
Mühle, Ramiswil **11** D2
Negrentino **40** C3
Nocturama/Papiliorama **21** F2
Palais des Nations (UNO) **46** C1
Panoramastrasse **24** B3
Papiliorama/Nocturama **21** F2
Payerneland **21** D4
Pierre Pertuis **9** F4
Ponte dei Salti **40** B5
Ponte, Bignasco **39** F4
Porte du Sex **34** C4
Rawil, Barrage du **36** B4
Salginatobelbrücke **28** C2
San Gian **31** E5
Santa Maria **41** D5
Schwanau **25** E1
Serravalle **40** C4
St. Martin, Zillis **28** A5

Sta. Petronilla **40** C4
Steinbogenbrücke, Hinterrhein **41** E2
Swiss Holiday Park, Morschach **25** F2
Swissminiatur **54** C4
Tellskapelle **25** F2
Teufelsbrücke, Etzelpass **14** A4
Teufelsbrücke, Schöllenenschlucht **25** E5
Tour de Gourze **34** B3
Tour de la Molière **20** C4
Urba **19** F4
Vacherie, Villars JU **9** E2
Village lacustre **20** C4
«Vogelwarte, Schweizerische; Sempach» **12** B4
Wildkirchli **16** A3
Winkelriedhaus **25** D2
Würzbrunnen **23** D3
Ziteil **28** B5
Zwinguri **26** A4

Naturschönheiten · Curiosités de la nature
Curiosities of the nature · Natuurschoon
Curiosità della natura · Atracciones de la naturaleza
Naturskönheter · Naturskønhed

Gletscher, Wasserfälle, Schluchten · Glaciers, cascades, gorges
Glaciers, waterfalls, gorges · Gletsjers, watervallen, kloven
Ghiacciai, cascate, gole · Glaciares, cataratas, gargantas
Glaciärer, vattenfall, raviner · Gletscher, vandfald, slugter

Aareschlucht **38** C1
Aletschwald **38** A4
Alp Grimmels **44** C1
Areuse, Gorges de l´ **20** B2
Areuse, Source de l´ **19** F3
Bärentritt **42** C1
Beatushöhlen **37** E1
Biaschina, Gola **40** B4
Birse, Gorges de la **10** B3
Blausee **37** D3
Brenets, Lac des (CH, F) **8** B5
Brissago, Isole di **54** A2
Buffalora, Ri de **41** E4
Carreratobel **27** F4
Cauma, Lag la **27** F3
Chapeau de Napoléon **19** F3
Cholerenschlucht **36** C3
Clemgiaschlucht **31** D3
Clos du Doubs **9** E2
Combe Grède **9** D4
Court, Gorges de **10** A3
Covatannaz, Gorges de **19** F3
Creux Genat **9** D2
Creux-du-Van **20** B2
Dalaschlucht **36** C4
Derborence, Lac de **35** F5
Durnand, Gorges du **49** E3
Dürsrütiwald **23** E2
Engstligenalp **36** C3
Engstligenfälle **36** C3
Fées, Grotte aux **49** D1
Flachsee **13** D2
Giessbachfälle **24** A4
Gletscherschlucht, Grindelwald **38** A2

Gondoschlucht **52** B2
Gornergletscher **51** E4
Grangettes, Les **34** C4
Griesschlucht **37** E2
Grosser Aletschgletscher **38** A4
Gruère, Etang de la **9** D3
Heidibrunnen **28** B1
Hohle Gasse **13** D5
Höllgrotten **13** E4
Hölloch **26** B2
Hudelmoos **6** B4
Illgraben **36** C5
Jardin alpin Florealpe, Champex **49** E3
Jardin alpin, Bourg-St-Pierre **49** F4
Jardin alpin, Rochers de Naye **35** D4
Jardin botanique alpin, Pont-de-Nant **49** E1
Joux, Lac de **19** D5
Jura Garten, Weissenstein **10** C3
Karrenfelder **23** E4
Kesslerloch **4** C2
Kinderzoo, Rapperswil **14** B3
Klus **26** B3
Laaxer-Tobel **27** E3
Labyrinthe **49** D2
Lattes, Bois des **20** B2
Linthschlucht **26** C3
Lonzaschlucht **37** D4
Lüderenalp **23** E2
Magadino, Bolle di **54** B2
Märjelensee **38** B3

Martinstobel **16** A1
Medelser Schlucht **40** B1
Monte San Giorgio **54** C4
Morteratsch, Vadret da **43** E3
Nationalpark **29** F5
Nidleloch **10** B3
Oensinger Klus **11** D3
Ofenloch **15** E3
Oltschibachfall **24** B4
Orbe, Gorges de l´ **19** E4
Orbe, Grotte de l´ **33** D1
Orbe, Source de l´ **33** D1
Pfäfers, Bad **28** A2
Pfynwald **36** C5
Pichoux, Gorges du **9** F3
Pissot, Gorges du **35** E3
Pochtenfall **37** E2
Pochtenkessel **36** C3
Poeta-Raisse, Gorges de la **20** A3
Pozzácio, Cascate di **54** A1
Préhisto Parc/Réclère, Grottes de **8** C2
Pyramides, Euseigne **50** B2
Rabiosaschlucht **28** B3
Räbloch **23** E3
Réclère, Grottes de/Préhisto Parc **8** C2
Reichenbachfall **38** B1
Rheinfall **4** C3
Rheinquelle **26** A5
Rheinschlucht **27** F3
Rhonegletscher **39** D2
Roflaschlucht **42** A2
Rosenlauischlucht **38** B1
Rütli **25** E2

Salines, Bex **35** D5
Saltinaschlucht **38** A5
Saut du Doubs **8** B5
Schatzalp **29** D3
Schinschlucht **42** B1
Schmadribachfall **37** F3
Schöllenenschlucht **25** E5
Schwarzwassergraben **22** B3
Schynige Platte, Alpengarten **23** F5
Sensegraben **22** A4
Siebenbrunnen **36** B4
Silser See **43** D3
Simmenfälle **36** B4
Simmitobel **15** F4
"Souterrain, Lac; St-Léonard" **50** B1
St. Petersinsel **9** E5
Staubbachfall **37** F2
Stäubifall **26** B3
Südrampe, Lötschberg **37** E5
Taminaschlucht **28** A2
Tätschbachfall **25** D4
Teufelsschlucht **11** E2
Trièges, Gorges du **49** D2
Trient, Gorges du **49** D2
Trift **39** D1
Trümmelbachfall **37** F2
Tschamberhöhle **2** B4
Tüfelschlucht **5** D5
Twannbachschlucht **9** E5
Ufenau **14** B3
Verzasca, Gola **54** B1
Via Mala **42** A1
Zügenschlucht **29** D4

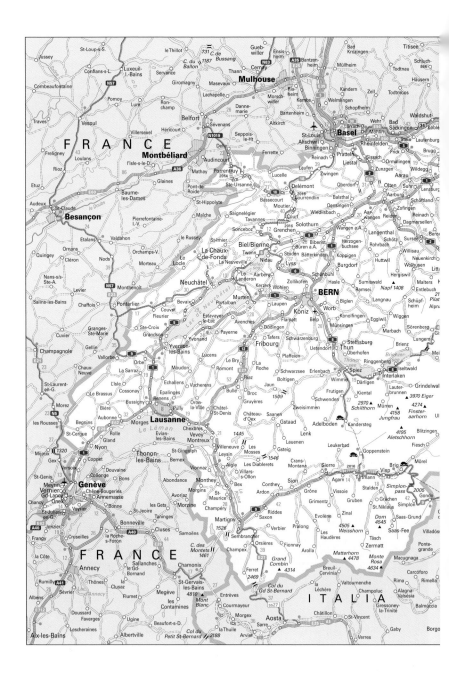

Schweiz/Suisse/Switzerland/Svizzera

 41 285 km^2 8 014 000 ● Bern

  ⇄

 200 | oder/ou/or 50 | oder/ou/or 250 g | 2 l | 1 l

max. CHF 300.– www.ezv.admin.ch

	☎→CH	←CH		☎→CH	←CH		☎→CH	←CH
A	+ 41	+ 43	FIN	+ 41	+ 358	NL	+ 41	+ 31
B	+ 41	+ 32	GB	+ 41	+ 44	P	+ 41	+ 351
BG	+ 41	+ 359	GR	+ 41	+ 30	PL	+ 41	+ 48
CH	–	–	H	+ 41	+ 36	RO	+ 41	+ 40
CZ	+ 41	+ 420	HR	+ 41	+ 385	S	+ 41	+ 46
D	+ 41	+ 49	I	+ 41	+ 39	SK	+ 41	+ 421
DK	+ 41	+ 45	IRL	+ 41	+ 353	SLO	+ 41	+ 386
E	+ 41	+ 34	N	+ 41	+ 352	TR	+ 41	+ 90
F	+ 41	+ 33	N	+ 41	+ 47	USA	011 41	+ 1

1 Schweizer Franken (CHF) = 100 Rappen / 1 franc suisse (CHF) = 100 centimes

CHF  1000 200 100 50 20 10 5 2 1 ½ MasterCard

Rappen/centimes 20 10 5 VISA

    → CHF 2013 (CHF 40.–)

50 km/h | 80 km/h | 100 km/h | 120 km/h

0,5 ‰ | SBB/CFF ☎ 0900 300 300 | Spikes / Pneus à clous / Pneumatici chiodati 24.10.–30.4./80 km/h →

Automobil-Club der Schweiz (ACS), Wasserwerkgasse 39, CH-3011 Bern, ☎ 031 / 328 31 11
Touring Club der Schweiz (TCS), Chemin de Blandonnet 4, CH-1214 Vernier, ☎ 0844 888 111

Schweiz Tourismus, Toedistrasse 7, CH-8027 Zürich
Internet: www.MySwitzerland.com, **E-Mail:** info@myswitzerland.com

Servicenummer / Numéro de service / Service number / Numero di servizio

A B CN CZ D DK E ☎ 00800 100 200 29

F FIN GB H I IRL L ☎ 00800 100 200 29

N NL P PL S USA ☎ 00800 100 200 29

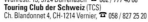 **Swisscamps / Verband Schweiz. Campings**
Bahnhofstr. 5 / Postfach, CH-3322 Schönbühl-Urtenen, ☎ 031 / 852 06 26
Schweiz. Camping- und Caravanning-Verband
Wührestr. 13, 5724 Dürrenäsch ☎ 062 / 777 40 08
Touring Club der Schweiz (TCS)
Ch. Blandonnet 4, CH-1214 Vernier, ☎ 058 / 827 25 20

⚡ 220 V 11.–3. MEZ 4.–10. MEZ +1 h

 Polizei Police 117 | 118 | 144 | 1414 | 0800 140 140

Politische Karte · Carte politique
Political map · Politieke kaart
Carta politica · Mapa político
Politisk karta · Politisk kort

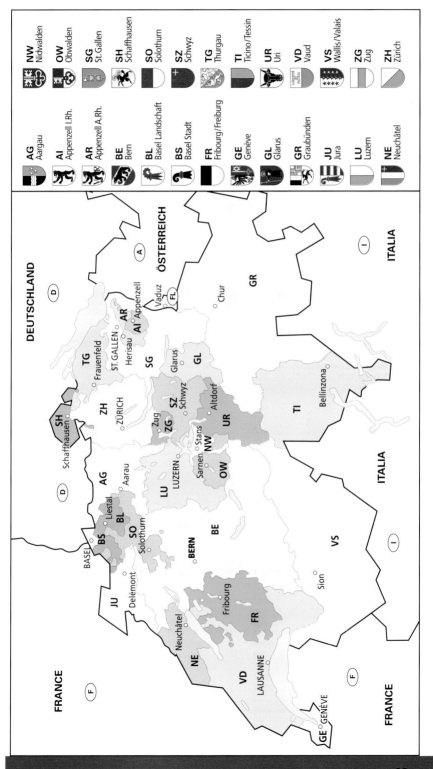

NW Nidwalden
OW Obwalden
SG St.Gallen
SH Schaffhausen
SO Solothurn
SZ Schwyz
TG Thurgau
TI Ticino/Tessin
UR Uri
VD Vaud
VS Wallis/Valais
ZG Zug
ZH Zürich

AG Aargau
AI Appenzell I.Rh.
AR Appenzell A.Rh.
BE Bern
BL Basel Landschaft
BS Basel Stadt
FR Fribourg/Freiburg
GE Genève
GL Glarus
GR Graubünden
JU Jura
LU Luzern
NE Neuchâtel

DEUTSCHLAND
ÖSTERREICH
ITALIA
FRANCE

Passstrassen · Cols accessibles en véhicule
Passes accessible for vehicles · Berijdbare passen
Passi accessibile ai veicoli · Puertos de montaña
Bergspassvägar · Pasveje

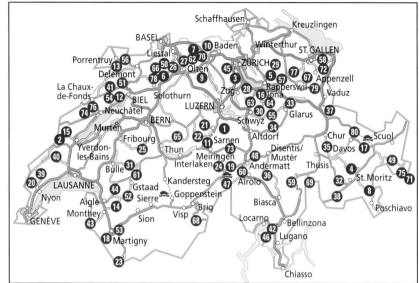

Nr.	Pass	Höhe		Nr.	Pass	Höhe
1	Aecherli	1458		41	Mont Crosin, Col du	1227
2	Aiguillon, Col de l´	1293		42	Monte Ceneri	554
3	Albispass	791		43	Morgins, Pas de	1369
4	Albula	2312		44	Mosses, Col des	1445
5	Bachtel	875		45	Mutschellen	551
6	Balmberg	1078		46	Néggia, Alpe di	1395
7	Benkerjoch	674		47	Nufenen	2478
8	Bernina	2328		48	Oberalp	2044
9	Böhler	611		49	Ofenpass	2149
10	Bözberg	569		50	Passwang	943
11	Brünig	1008		51	Pierre Pertuis	827
12	Chasseral, Col de	1502		52	Pillon, Col du	1546
13	Croix, Col de la (JU)	789		53	Planches, Col des	1411
14	Croix, Col de la (VD)	1778		54	Pontins, Col des	1110
15	Etroits, Col des	1152		55	Pragel	1550
16	Etzel	950		56	Rangiers, Les	856
17	Flüela	2383		57	Ricken	794
18	Forclaz, Col de la	1526		58	Ruppen	1003
19	Furka	2431		59	S. Bernardino, Passo	2065
20	Givrine, Col de la	1228		60	St. Gotthard	2108
21	Glaubenberg	1543		61	Saanenmöser	1279
22	Glaubenbielen	1611		62	Salhöhe	779
23	Grand St-Bernard	2469		63	Sattel	932
24	Grimsel	2165		64	Sattelegg	1190
25	Gurnigel	1608		65	Schallenberg	1167
26	Hauenstein, Oberer	731		66	Schelten	1051
27	Hauenstein, Unterer	691		67	Schwägalp	1278
28	Hirzel	682		68	Simplon	2005
29	Hulftegg	953		69	Splügen	2113
30	Ibergeregg	1406		70	Staffelegg	621
31	Jaun	1509		71	Stilfser Joch	2757
32	Julier	2284		72	Stoss	942
33	Kerenzerberg	743		73	Susten	2224
34	Klausen	1948		74	Tourne, La	1170
35	Lenzerheide	1547		75	Umbrail	2501
36	Lukmanier	1914		76	Vue des Alpes	1283
37	Luziensteig	713		77	Wasserfluh	843
38	Maloja	1825		78	Weissenstein	1279
39	Marchairuz, Col du	1447		79	Wildhaus	1090
40	Mollendruz, Col du	1180		80	Wolfgang	1631

Transitpläne · Plans de transit
Transit maps · Transitkaarten
Piante di transito · Mapas de tránsito
Genomfartskartor · Transitkort

Transitpläne · Plans de transit
Transit maps · Transitkaarten
Piante di transito · Mapas de tránsito
Genomfartskartor · Transitkort

Bezeichnung der Ausfallstrassen
Indication of arterial roads
Indicazione delle strade di uscita
Beteckning för utfartsleder

Indication des routes de sortie
Aanduiding van uitvalswegen
Denominación de carreteras de salida
Betegnelse for udfaldsveje

Informationsbüro · Polizei
Information centre · Police
Ufficio d' informazione · Polizia
Turistinformation · Polis

Office de tourisme · Police
Informatie voor toeristen · Politie
Oficina de turismo · Policía
Turistbureau · Politi

Post · Jugendherberge
Post office · Youth hostel
Posta · Ostello della gioventù
Post · Vandrarhem

Poste · Auberge de jeunesse
Postkantoor · Jeugdherberg
Correos · Albergue juvenil
Post · Vandrerhjem

Bahnhof · Autoreisezug
Railway station · Car transporting train
Stazione · Servizio navetta per auto
Järnvägsstation · Biltåg

Gare · Service auto-train
Station · Autoslaaptrein
Estación · Servicio auto-tren
Banegård · Biltog

Schiffsanlegestelle · Jachthafen
Docking · Yacht harbour
Debarcadero · Porto per i panfili
Båtbrygga · Hamn för fritidsbåtar

Débarcadère · Port de plaisance
Aanlegplaats voor schepen · Jachthaven
Desembarcadero · Puerto deportivo
Anløbssted · Lystbådehavn

Bad · Hallenbad
Bathing · Swimming-pool
Bagno all' aperto · Piscina coperta
Bad · Simhall

Baignade · Piscine couverte
Zwemgelegenheid · Overdekt zwembad
Playa · Piscina cubierta
Bad · Svømmehal

Spital · Theater
Hospital · Theatre
Ospedale · Teatro
Sjukhus · Teater

Hôpital · Théâtre
Ziekenhuis · Theater
Hospital · Teatro
Sygehus · Teater

Botanischer Garten · Zoo
Botanical garden · Zoo
Giardino botanico · Zoo
Botansk trädgård · Zoo

Jardin botanique · Zoo
Botanische tuin · Dierentuin
Jardín botánico · Zoo
Botanisk have · Zoologisk have

Wochentage (Montag - Sonntag)
Weekdays (Monday - Sunday)
Giorni della settima (Lunedi - Domenica)
Veckodagen (Måndag - Söndag)

Jours ouvrables (Lundi - Dimanche)
Weekdagen (Maandag - Zondag)
Días laborables (Lunes - Domingo)
Ugedagen (Mandag - Søndag)

Altstadt
Old city
Città vecchia
Gamla stad

Vieille ville
Oude stad
Ciudad antigua
Gamle by

Hallwag
INTERNATIONAL

⊠ 2500/✆ 032

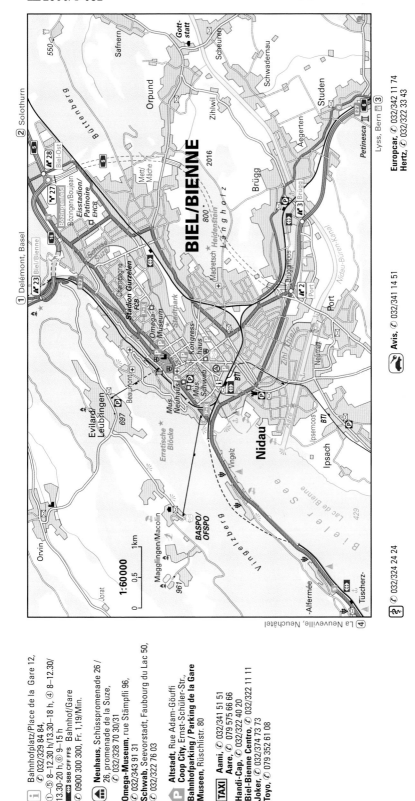

① Delémont, Basel ② Solothurn

④ La Neuveville, Neuchâtel

Lyss, Bern 🚗 ③

Europcar, ✆ 032/342 11 74
Hertz, ✆ 032/322 33 43

Avis, ✆ 032/341 14 51

✆ 032/324 24 24

ℹ Bahnhofplatz/Place de la Gare 12,
✆ 032/329 84 84,
①–⑤ 8–12.30 h/13.30–18 h, ④ 8–12.30/
13.30–20 h,⑥ 9–15 h
🚆 SBB CFF FFS Bahnhof//Gare
✆ 0900 300 300, Fr. 1,19/Min.

🏛 **Neuhaus,** Schüsspromenade 26 /
26, promenade de la Suze,
✆ 032/328 70 30/31
Omega-Museum, rue Stämpfli 96,
✆ 032/343 91 31
Schwab, Seevorstadt, Faubourg du Lac 50,
✆ 032/322 76 03

🅿 **Altstadt,** Rue Adam-Göuffi
Coop City, Ernst-Schüler-Str.,
**Bahnhofparking / Parking de la Gare
Museen,** Rüschlistr. 80

🚕 **Aami,** ✆ 032/341 51 51
Aare, ✆ 079 575 66 66
Handi-Cap, ✆ 032/322 40 20
Biel-Bienne Centro, ✆ 032/322 11 11
Joker, ✆ 032/374 73 73
Toyo, ✆ 079 352 61 08

Basel

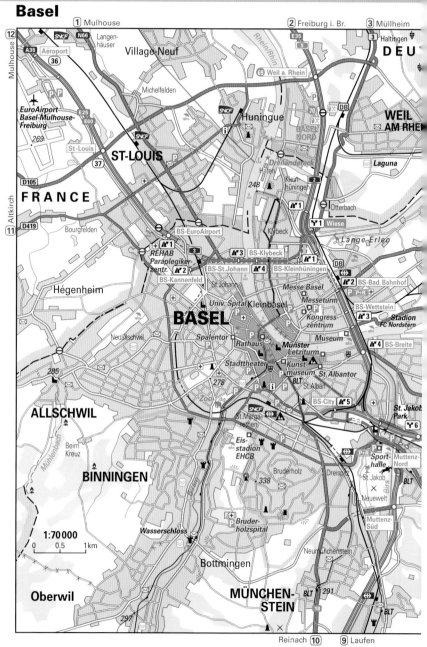

① Mulhouse ② Freiburg i. Br. ③ Müllheim
⑩ Reinach ⑨ Laufen

1:70 000

0   0.5   1km

Bahnhof SBB u. Stadtcasino
am Barfüsserplatz
℡ 061/268 68 68
①–⑤ 8.30–18.30 h,
⑥ 9–17 h, ⑦ 9–15 h

🚄 SBB CFF FFS
℡ 0900 300 300, Fr. 1,19/Min.
DB ℡ 0180 599 66 33, € 0.42/Min

✈
swiss schweiz suisse svizzera swiss
℡ 0848 700 700
Flughafen, ℡ 061/325 31 11

℡ 061/261 15 15

Anatomisches Museum,
Pestalozzistr. 20, ℡ 061/267 35 35
Antikenmus. und Sammlung Ludwig,
St.Alban–Graben 5,
℡ 061/201 12 12
Architekturmuseum,
Steinenberg 7, ℡ 061/261 14 13
Fondation Beyeler,
Baselstr. 101, 4125 Riehen
℡ 061/645 97 00

Historisches Museum Basel:
– **Barfüsserkirche,** Steinenberg 4,
  ℡ 061/205 86 00
– **Haus zum Kirschgarten,**
  Elisabethenstr. 27,
  ℡ 061/205 86 78
– **Kutschenmuseum,**
  Im botanischen Garten
  Brüglingen,
  ℡ 061/205 86 00
– **Musikmuseum,**
  Im Lohnhof 9,
  ℡ 061/264 91 60

Museum für Gegenwartskunst,
St.Alban-Rheinweg 60,
℡ 061/206 62 62

Aeschen,
Aeschengraben 9, **97 Plätze**
Anfos,
Henric-Petri-Strasse 21, **166**
Bahnhof Süd,
Güterstrasse 115, **100**
Bad. Bahnhof,
Schwarzwaldstr. 160, **300**
Centralbahnparking,
Gartenstrasse 150, **286**
City-UBS, Klingelbergstr. 20,
Schanzenstrasse 48, **980**
Claramatte,
Klingentalstrasse 25, **100**
Elisabethen,
Steinentorberg 5, **840**
Europe,
Hammerstrasse 68, **120**
Gundeli Park,
J.J. Balmerstrasse 8, **300**
Hilton,
Aeschengraben 31, **60**
Rebgasse, Rebgasse 20, **250**
Messe Basel,
Riehenstr. 101, **600**
Post Basel,
Gartenstrasse 143, **72**
Steinen,
Steinenschanze 5, **520**
Storchen,
Fischmarkt 10, **130**
St.Jakob-Park,
Gellert-/Birsstrasse 31, **680**
St.Jakobshalle,
Brüglingerstrasse 17, **1465**

www.parkleitsystem-basel.ch

Avis, ☎ 061/206 95 45,
✈ ☎ 061/325 28 40
Europcar, ☎ 061/378 99 66,
✈ ☎ 061/325 29 03
Hertz, ☎ 061/205 92 22,
✈ ☎ 061/325 27 80
Settelen AG, ☎ 061/307 38 00

TAXI

Airport Taxi, ☎ 061/325 27 00
Blitz Taxi, ☎ 061/692 77 77
Kiraly, ☎ 061/692 13 72
Metro-Taxi, ☎ 061/312 44 44
Stern Taxi, ☎ 061/691 44 44
Taxiphon, ☎ 061/444 44 44
Taxizentrale, ☎ 061/222 22 22
33er Taxi, ☎ 061/333 33 33

Jüdisches Museum der Schweiz,
Kornhausgasse 8,
☎ 061/261 95 14
Karikatur- & Cartoon Mus. Basel,
St.Alban-Vorstadt 28,
☎ 061/226 33 60
Museum Kleines Klingental,
Unterer Rheinweg 26,
☎ 061/267 66 25
Museum der Kulturen,
Münsterplatz 20,
☎ 061/266 56 00
Kunsthalle,
Steinenberg 7,
☎ 061/206 99 00
Kunstmuseum, St.Alban Graben 16,
☎ 061/206 62 62

Kupferstichkabinett und Bibliothek,
Kunstmuseum, St.Alban-Graben 16,
☎ 061/206 62 62
Naturhistorisches Museum,
Augustinergasse 2,
☎ 061/266 55 00
Basler Papiermühle,
St.Alban-Tal 37,
☎ 061/225 90 90
Schweiz. Pharmazie-Historisches
Museum, Totengässlein 3,
☎ 061/264 91 11
Puppenhausmuseum,
Steinenvorstadt 1,
☎ 061/225 95 95

Skulpturhalle, Mittlere Str. 17,
☎ 061/261 52 45
Spielzeugmuseum,
Baselstr. 34, 4125 Riehen,
☎ 061/641 28 29
Schweiz. Sportmuseum,
Reinacherstr. 1, Münchenstein
☎ 061/261 12 21
Verkehrsdrehscheibe Schweiz
«Unser Weg zum Meer»,
Westquaistr. 2, Rheinhafen
Kleinhüningen, ☎ 061/631 42 61
Museum Jean Tinguely
Paul Sacher–Anlage 2
☎ 061/681 93 20
Zoo Basel,
Binningerstr. 40, ☎ 061/295 35 35

Bern

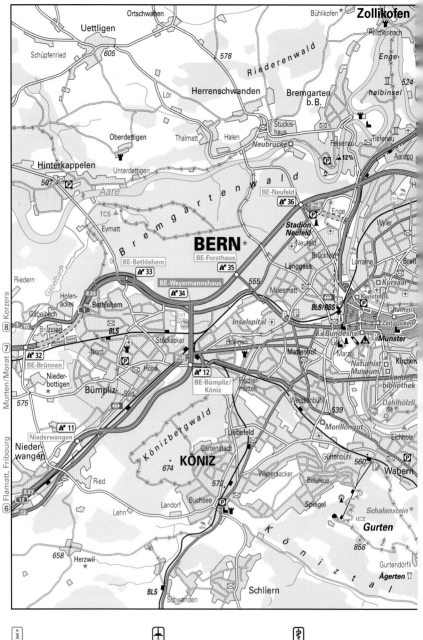

✉ 3000/✆ 031

① Biel, Solothurn   ② Basel, Zürich

Bahnhof,
Parkterrasse 14, **622 Plätze**
BEAbern expo,
Bolligenstrasse 61, **720**
City-West,
Effingerstrasse 20, **430**
Insel, Murtenstrasse 12, **480**
Metro-Autopark,
Waisenhausplatz 19, **425**
Mobiliar-Parking,
Bundesgasse 35, **90**
Neufeld (Park+Ride),
Neubrückstrasse 166, **255**
Parking Casino,
Kochergasse 1, **481**
Rathaus,
Postgasshalde 50, **586**

www.parking-bern.ch

Avis, ✆ 031/378 15 15
Bantiger Rent-a-Car,
✆ 031/721 62 60
Europcar, ✆ 031/381 75 55
Hertz, ✆ 031/318 21 60
Park + Fly, (✆ 031/960 22 66
Sixt, ✆ 031/371 71 00

TAXI
Tag+Nacht Taxi, ✆ 079/823 23 23
Bären Taxi, ✆ 031/371 11 11
✈ Airport-Taxi, ✆ 031/961 74 84
Taxiservice Bern, ✆ 031/351 70 70
Hallo-Taxi, ✆ 031/333 55 55
Kombitaxi, ✆ 031/332 26 06
Nova Taxi, ✆ 031/331 33 13
Sollberger, ✆ 079/651 72 72

Alpines Museum, Helvetiaplatz 4,
✆ 031/350 04 40
Antiken-Sammlung,
Hallerstr.12, ✆ 031/631 89 92
Botanischer Garten,
Altenbergrain 21,
✆ 031/631 49 45
Einstein-Haus, Kramgasse 49,
✆ 031/312 00 91
Historisches Museum,
Helvetiaplatz 5, ✆ 031/350 77 11
Käfigturm, Marktgasse 67,
✆ 031/322 75 00
Kornhausforum,
Kornhausplatz 18,
✆ 031/312 91 10

Kunsthalle, Helvetiaplatz 1,
✆ 031/350 00 40
Kunstmuseum, Hodlerstr. 8-12,
✆ 031/328 09 44
Museum für Kommunikation,
Helvetiastr. 16, ✆ 031/357 55 55
Naturhistorisches Museum,
Bernastr. 15,
✆ 031/350 71 11
Zentrum Paul Klee,
Monument im Fruchtland 3,
✆ 031/359 01 01
Schweizerisches Schützenmuseum,
Bernastr. 5,
✆ 031/351 01 27
Schweizerische Theatersammlung,
Schanzenstr. 15,
✆ 031/301 52 52

Tierpark Dählhölzli,
Tierparkweg 1,
✆ 031/357 15 15
Sommer/Eté/Summer/Estate,
①–⑦ 8.30–19.00 h
Winter/Hiver/Winter/Inverno,
①–⑦ 9–17 h

Genève

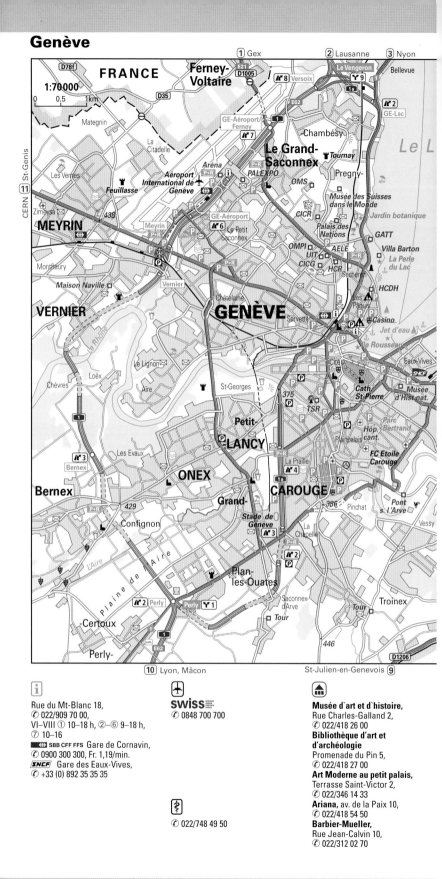

1:70000

0 0.5 1km

FRANCE

Ferney-Voltaire

① Gex ② Lausanne ③ Nyon

⑩ Lyon, Mâcon St-Julien-en-Genevois ⑨

MEYRIN
VERNIER
GENÈVE
LANCY
ONEX
Bernex
CAROUGE
Petit-Lancy
Grand-Lancy
Plan-les-Ouates
Certoux
Perly-
Confignon

Le Grand-Saconnex
Chambésy
Pregny-
Bellevue
Versoix
Le Vengeron

ℹ️ Rue du Mt-Blanc 18,
☏ 022/909 70 00,
VI–VIII ① 10–18 h, ②–⑥ 9–18 h,
⑦ 10–16
🚆 SBB CFF FFS Gare de Cornavin,
☏ 0900 300 300, Fr. 1,19/min.
SNCF Gare des Eaux-Vives,
☏ +33 (0) 892 35 35 35

swiss
☏ 0848 700 700

☏ 022/748 49 50

🏛️ **Musée d'art et d'histoire,**
Rue Charles-Galland 2,
☏ 022/418 26 00
**Bibliothèque d'art et
d'archéologie**
Promenade du Pin 5,
☏ 022/418 27 00
Art Moderne au petit palais,
Terrasse Saint-Victor 2,
☏ 022/346 14 33
Ariana, av. de la Paix 10,
☏ 022/418 54 50
Barbier-Mueller,
Rue Jean-Calvin 10,
☏ 022/312 02 70

✉ 1200/✆ 022

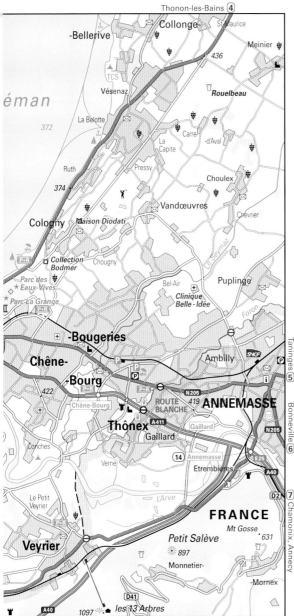

Aéroport,
Cointrin, **2400 Places**
Arcades, rue des Alpes, **300**
Alpes, 12, rue Thalberg, **350**
Balexert,
27, av. Louis-Casai, **150**
Cornavin,
place de Cornavin, **910**
David Dufour,
rue David-Dufour, **440**
Eaux-Vives 2000,
5, rue Jargonnant, **190**
Genève-Plage (P+R),
quai de Cologny, **900**
Grand Hotel Kempinski,
Rue de la Cloche, **500**
Grenus, place Grenus, **300**
Hôtel des Finances,
26, rue du Tir, **340**
ICC, Route de Pré-Bois, **1586**
Lombard,
8, rue Lombard, **650**
Mont Blanc,
quai Général-Guisan, **1500**
CFF-Montbrillant,
rue de Montbrillant, **200**
Palexpo,
Route des Batailleux, **1050**
Place des Nations,
rue de Varembé, **1060**
Plainpalais, av. du Mail, **800**
Ramada Park Hotel,
Av. Louis - Casaï, **150**
Rive Centre,
31, bd. Helvétique, **500**
Seujet,
18 quai du Seujet, **530**
World Trade Center II,
Route de Pré-Bois, **1250**

Rental
✈✆ 022/717 84 30
Avis, ✆ 022/731 90 00
✈✆ 022/929 03 30
Budget
✈✆022/731 90 60
Europcar, ✆ 022/909 69 90,
✈✆ 022/717 81 10
Hertz, ✆ 022/716 30 80,
✆ 022/717 80 80

TAXI
AA-New-Cab, ✆ 022/320 20 20
Central Taxi, ✆ 022/331 41 33
Taxi-Phone Centrale SA,
✆ 022/331 41 33

Fondation Martin Bodmer,
Route du Guignard 19–21,
Cologny, ✆ 022/ 707 44 33
Bibliothèque municipale,
Rue de la Tour-de-Boël 10,
✆ 022/418 32 50
Cern Exposition Microcosm,
✆ 022/767 76 76
Collections Baur,
Rue Munier-Romilly 8,
✆ 022/704 32 82
Croix-Rouge et Croissant-Rouge,
av. de la Paix 17,
✆ 022/748 95 02
Ethnographie,
Boulevard Carl-Vogt 65-67
✆ 022/418 45 50

Art en Ile
Place de l`Ile 1,
✆ 022/312 12 30
Horlogerie, Route de Malagnou 15,
✆ 022/418 64 70
Histoire Naturelle,
Rte de Malagnou 1,
✆ 022/418 63 00
International de l'Automobile
Rte François Peyrot 30,
1218 Gd-Saconnex,
✆ 022/761 11 11
Espace Rousseau,
Grand-Rue 40, ✆ 022/310 10 28
Site Archéologique de St-Pierre,
Cours Saint-Pierre 6,
✆ 022/311 75 75

Suisses dans le Monde,
Château de Penthes,
Ch. de l'Impératrice 18,
1292 Pregny
✆ 022/734 90 21
**MAMCO Art Moderne et
Contemporain,**
Rue des Vieux-Grenadiers 10
✆ 022/320 61 22
Maison Tavel,
R. Puits-St-Pierre 6,
✆ 022/418 37 00
Voltaire, Rue des Délices 25,
✆ 022/344 71 33
Musée Rath,
Place Neuve 2,
✆ 022/418 33 40

Lausanne

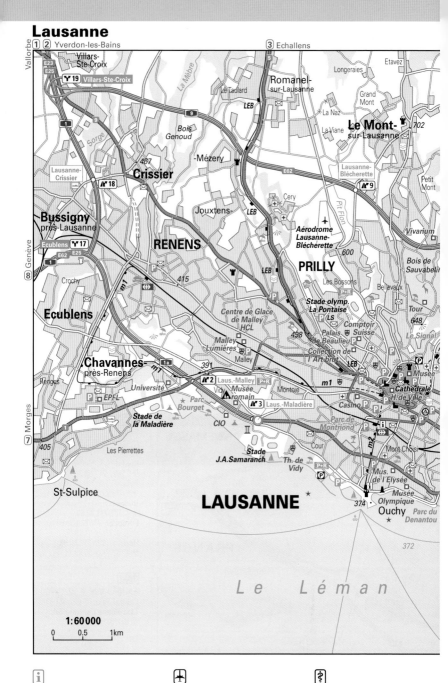

1:60 000

0   0.5   1km

ℹ
☎ 021/613 73 73,
Gare CFF ①–⑦ 9–19 h,
Ouchy, Place de la Navigation
IV-IX ①–⑦ 9–19 h
X-III ①–⑦ 9–18 h
Avenue de Rhodanie 2
①–⑤ 8–17 h

✈
swiss
☎ 0848 700 700

⚕
☎ 144

⇔ SBB CFF FFS Lausanne-Gare,
☎ 0900 300 300, Fr. 1,19/min.

⊠1000/☎ 021

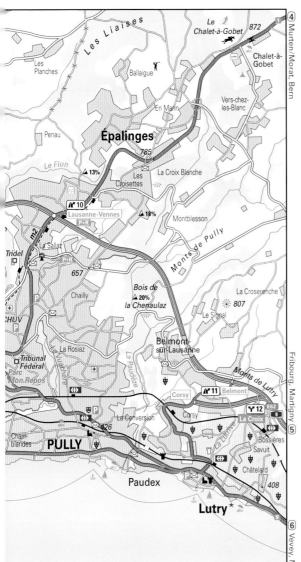

P

Bellefontaine,
rue Bellefontaine 3, **325 Places**
Chauderon, Pl. chauderon 9, **314**
Hôpitaux,
av. de Beaumont 25, **492**
Métropole,
rue des Terreaux 23, **225**
Mon-Repos,
av. Mon-Repos 5, **371**
Montbenon,
ch. de Mornex 36, **960**
Palais de Beaulieu,
av. Bergières 10, **580**
Parking du centre,
rue de Genève 31, **910**
Port d'Ouchy,
pl. Navigation 3, **846**
Riponne, pl. Riponne 12, **1190**
Rôtillon, rue Centrale 28, **180**
Royal-Savoy,
av. d'Ouchy 40, **175**
Saint-François,
rue Grand-Chêne 10, **196**
Gare de Lausanne,
rue du Simplon 32, **403**

Avis, ☎ 021/340 72 00
Europcar, ☎ 021/319 90 40
Hertz, ☎ 021/312 53 11

TAXI
Taxi Services Sàrl,
☎ 021/621 77 77
Allô Taxis, ☎ 0800 907 907
Auto-Location et Taxis,
☎ 021 616 25 25
Coopérative Taxiphone,
☎ 0800 810 810
Lausannois SA, ☎ 021/646 11 11

Collection de l`Art Brut ,
Av. des Bergières 11,
☎ 021/315 25 70
Archéologie et Histoire,
Palais de Rumine, pl. Riponne 6,
☎ 021/316 34 45
Beaux-Arts, Place de la Rippone 6,
☎ 021/316 34 30
l'Elysée, av. de l'Elysée 18,
☎ 021/316 99 11
Fondation de l'Hermitage,
Route du Signal 2,
☎ 021/320 50 01
Géologie, Direction BFSH2,
☎ 021/692 44 70

Jardin botanique, av. de Cour 14 bis,
☎ 021/316 99 88
Zoologie, Palais de Rumine, Pl. de la
Riponne 6 ☎ 021/316 34 60
Historique de Lausanne,
pl. Cathédrale 4,
☎ 021/315 41 01
Olympique, 1, quai d'Ouchy,
☎ 021/621 65 11
Romain de Vidy,
ch. Bois-de-Vaux 24,
☎ 021/315 41 85
Cabinet des Médailles,
Place de la Riponne,
☎ 021/316 39 90
Vivarium, 82, ch. Boissonnet 82,
☎ 021/652 72 94

MUDAC,
6, place de la Cathédrale,
☎ 021/315 25 30

Lugano

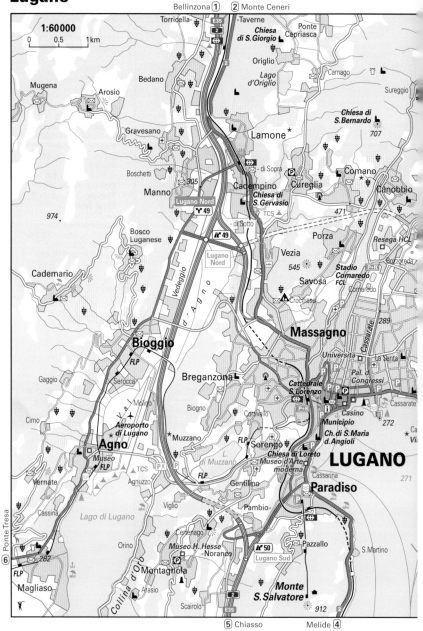

1:60000

0   0.5   1km

Bellinzona 1   2 Monte Ceneri

Torricella-

Taverne

Chiesa di S.Giorgio

Ponte Capriasca

Origlio

Lago d'Origlio

Carnago

Mugena

Arosio

Bedano

Sureggio

Lamone

Chiesa di S.Bernardo

707

Gravesano

Boschetti

di Sopra

Comano

974

Manno

305

Cadempino

Chiesa di S.Gervaso

Cureglia

Canobbio

Lugano Nord

TCS

471

Resega HCL

Bozzoreda

Bosco Luganese

di Sotto

Porza

Lugano Nord

Vezia

545

Savosa

Stadio Cornaredo FCL

Cademario

Cornaredo

289

Crocifissa

Massagno

Bioggio

FLP

Breganzona

Università

La Santa

Pal. d. Congressi

Cassarate

Gaggio

Serocca

Biogno

Cattedrale S.Lorenzo

Cimo

Molino

Corvallo

Aeroporto di Lugano

Muzzano

FLP

Sorengo

Casino

Municipio

272

Ca

Vi

Agno

FLP

Museo

TCS

L. di Muzzano

FLP

Ch. di S.Maria d. Angioli

LUGANO

271

Vernate

Agnuzzo

Gentilino

Chiesa di Loreto

Museo d'Arte moderna

Cassarina

Cassina

Viglio

Pambio

Paradiso

Lago di Lugano

Certenago

Pazzallo

S.Martino

Orino

Museo H.Hesse

-Noranco

Lugano Sud

Ponte Tresa

282

FLP

Magliaso

Montagnola

Arasio

Scairolo

Monte S.Salvatore

912

5 Chiasso

Melide 4

Lugano

Palazzo Civico, ✆ 091/913 32 32,
①–⑤ XI–III 9–12 h/13.30 –17.30 h,
IV–X 9–19 h
⑥ XI–III 10–12.30h/13.30–17h
IV–X 9–17h, V–IX 9–18h
⑦ IV–X 10–17h, V–IX 10–18h

swiss ✆ 0848 700 700

✆ 091/811 61 11

SBB CFF FFS Stazione,
✆ 0900 300 300, Fr. 1,19/min.

⊠ 6900/℡ 091

Central Park,
Via Antonio Caccia 1a
Centro Bettydo,
Via Cantonale
Comunale Balestra,
Via Serafino Balestra, **489 Posti**
Comunale Motta,
Via Motta, **278**
Comunale Paradiso,
Via delle scuole, **340**
Piazza Castello
Ospedale Civico

Avis, ℡ 091/913 41 51
✈ ℡ 091/605 54 59
Europcar, ℡ 091/971 01 01
Hertz, ℡ 091/923 46 75

TAXI
AABC, ℡ 091/971 91 91
Nuovo Taxi, ℡ 091/993 16 16
Pronto Taxi, ℡ 091/600 06 06
Tele-Taxi, ℡ 091/971 21 21

Museo cantonale d'arte,
via Canova 10,
℡ 091/910 47 80
Museo civico di belle arti,
Parco Civico,
℡ 058/866 71 98
Museo d'Arte Moderna,
Villa Malpensata,
riva Antonio Caccia 5,
℡ 058/866 68 00
Storia Naturale,
viale Carlo Cattaneo 4,
℡ 091/815 47 61

Umgebung/Environs/
Surroundings/Dintorni:

Archivio storico,
strada di Gandria 4,
6976 Castagnola,
℡ 058/866 68 50
Galeria Gottardo, 6979 Brè,
Viale Franscini 12,
℡ 091/808 19 88
Museo Doganale,
6978 Cantine di Gandria,
℡ 091/910 48 11
Museo delle Culture Extraeuropee,
Villa Heleneum, via Cortivo 24,
6976 Castagnola, ℡ 058/866 69 60

Luzern

✉ 6000/✆ 041

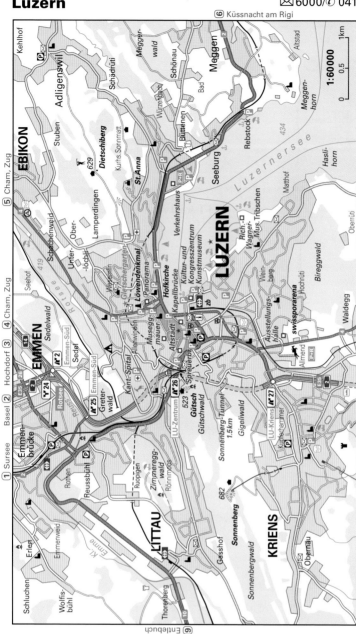

⑥ Küssnacht am Rigi

1:60000

Kehlhof

Adligenswil

MEGGEN

Meggen

Luzernersee

EBIKON

EMMEN

LUZERN

LITTAU

KRIENS

※ Pilatus 2120m

⑨ Entlebuch

① Sursee ② Basel ② Hochdorf ③ ④ Cham, Zug ⑤ Cham, Zug

Gotthard ⑧ Horw ⑦

ℹ Zentralstrasse 5, ✆ 041/227 17 17,
①–⑤ 8.30–19.00 h, ⑥ 9.00–19.00 h,
⑦ 9.00–17.00 h

🚉 SBB CFF FFS Bahnhof,
✆ 0900 300 300, Fr. 1,19/Min.

🏛 **Alpineum**, Denkmalstrasse 11,
✆ 041/410 62 66
Gletschergarten, Denkmalstrasse 4,
✆ 041/410 43 40
Historisches Museum, Pfistergasse 24,
✆ 041/228 54 24
Kunstmuseum, Europaplatz 1,
✆ 041/226 78 00
Natur-Museum, Kasernenplatz 6,
✆ 041/228 54 11
Bourbaki-Panorama, Löwenplatz 11,
✆ 041/412 30 30
Richard-Wagner, Richard-Wagner-Weg 27,
✆ 041/360 23 70,
Montag geschlossen/fermé/closed/chiuso
Rosengart, Pilatusstrasse 10,
✆ 041/220 16 60
Verkehrshaus der Schweiz, Lidostrasse 5,
✆ 0848 85 20 20

🅿 **Altstadt**, Baselstrasse 4, **462**
Am Gütsch, Baslerstrasse 61, **220 Plätze**
Bahnhof P1+P2, Bahnhofplatz 2, **467**
Bahnhof P3, hinter dem Bahnhof, **487**
Casino Palace, Haldenstrasse 6, **250**
City Parking, Zürichstrasse 31-35, **400**
Hirzenmatt, Winkelriedstrasse 36, **54**
Kantonalbank, Pilatusstrasse 12, **254**
Kesselturm, Burgerstrasse 20, **350**
Löwen-Center, Löwenplatz, **355**
Schweizerhof, Schweizerhofquai 3, **350**

www.pls-luzern.ch

🚕 **Bahnhoftaxi**, ✆ 041/210 33 33
ABC-Taxi, ✆ 041/210 10 10

🚗 **Avis**, ✆ 041/310 16 16
Europcar, ✆ 041/210 57 22

Hertz, ✆ 041/420 02 77
Miecar AG, ✆ 041/210 00 44

📞 ✆ 041/211 14 14

St.Margrethen

1:60000

0   0,5   1km

ST. GALLEN

Rorschach ① ②

③ Appenzell

④ Herisau

Gossen ⑤ ⑥ Winterthur

🚗 Bahnhofplatz 1a, ✆ 071/227 37 37,
①–⑤ 9–18 h,

🚆 SBB CFF FFS Hauptbahnhof,
✆ 0900 300 300, Fr. 1,19/Min.

♿ **Historisches und Völkerkundemuseum,**
Museumstr. 50, ✆ 071/242 06 42
Lapidarium der Stiftskirche, Klosterhof 6d,
✆ 071/227 34 16
Naturmuseum, Museumstr. 32,
✆ 071/242 06 70
Museum im Lagerhaus, Davidstr. 44,
✆ 071/223 58 57
Historisches und Völkerkundemuseum,
Museumstr. 27, ✆ 071/242 06 42
Kunst Halle, Davidstr. 40,
✆ 071/222 10 14
Textilmuseum, Vadianstr. 2,
✆ 071/222 17 44

P **Brühltor,** Torstrasse 12, **504 Plätze**
Burggraben, 295
Manor, Vadianstrasse 29, **137**
Neumarkt, Vadianstrasse, **291**
Oberer Graben, Oberer Graben 37, **143**
Olma Messen, Sonnenstrasse, **59**
Raiffeisen-Zentrum, Gartenstrasse, **103**
Rathaus, Bahnhofstrasse, **84**
Spisertor, 52
Sporthalle Kreuzbleiche, Bogenstr., **367**
Stadtpark, Torstrasse 12, **183**
Unterer Graben, Unterer Graben 21-25, **92**

www.pls-sg.ch

TAXI   **Gallus,** ✆ 071/222 50 50
Herold Taxi, ✆ 071 222 27 77
Sprenger, ✆ 071/333 33 33
Taxi-Zentrale, ✆ 0800 82 27 77

✈ **Avis,** ✆ 071/279 30 30   **Hertz,** ✆ 071/278 84 74
Europcar, ✆ 071/222 11 14

swiss ✆ 0848 700 700

📞 ✆ 0900 144 144

109

Zürich

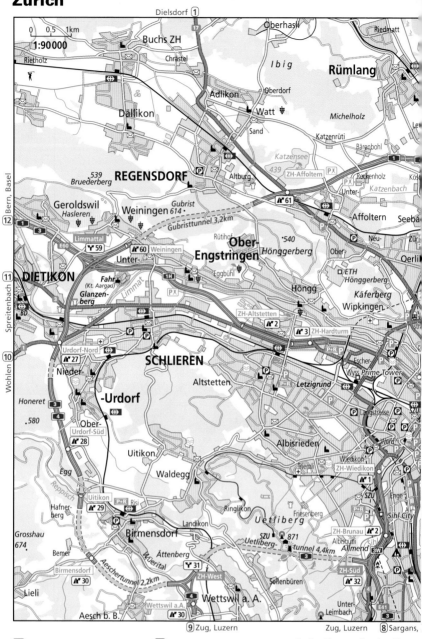

Touristservice Hauptbahnhof,
☎ 044/215 40 00,
XI–IV ①–⑥ 8.30–19 h,
⑦ 9–18 h,
V–X ①–⑥ 8–20.30 h,
⑦ 8.30–18.30 h

━━ SBB CFF FFS Hauptbahnhof,
☎ 0900 300 300, Fr. 1,19/Min.

swiss
schweiz
suisse
svizzera
svizra

☎ 0848 700 700
Flughafen, ☎ 0900 300 313,
Fr. 1.99/Min

☎ 044/421 21 21

Schweiz. Landesmuseum,
Museumstr. 2, ☎ 044/218 65 11
Museum für Wohnkultur,
Bärengasse 20-22, ☎ 044/211 17 16
Archäologische Sammlung
Rämistr. 73, ☎ 044/634 28 11

Coninx-Museum, Heuelstr. 32,
☎ 044/252 04 68
Haus «Zum Rech» Baugeschichtl.
Archiv/Stadtarchiv, Neumarkt 4,
☎ 044/266 86 -86/-46
Zentralbibliothek, Zähringerplatz 6,
☎ 044/268 31 00
Thomas-Mann-Archiv der ETH,
Schönberggasse 15,
☎ 044/632 40 45
Spielzeugmuseum,
Fortunagasse 15,
☎ 044/211 93 05
Kunsthaus, Heimplatz 1,
☎ 044/253 84 84
Museum Rietberg,
Gablerstr. 15, ☎ 044/206 31 31

Bülach ②　　Embrach

Kloten-Nord ⚑4 🅱1
Flughafen Zürich
Birchwil
⚑5 Flughafen ☒ P+R
⚑6
Flugh.-Werft
⚑7
★ **KLOTEN**
Bassersdorf
Glatt
Kolping Arena Kloten Flyers
ZH-Seebach
⚑62
Glattbrugg Glattbrugg ⚑8
H a r d
OPFIKON
⚑9 Opfikon
Dietlikon
ZH-Nord ⛾63
Brüttisellen
Glattpark
SF DRS
WALLISELLEN
Brüttisellen
n-Nord
⛾64 ZH-Ost
Messe
Hallenst./ZSC-Lions
Glatt-zentrum
⚑4 E41 E60
1L ZH-Aubrugg
Wallisellen
Flugplatz Dübendorf
ZH-Unterstrass
⚑2
⚑3 ZH-Schwamendingen
⚑65
ZH-Schwamendingen
Universität Irchel
Schwamendingen
.631
Oberstrass
Milchbucktunnel
1,9km
Zürichberg
Stettbach
Wil
⚑1 ZH-Letten
Weinbergtunnel im Bau
Zoo Zürich
Klösterli
Gockhausen
DÜBENDORF
Schweiz.
Landesmuseum
Univ.-Spital
Fluntern
Dübelstein
ETH
ZÜRICH
Hottingen
Geeren
Geissberg
Grossmünster
Kunst-haus
A d l i s b e r g
Loorenkopf
Pfaffhausen
Hirslanden
Kongress-haus
Seefeld
Centre le Corbusier
Öschbrig
Binz
Chinagarten
Weinegg
Zürichhorn
P+R
Witikon
Rehalp
Seepolizei
Whof
Sennhof
Wollishofen
ZOLLIKON
Zollikerberg
Zürichsee
406
Waltikon
S a l s t e r
Zumikon
Gössikon

Chur ⑦Thalwil, Horgen　⑥Meilen, Rapperswil-Jona　Forch, Rüti ⑤

Winterthur, St. Gallen ③　Uster ②　Uster ④

Accu,
Otto-Schütz-Weg, **194 Plätze**
Bleicherweg,
Beethovenstr. 35, **275**
Center Eleven,
Sophie-Täuber-Str. 4, **342**
Central, Seilergraben, **50**
Cityport, Affolternstr. 56, **153**
Dorflinde,
Schwamendingerstr. 41, **98**
Feldegg, Riesbachstr. 7, **346**
Gessnerallee,
Gessnerallee 14, **620**
Globus, Löwenstr. 50, **178**
Hohe Promenade,
Rämistr. 22a, **568**
Jelmoli,
Steinmühleplatz 1, **230**
Jungholz, Jungholzstr. 19, **124**
Max-Bill-Platz,
Armin-Bollinger-Weg, **59**
Messe, Andreasstr. 65, **2000**
Nordhaus, Dörflistr. 120, **175**
Nova Parking,
Badenerstr. 420, **520**
Octavo, Brown-Boveri-Str. 2, **123**
P West, Förrlibuckstr. 151, **1000**
Park Hyatt, Beethovenstr. 21, **267**
Parkside,
Sophie-Täuber-Str. 10, **38**
Sihlquai, Sihlquai 41, **187**
Stampfenbach,
Niklausstr. 1, **237**
Talgarten,
Nüschelerstr. 31, **110**
Uni-Irchel,
Winterthurerstr. 181, **1227**
Urania, Uraniastr. 3, **607**
Utoquai, Färberstr. 6, **175**
Züri11 Shopping,
Nansenstr. 5/7, **60**
Zürichhorn, Dufourstr. 142, **245**

www.pls-zh.ch

TAXI

Jung, ☎ 044/271 11 88
Alpha Taxi AG, ☎ 044/777 77 77
Taxi 444 AG, ☎ 044/444 44 44
Züritaxi, ☎ 044/222 22 22

Sammlung E.G.Bührle,
Zollikerstr.172,
☎ 044/422 00 86
Haus Konstruktiv,
Selnaustr. 25, ☎ 044/217 70 80
Grafische Sammlung ETH,
Rämistr.101, ☎ 044/632 40 46
Helmhaus, Limmatquai 31,
☎ 044/251 61 77
Kunsthalle, Limmatstr. 270,
☎ 044/272 15 15
Museum für Gestaltung, Ausstel-
lungsstr. 60, ☎ 043/446 67 67
Bellerive, Höschgasse 3
☎ 043/446 44 69
Völkerkundemuseum, Pelikanstr. 40,
☎ 044/634 90 11

Nordamerika Native Museum,
Seefeldstr. 317,
☎ 044/413 49 90
Zoologisches Museum,
Karl-Schmid-Str. 4,
☎ 044/634 38 38
Anthropologisches Museum,
Winterthurerstr. 190,
☎ 044/635 49 54
Paläontologisches Museum,
Karl-Schmid-Str. 4,
☎ 044/634 38 38
Medizinhistorisches Museum,
Rämistr. 69, ☎ 044/634 20 71
Zoo Zürich,
Zürichbergstr. 221,
☎ 044/254 25 05

Botanischer Garten,
Zollikerstr.107,
☎ 044/634 84 61
Uhrenmuseum Beyer,
Bahnhofstr. 31,
☎ 043/344 63 23

Avis, ☎ 044/296 87 87
✈☎ 044/800 77 33
Zodiac, ✈☎ 044/813 31 31
Europcar, ☎ 044/271 56 56,
✈☎ 043/255 56 56
Hertz, ☎ 043/444 40 00,
✈☎ 043/816 32 55
Sixt, ✈☎ 043/816 35 23

Winterthur

✉ 8400/☎ 052

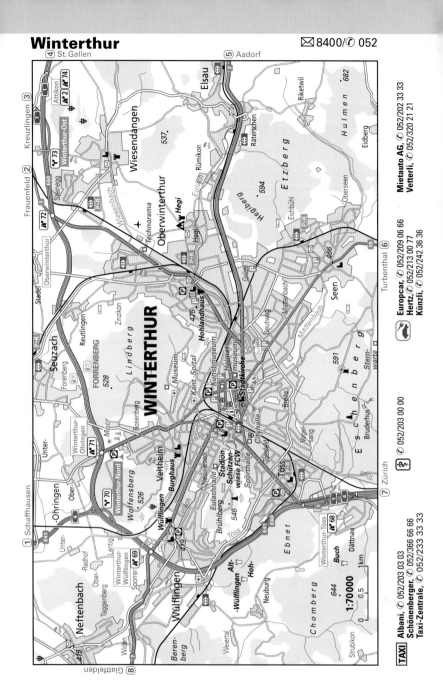

1 km
1:70000
0   0.5

ℹ **Hauptbahnhof,** ☎ 052/267 67 00,
①–⑤ 8.30–18.30 h, ⑥ 8.30–16 h
🚌 SBB CFF FFS
☎ 0900 300 300, Fr. 1,19/Min.

ℹ **Sammlung Oskar Reinhart**
«am Römerholz», Haldenstr. 95,
☎ 052/269 27 40
Museum Oskar Reinhart, Stadthausstr. 6,
☎ 052/267 51 72
Kunstmuseum, Museumstr. 52,
☎ 052/267 51 62
Kunsthalle, Marktgasse 25,
☎ 052/267 51 32
Lindengut, Römerstr. 8,
☎ 052/213 47 77 Montag und Freitag
geschlossen/fermé/closed/chiuso
Technorama, Technoramastr. 1,
☎ 052/244 08 44
Museum Briner und Kern,
Marktgasse 20,
☎ 052/267 51 26
Münzkabinett und Antikensammlung,
Lindstr. 8, ☎ 052/267 51 46
Gewerbemuseum, Kirchplatz 14,
☎ 052/267 51 36
Villa Flora/Sammlung Hahnloser,
Tösstalstr. 44, ☎ 052/212 99 66
Fotomuseum, Grüzenstr. 44 + 45,
☎ 052/234 10 60

🅿 **AXA Winterthur,**
Museumstrasse, **80**
Bahnhof, 480
Coop/Manor, Merkurstrasse, **445**
Neuwiesen, Strickerstrasse, **520**
Technikum Nord, Technikumstrasse, **170**
Technikum Süd, Wildbachstr., **70**
Stadttheater,
Museumstrasse, **160**

🚖 **Albani,** ☎ 052/203 03 03
Schönenberger, ☎ 052/366 66 66
Taxi-Zentrale, ☎ 052/233 33 33

🔧 **Europcar,** ☎ 052/209 06 66
Hertz, ☎ 052/213 00 77
Künzli, ☎ 052/242 36 36

Mietauto AG, ☎ 052/202 33 33
Vetterli, ☎ 052/320 21 21

☎ 052/203 00 00